Microsoft®
Project Fundamentals
Microsoft Project Standard 2021, Professional 2021, and Project Online Editions

Teresa S. Stover

SYBEX®
A Wiley Brand

Library of Congress Control Number: 2021950187

For Mom—Song Ai Soon Remhof—and our continuing moments of joy.

Acknowledgments

Many thanks go to my ever-steady and ever-ready editorial team, including Jan Lynn, Joyce Nielsen, Barath Kumar Rajasekaran, Christine O'Connor, Devon Cajas, and Jim Minatel, along with the many others working behind the scenes. As the model of a project team at its very best, you all worked your magic to bring this book to life and make it the best it could be.

I applaud the conscientious and painstaking work of the Project team at Microsoft, past and present, for creating in Microsoft Project a brilliant tool for project managers in a variety of industries with a range of requirements.

Cheers to Bonnie Biafore for her continuing work in teaching and guiding the next generation of project managers. I value our past collaborations as well as our friendship through the years.

Tons of respect and admiration to Kate Lasky and Rebecca Stoltz for our current work at Josephine Community Library. The upcoming library construction projects will test our project management chops and will result in amazing information services and programs that will expand horizons, enrich experiences, and build community.

My highest esteem goes to all those inspirational and dedicated individuals and groups who work toward justice in our world. It's hard work, and it's slow work, but it pays off with a society that works well for everyone.

All my love and gratitude to Craig Stover, for being my voice of reason, my best friend, and my rock.

About the Author

"What a Difference a Plan Makes" could be Teresa Stover's adapted theme song. To her, planning and implementing a project—while keeping a mindful eye on the prize of the project's outcomes—creates special excitement and satisfaction.

As the technical publications supervisor for a Silicon Valley startup more than 20 years ago, Teresa came face to face with the art and science of project management. Keen to know who needed to be working on which tasks daily to meet competing deadlines on multiple projects, she discovered the power of project management.

Since then, Teresa has worked as a technical communications and project management consultant for software creators, manufacturing, business, and education. She specializes in project management for entrepreneurial startups, nonprofit organizations, and content development enterprises. She has authored or co-authored 15 books on Microsoft Project, project management, and business productivity software. Recent achievements include helping start up a new library district and serving as a nonprofit foundation's interim executive director, in both cases setting up systems and structures for organizational development and success.

Teresa lives in southern Oregon with her husband, Craig Stover, and her German Shepherd, Dante's Inferno der Wunderhund. Teresa welcomes emails from readers sent to teresa@stoverwriting.com.

About the Technical Editor

Joyce J. Nielsen has worked in the publishing industry for more than 30 years as a technical writer/editor, development editor, and project manager, specializing in Microsoft Office, Windows, Internet, and general technology content for leading educational, retail, and online publishers. She is the author or co-author of more than 50 computer books and 2,100 online articles. Joyce holds a Bachelor of Science degree in Quantitative Business Analysis from Indiana University's Kelley School of Business in Bloomington, Indiana. She currently resides in Arizona.

Contents at a Glance

Introduction   *xiv*

Part I   **Manage Your Projects with Microsoft Project**   **1**

Lesson 1   Project Management Basics   3
Lesson 2   Introducing Microsoft Project   17

Part II   **Plan Your Project**   **35**

Lesson 3   Establish a Strong Foundation   37
Lesson 4   Set Up the Project and Tasks   47
Lesson 5   Build the Schedule   69
Lesson 6   Set Up Resources   97
Lesson 7   Assign Resources to Tasks   115
Lesson 8   Check and Adjust the Project   137

Part III   **Monitor and Control Your Project**   **163**

Lesson 9   Track Project Information   165
Lesson 10   View Project Information   183
Lesson 11   Customize Project Information   207
Lesson 12   Report Project Information   219

Part IV   **Close Your Project**   **231**

Lesson 13   Obtain Project Acceptance   233
Lesson 14   Retain Project History   241
Appendix   Answers to the Review Questions   251

Index   *263*

Contents

Introduction   *xiv*

Part I   **Manage Your Projects with Microsoft Project**   **1**

Lesson 1   **Project Management Basics**   **3**

Projects and Project Managers   4
    What Is a Project?   4
    What Is a Project Manager?   5
The Project Triangle   6
Project Processes   7
    Initiating   7
    Planning   7
    Executing   8
    Monitoring and Controlling   8
    Closing   8
Project Management Methodologies   9
    Waterfall Project Management   9
    Agile Project Management   10
    Other Methodologies   10
More About Project Management   11
Key Terms   11
Review Questions   13

Lesson 2   **Introducing Microsoft Project**   **17**

How Microsoft Project Helps   18
    Manage the Schedule   18
    Calculate Costs   19
    Balance Resources   20
    Communicate Progress   21
    Respond to Changes   21
Microsoft Project Solutions   22
Touring the Microsoft Project App   24
    Browse Task and Resource Views   25
    Browse Reports   26
    Click Through the Ribbons   26
    Go Backstage   27
Get Help with Project   29
    Help Within Project   29
    Help Outside Project   31
Key Terms   32
Review Questions   33

Part II   **Plan Your Project**   **35**

Lesson   3   **Establish a Strong Foundation**   **37**

                     Initiate the Project   38
                         Identify the Stakeholders and Project Sponsor   39
                         Authorize the Project Charter   39
                     Start Planning   40
                         Collect Requirements   41
                         Define the Scope   42
                     Organize Project Plan Documents   43
                     Key Terms   45
                     Review Questions   46

Lesson   4   **Set Up the Project and Tasks**   **47**

                     Start a New Project Plan   48
                         Create a New Blank Project   48
                         Copy an Existing Similar Project   49
                         Adapt a Project Template   50
                     Set the Project Start Date   51
                     Enter Task Names   53
                         Where Do Task Names Come From?   54
                         Name Your Tasks   55
                         Explore Task Views   56
                         Work with Tasks in the Task Sheet   57
                         Work with Tasks on the Task Board   60
                     Sequence Tasks   62
                         Reorder Tasks in the Task Sheet   62
                         Reorder Tasks on the Task Board   63
                     Organize the Task Outline   63
                     Key Terms   67
                     Review Questions   68

Lesson   5   **Build the Schedule**   **69**

                     Decide on Automatic Scheduling   70
                         Change All Tasks to Automatic Scheduling   71
                         Set Any New Tasks to Automatic Scheduling   72
                         Switch from Automatic to Manual Scheduling   72
                         Switch from Manual to Automatic Scheduling   72
                     Get to Know the Gantt Chart   73
                     Enter Task Durations   75
                         Enter Durations in the Gantt Chart   76
                         View Durations on the Task Board   77

Set Milestones   79
Link Dependent Tasks   80
    Set Up Task Dependencies   81
    View Dependencies on a Task Board   82
Schedule Sprints for an Agile Project   83
    Add Sprints to Your Project   84
    Add Tasks to Your Sprints   85
    Modify Sprint Information   86
Identify Any Hardwired Dates   87
Enter Deadline Reminders   89
Use Project and Task Calendars   90
    Review and Change the Project Calendar   91
    Apply a Task Calendar   91
Key Terms   92
Review Questions   93

Lesson 6   Set Up Resources   97

Add Resources to the Plan   98
    Define Human and Equipment Resources   99
    Define Material Resources   99
    Define Cost Resources   100
Enter Resource Costs   101
    Specify Work Resource Costs   102
    Specify Material Resource Costs   103
    Specify Cost Resource Costs   103
Refine Resource Unit Availability   104
    Change Resource Units   105
    Specify Differing Availability Over Time   105
Customize Resource Calendars   106
    Switch the Base Calendar   108
    Change the Work Week in a Resource Calendar   108
    Specify an Exception to a Resource Calendar   110
Key Terms   112
Review Questions   113

Lesson 7   Assign Resources to Tasks   115

Assign Work Resources to Tasks   116
Assign Material Resources to Tasks   118
Assign Cost Resources to Tasks   120
Review Resource Assignments   122
See Task Costs from Assignments   125
    Review Task Costs   126
    Review Task Costs on an Agile Planning Board   127
    Review the Overall Project Cost Estimate   127

Change Assignments   128
    Replace a Resource Assignment   129
    Add or Remove a Resource Assignment   129
    Change Duration on Tasks with Assignments   132
Key Terms   133
Review Questions   134

Lesson   8   Check and Adjust the Project   137

Check the Project Finish Date   138
    Review the Project Finish Date   139
    Bring In the Project Finish Date   142
Check Costs   145
    Review the Total Project Cost   145
    Reduce Costs   146
Check Resource Assignments   153
    Resolve Overallocations in a Task Sheet   154
    Resolve Assignment Problems in Team Planner   155
Set the Project Baseline   157
Key Terms   159
Review Questions   161

Part III   Monitor and Control Your Project   163

Lesson   9   Track Project Information   165

Collect Progress Information   167
Enter Actuals in a Waterfall Project   168
    Enter Progress as Expected   168
    Enter Different Types of Progress Information   169
    Distinguish Baseline, Scheduled, and Actual Values   170
Update Status in an Agile Project   172
    Enter Progress on the Task Board   172
    Enter Progress in the Task Board Sheet   173
    Specify Percent Complete on the Task Board   174
    Enter Progress on the Current Sprint   176
    Move Tasks from One Sprint to Another   177
Respond to Changes   178
    Check the Project Finish Date   178
    Check the Project Cost   179
    Check Resource Allocations   179
Key Terms   180
Review Questions   181

Lesson   10   View Project Information   183

See the Data You Need   184
    Zoom a View In or Out   184
    Adjust the Timescale   185
    Show a Specific Outline Level   186
    Sort Project Information   187
    Group Project Information   188
    Filter Project Information   188
    Highlight Project Information   189
Change Columns in a Sheet View   190
    Add a Column   190
    Move a Column   192
    Hide a Column   192
Print a View   193
Work with More Views   194
    Browse Graphical Views   195
    Browse Combination Views   199
Key Terms   202
Review Questions   204

Lesson   11   Customize Project Information   207

Customize a Sheet View   208
Customize a Gantt View   210
Customize a Board View   212
    Modify Board View Columns   212
    Modify Task Cards   213
Set Options and Preferences   214
Key Terms   215
Review Questions   216

Lesson   12   Report Project Information   219

Work with Reports   220
    Run a Report   221
    Adjust the Design of a Report   222
Work with Dashboards   223
Create a New Report or Dashboard   224
Print a Report   226
Key Terms   228
Review Questions   229

Part IV		Close Your Project	231
Lesson	13	**Obtain Project Acceptance**	**233**
		Present the Project to the Sponsor	234
		Secure Official Project Sign-Off	236
		Complete Final Refinements	236
		Have the Sponsor Sign Off on the Project	238
		Celebrate With Your Team	238
		Key Terms	239
		Review Questions	240
Lesson	14	**Retain Project History**	**241**
		Document Lessons Learned	242
		Identify the Information You Can Use	243
		Gather Lessons Learned	243
		Document and Share the Lessons Learned	244
		Archive Project History	245
		Clean Up Your Project Plan	245
		Add Key Documents to the Project Plan	247
		Organize the Archive File Structure	247
		Key Terms	248
		Review Questions	249
Appendix		**Answers to the Review Questions**	**251**
Index			*263*

Introduction

Welcome to *Microsoft Project Fundamentals*. You're about to embark on a journey through the basics of Microsoft Project capabilities that can help you effectively manage your projects. This book focuses on the best and easiest ways to use Project to plan, schedule, manage resources, track progress, and view and report project information. Along the way, you'll also pick up core principles of project management, like the project triangle of scope, time, and cost, as well as the five project phases or processes.

The procedures, examples, and screenshots in this book are based on Microsoft Project Online Desktop Client as implemented in October 2021. Project Online Desktop Client is part of the Microsoft "Project Plan 3" subscription for cloud-based project management solutions. If you are working with Microsoft Project Professional 2019 or 2021, the perpetual (nonsubscription) version, you should be able to follow along with this book just fine.

Who Will Benefit Most from This Book

This book is an essential resource if you're new to Microsoft Project and project management. Whether you're a student in school or a practitioner in the field, you'll find this book valuable to your project management journey.

For others of you who have used previous versions of Microsoft Project, this book can reintroduce you to the tool and its new capabilities, especially for managing agile projects as well as traditional waterfall projects.

Looking Ahead in This Book

This book consists of 14 lessons, each of which includes learning objectives, major concepts, and step-by-step procedures, key terms, and review questions to help you test and cement your new skills. The following summarizes each lesson:

Lesson 1, "Project Management Basics," introduces the work of projects and project managers, the project triangle, the six project phases or processes, and project management methodologies, including waterfall and agile.

Lesson 2, "Introducing Microsoft Project," explains how Microsoft Project helps manage your schedule, calculate costs, balance resources, and more. This lesson also describes the various Microsoft Project editions, and offers a tour of the application's user interface.

Lesson 3, "Establish a Strong Foundation," covers basic best practices for initiating a new project. These include identifying the project sponsor, having your project charter authorized, defining the scope, and organizing project plan documents.

Lesson 4, "Set Up the Project and Tasks," moves the project from the initiating to the planning process. This lesson demonstrates how to use Microsoft Project to start a new project plan, and how to enter and organize tasks in a task sheet view for a waterfall project or a task board view for an agile project.

Lesson 5, "Build the Schedule," describes automatic versus manual scheduling and explains the Gantt Chart. The lesson walks you through entering task durations, setting milestones, linking dependent tasks, and identifying deadlines. It also shows how to schedule sprints for an agile project.

Lesson 6, "Set Up Resources," explains the different types of project resources: human, equipment, material, and cost resources. This lesson shows how to add resources to your project plan, enter resource costs, and specify resource availability with units as well as calendars.

Lesson 7, "Assign Resources to Tasks," steps you through assigning work, material, and cost resources to tasks. This lesson also shows how to review resource costs for a specific task, and how to add, replace, or remove resources on assignments.

Lesson 8, "Check and Adjust the Project," systematically demonstrates how you can optimize your plan for the project finish date, for the total budget amount, and for the best use of available resources, all while fulfilling the stated project scope. This lesson also introduces the use of the project baseline.

Lesson 9, "Track Project Information," transitions your project from the planning process to the monitoring and controlling processes, in which the project starts to be implemented. You learn how to collect and enter progress information, as well as how to adjust for inevitable changes and challenges.

Lesson 10, "View Project Information," covers how to see the data you need by zooming, sorting, grouping, filtering, or highlighting information in a Project view. This lesson also describes how to work with columns in a sheet view and how to print a view.

Lesson 11, "Customize Project Information," introduces basic customizing for a sheet view, a Gantt view, and a board view so you can access the information you need in your Project views. This lesson also offers a tour of some basic Project options and preferences you can set.

Lesson 12, "Report Project Information," shows how to run a report or dashboard to share key project progress with stakeholders. The lesson also works through creating a new, custom report, as well as printing a report on paper or to a PDF file to share with others.

Lesson 13, "Obtain Project Acceptance," shifts your project from the monitoring and controlling processes to the final closing process. This lesson specifies how to present the finished project to the sponsor and obtain final project sign-off.

Lesson 14, "Retain Project History," describes techniques for gathering and documenting lessons learned through a final project review. This lesson also specifies best practices for archiving project history to ensure that solid information is available for people working on similar future projects.

"Appendix" contains answers to the Review Questions in each lesson.

Features

This book uses certain conventions in order to help you quickly identify important information. In particular, look for the following text segments:

In-line boxes further expand on some aspect of a topic, without interrupting the flow of the narrative.

Located throughout are small general discussions that deserve special emphasis or that have relevance beyond the immediately surrounding content. These are found in the general sidebar notes.

Instructor Materials

Instructors using this book as a text for their classes can find bonus digital content at www.wiley.com/go/microsoftprojectfundamentals. This content includes a syllabus, an assessment test, and a presentation slide deck.

Syllabus   The syllabus contains course learning objectives, topics, and a chapter reference guide. It's provided as a PDF as well as in Microsoft Word (.docx) format so that it can be easily customized for instructor needs.

Assessment Test Questions   The assessment test contains a subset of the questions included at the end of each lesson in this book. Instructors can use this as a pre-test and post-test for their class or adapt it for other purposes. The test questions are provided in PDF as well as in Microsoft Word (.docx) format.

Presentation Slide Deck   Instructors can use or adapt the robust series of presentation slides for their course lectures based on the content in this book. The deck is provided in Microsoft PowerPoint (.pptx) format as well as in PDF.

Manage Your Projects with Microsoft Project

Lesson
1

Project Management Basics

LESSON OBJECTIVES

✓ Identify a project versus an operation.

✓ Label the three sides of the project triangle.

✓ List the six project stages or processes.

✓ Explain project manager duties in each project process.

✓ Name two prevalent project management methodologies.

✓ Assess the project types best for the two methodologies.

When you decide to use Microsoft Project as a key tool in managing your projects, you also want to include a solid grounding in project management principles in that toolbox.

This lesson introduces you to the basics of projects and project manager responsibilities, including project management knowledge areas. You'll see the project triangle and the processes within the project life cycle. You'll review waterfall and agile project management methodologies.

Through all this, you'll preview how Microsoft Project can assist you in your responsibilities as a skilled project manager so that you can deliver your well-scoped project on deadline and within budget.

Projects and Project Managers

So what actually characterizes a project as such, rather than other activities we do like operations or task lists? And what are the responsibilities of the project manager? Let's break them down now.

What Is a Project?

A *project* is a unique activity that has a distinct starting point and a distinct finishing point. Here are some examples of projects:

- Remodeling an office
- Developing a new training program
- Launching an awareness campaign
- Hosting a conference and trade show
- Designing a new product

Each of these examples are unique—the specific office being remodeled, the topic of the training program or awareness campaign, the locale and speakers involved in the conference, or the specific qualities that go into designing a new product.

None of these projects are ongoing, meaning that they each have a start and an end date. Although some projects like designing a new product or building a high rise might take several years, they proceed through different phases through those years until the project's completion.

In contrast, ongoing activities that are repeated and that don't have distinct start and finish dates are considered *operations*. Some examples of operations are as follows:

- Maintaining information on a website
- Running payroll twice each month
- Sending weekly e-news to customers and prospects
- Preparing packets for the monthly board of directors meeting
- Posting daily items on social media

These are routine activities that take place on an ongoing basis as part of the regular business of an organization.

Projects can become operations, or operations can be a result of finished projects. For example, after the project of developing a new training program is complete, delivering a set of classes each month can become part of the organization's regular operations.

Projects can repeat in certain ways but still not be considered an operation. For example, your organization might follow a certain project template for product development that includes research, prototyping, testing, manufacturing, marketing, and launch. Its uniqueness lies in the difference in the product under development.

Whether small, medium, or large, projects are often characterized by the following:

- A scope of work defining the project boundaries and standards
- Part- or full-time team members who are assigned to the project
- Equipment and materials earmarked for the project, if applicable
- A budget dedicated to the project
- At least one expected deliverable or outcome at the project end

What Is a Project Manager?

Some people become professional *project managers* as a result of strategic career planning, whether they majored in it in college or discovered it in the working world and then climbed the project management ladder. Many just get themselves assigned one day as a project manager and then must figure out what it's all about.

A project manager is the point person responsible for carrying out a project and delivering the desired outcomes—the *scope* of the project. As the project manager, you balance the constraints of the project *budget* and the deadline with the elements of the project scope. You continually check in with the team members working on their assigned project tasks, track and analyze the progress, prevent or solve any problems that arise, and report overall project progress to the project sponsor and other stakeholders.

As the project manager, you have your finger on the pulse of the overall project at any given moment. While individual team members might be working on their own specific part of the project, the project manager always sees the project as a whole and knows in what direction it is heading.

According to the *Project Management Book of Knowledge (PMBOK©)*, a successful and well-rounded project manager functions within the following nine disciplines, or *knowledge areas*:

1. Integration management
2. Scope management
3. Schedule management
4. Cost management
5. Quality management
6. Resource management
7. Communications management
8. Risk management
9. Procurement management
10. Stakeholder management

The Project Triangle

Project management is a constant balancing act of managing the tension between project deadlines and costs deadlines to deliver the intended project scope. You might have heard the old saying, "Cheap, fast, or good. Pick two." This illustrates the *project triangle*, which is also known as the project management triangle, triple constraint, or the iron triangle.

Suppose your project is to develop a new website. If you have a spare budget and need to launch it in two weeks, the website might be more minimal with fewer features. But if you have an ample budget and several months of development time, the site might contain all the information and features that the project sponsor wants. If your customer wants the website in two weeks and is adamant that all the information and features are included without delay, it will be more expensive.

Therefore, the two triangle sides that are non-negotiable, and the one side that's flexible, determines the constraints of your project and where your project has some "give."

Several interpretations of the project triangle exist. One version is the triangle sided with time, cost, and quality, with scope in the center. You might see it as a project rectangle with scope, schedule, budget, and quality. Another version is a six-sided project star with scope, schedule, budget, risk, resources, and quality. Figure 1.1 illustrates the concept of a good interpretation of the project triangle with time, cost, and scope.

Depending on the interpretation, a budget can include all *resources* that cost money including staff, *equipment*, and *materials*. Scope might include quality.

While project managers can and do argue about the "right" project triangle, the important thing is to simply keep the model in mind as you manage your projects. Your job as project manager is to know the ranked priorities and constraints of your project and to make adjustments accordingly.

FIGURE 1.1   A project triangle

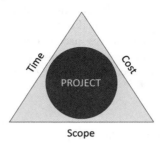

Project Processes

With its explicit start and finish dates, any project has its own life cycle. The project life cycle consists of six specific *stages*, or *project processes*. Figure 1.2 illustrates the project processes along the project life cycle.

FIGURE 1.2   The processes in the project life cycle

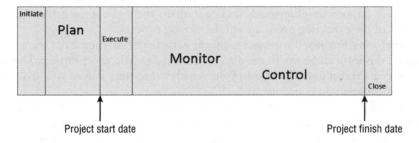

Initiating

Also considered preplanning or scoping, the project is conceived, its scope is defined, and a preliminary budget is drafted during the *initiating process*. The powers that be—that is, the customer, executive, or other *project sponsor* paying for the project—agree to the project objectives and requirements.

The initiating stage is also the stage when a project manager is assigned, the business case for the project is outlined, and any other *stakeholders* and their expectations are identified.

Planning

The project manager works during the *planning process* to transform the goals and constraints defined in the initiating process into a roadmap for achieving those goals, step by step and task by task. To do this, the project manager lays out the tasks in the *work breakdown structure (WBS)*, determines the duration and dependency of those tasks, assigns resources to the tasks, and estimates costs for those resources.

This effort defines the project schedule, resource requirements, and costs with a greater degree of certainty. With its scheduling engine, resource planner, and costing formulas, Microsoft Project steps up as the project manager's key partner in this planning process.

Executing

When planning is complete and the funding and resources are secured and ready to work, the project manager can press that figurative "GO" button. This represents the start of the *executing process*.

The project starts and all resources begin working on their assigned tasks in the work breakdown structure. The clock is ticking and the budget is depleting. The project manager can now use Microsoft Project to track actual progress against the scheduled projections in the plan.

Monitoring and Controlling

As soon as project execution begins, the project shifts to the monitoring and controlling processes, which happen simultaneously and continually throughout the project life cycle from the start of the executing process until the closing process.

In the *monitoring process*, the project manager gathers information from team members and compares this information with the plan represented in Microsoft Project. Think of as if you've entered a travel destination into your vehicle's map app, and as you drive, you're watching your progress on your itinerary.

In the *controlling process*, the project manager makes decisions and adjustments when actual experience differs from the project plan. These adjustments are corrections to the plan to maintain the project triangle balance of time, cost, and quality within the project scope. Again, it's as if you're trying to follow your vehicle's map app, but you've run into a traffic jam or spent more money at a roadside attraction than planned. You must then adjust your travel itinerary to account for the time delay or the unexpected cost.

Closing

When the final project tasks are completed, the deliverables are submitted, and the goals are met, the project's *closing process* happens. The project manager deals with the final details, especially ensuring that the project sponsor accepts the project as complete.

The closing process also includes documenting processes, archiving files, and conducting a project review, or *lessons learned* exercise, with the project team before they all move to their next projects. This review process ensures that the project ends as it intentionally began, and that important institutional knowledge is captured to help future projects be more successful.

Project Management Methodologies

The waterfall and agile project management methodologies are two major approaches to project management. Both methods are widely used and both are supported by Microsoft Project.

Waterfall Project Management

Waterfall project management is also known as traditional project management or the *Critical Path Method (CPM)*. This method identifies project activities into sequential phases, where each phase depends on the completion of previous phases. Progress flows mostly in one direction, like a waterfall, through the various phases (see Figure 1.3).

FIGURE 1.3   Bars on a Gantt chart illustrate waterfall project management.

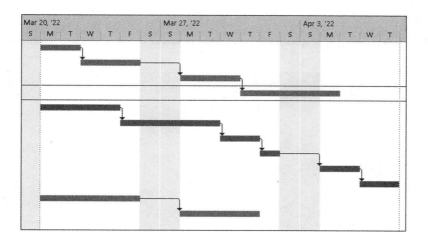

More specifically, this method relies on the duration of all activities required to complete the project and the dependencies between those activities. The tasks and their dependencies create multiple paths throughout the project. The longest path is known as the *critical path*. If any task component on the critical path is delayed, the entire project is also delayed.

The waterfall method or CPM is typically used in manufacturing and construction—that is, in structured physical environments in which changes even early in the project are very expensive.

Agile Project Management

Agile project management is a type of iterative or incremental project management that allows for more experimentation, exploration, and discovery. Designed for the software industry, it has been adopted in other industries that center on knowledge-based (rather than physically based) creative work.

In work such as software development, the phased waterfall approach is not well suited because requirements are often loosely defined at first, or technologies in use are quickly changing.

In agile or iterative project management, the details of the entire project are not planned from the start. Instead, the plan focuses on iterations, often called *sprints*. After the start of the project, the iteration or sprint is planned, executed, monitored, controlled, and closed. Each one is like a mini-project within the project. A deliverable, perhaps a prototype or a section of code, is produced at the end of the iteration and offered to the customer or other project sponsor for feedback. Based on that feedback, additional iterations are planned and executed. In this way, the solution the project is seeking evolves through each sprint (see Figure 1.4).

FIGURE 1.4   An agile project uses task board views to schedule project iterations.

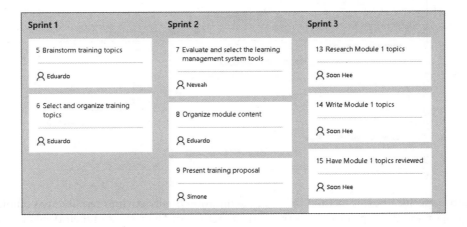

Although Microsoft Project was originally designed for the waterfall method, it now highlights features and views designed specifically for agile projects as well.

Other Methodologies

Although waterfall and agile are the most widely used project management methodologies and the only two discussed in this book, there are several others. Examples include critical chain, earned value management, lean project management, and benefits realization.

As the project manager, you are in the best position to determine which methodology is best for the project under consideration. This determination should be done during the initiating process, when the project scope, resources, and tools are all being defined.

When you know the nature of the project, its requirements, and the team, you'll have a better idea of the best methodology to employ for greater chances of the project's success. You might find yourself advocating for a different methodology, especially if one has been the norm or the trend in your organization but not necessarily the best choice.

More About Project Management

The more you expand your knowledge on project management principles and best practices, the more adept and effective you'll become as a project manager.

An especially valuable resource is the Project Management Institute (*PMI©*), a professional association for project managers. It publishes the *Project Management Book of Knowledge* (PMBOK©) and hosts annual conferences and other training opportunities. It administers the Project Management Professional (*PMP©*), *Certified Associate in Project Management (CAPM©)*, and Disciplined Agile Scrum Master (DASM™) certification exams, among several others. Learn more at `www.PMI.org`.

Learning project management principles and how to use the tools and features in Microsoft Project go hand in hand. Together, they both can help you become a more successful project manager: one who plans deliberately, communicates well, solves problems, balances the triangle, satisfies stakeholders, closes out strong, and moves on to the next project challenge with confidence and enthusiasm.

Key Terms

agile project management

budget

Certified Associate in Project Management (CAPM©)

closing process

controlling process

critical path

Critical Path Method (CPM)

equipment

executing process

Disciplined Agile Scrum Master (DASM)

initiating process
knowledge areas
lessons learned
materials
monitoring process
operation
planning process
project
Project Management Book of Knowledge (PMBOK©)
Project Management Institute (PMI©)
Project Management Professional (PMP©)
project manager
project processes
project sponsor
project triangle
resources
scope
sprints
stage
stakeholder
waterfall project management
work breakdown structure (WBS)

Review Questions

1. A nonprofit organization, which has worked with volunteers for many years, has decided to develop the curriculum and materials for a new quarterly volunteer-training program and then train the trainers—the various department heads—in conducting their training modules. Is this considered a project or an operation?

   A. It's a project because although it's conducted quarterly, it will be done by different volunteers each time, and possibly by different trainers.

   B. It's a project because developing the curriculum and materials for the new training program is a new and unique activity for the organization.

   C. It's an operation because it's not unique to the organization, as it has been training and working with volunteers for years.

   D. It's an operation because training will be conducted quarterly as part of regular business.

2. A startup technology company has just finished developing its branding and marketing materials, including the design of its e-newsletter. After conducting a pilot and making adjustments with a few test issues, the company is now writing and disseminating the e-newsletter at the first of each month. Is this a project or an operation?

   A. It's a project because although the e-newsletters go out monthly, each one contains different content from the previous month.

   B. It's a project because the development of the branding and marketing materials had specific start and finish dates.

   C. It's an operation because producing the e-newsletter is an ongoing process that happens once every month with no end date.

   D. It's an operation because producing the e-newsletter has a start date but no finish date.

3. The discussion in this lesson indicates that the three sides of the project triangle are time, cost, and scope. Regardless of different opinions about which elements belong where on the project triangle, what is the point that a project manager should always keep in mind?

   A. That the budget is always the fixed element of any project, and other elements like time and scope must flex around the budget as needed

   B. That time is always the fixed element of any project, and other elements like budget and scope must flex around the schedule as needed

   C. That there are always two fixed elements of any project, and the third element can flex as necessary to maintain the project scope

   D. That each project will have different priorities for time, cost, and scope, and when one of these elements changes, the other elements must flex to compensate

4. You're the project manager of an office remodeling project that has a limited budget and an absolutely fixed finish date of September 1. As conditions change throughout the life of the project, what adjustments can you make to the project without running out of money or jeopardizing that set finish date?

   A. You can only reduce the project scope.

   B. You can only adjust the budget.

   C. You can increase the budget and extend the project finish date.

   D. You can only extend the project finish date.

5. What are the first three processes in the project life cycle?

   A. Initiating, planning, and controlling

   B. Initiating, planning, and executing

   C. Planning, executing, and monitoring

   D. Planning, controlling, and monitoring

6. Monitoring and controlling happen at the same time in the project life cycle. What's the difference between the two processes?

   A. Monitoring is about collecting information about project progress and comparing it against the project plan. Controlling is about adjusting the project based on that comparison.

   B. Monitoring is about collecting status information from team members daily. Controlling is about helping team members stay on schedule.

   C. Monitoring is about working with the appropriate Microsoft Project views. Controlling is about entering the right information in the right views.

   D. Monitoring is about designing and generating reports for the team and stakeholders. Controlling is about watching the project schedule and budget.

7. What are two of the most important aspects of the closing process of a completed project?

   A. Archiving project files and celebrating with the team

   B. Documenting processes developed as part of the project and writing team member evaluations

   C. Obtaining project sponsor acceptance and conducting a lessons learned meeting

   D. Collecting all project deliverables and debriefing with your manager

8. You are the project manager for equipment retrofit of a manufacturing line. Which of the following project characteristics lead you to advocate for using the waterfall project management methodology?

   A. The project requirements are very well defined before the project starts.

   B. The project scope is vague and can benefit from experimentation, prototyping, and iterations of solutions and deliverables.

    C. The project is in a more structured, physical environment and even early changes to the project can be prohibitively expensive.

    D. A and C

    E. B and C

9. You've been assigned as project manager for an ambitious website design initiative. Which of the following characteristics might lead you to recommend using the agile project management methodology?

    A. The project requirements are very well defined before the project starts, and the project sponsor will not be frequently engaged.

    B. The project scope is more vague and can benefit from experimentation, prototyping, and iterations of solutions and deliverables.

    C. The project is centered on knowledge-based work done by a highly collaborative creative team, and the project customers are enthusiastic about frequent reviews and feedback.

    D. A and C

    E. B and C

Lesson 2

Introducing Microsoft Project

LESSON OBJECTIVES

✓ Describe three of the five major ways that Microsoft Project helps you manage projects.

✓ List three of several Microsoft Project editions you can choose from as your project management solution.

✓ Explain the pros and cons of two different Microsoft Project editions.

✓ Select the Microsoft Project edition that is best suited to your projects, team, and organization.

✓ Navigate the Microsoft Project window.

✓ Name three sources for getting help with your Microsoft Project edition.

Although it doesn't manage your projects for you, Microsoft Project is your quick and clever assistant in estimating schedules, calculating costs, balancing resources, displaying progress, and testing what-if scenarios.

Microsoft offers several *editions* of Project, from basic to full-featured, and from traditional desktop to online cloud-based applications. In this lesson, you'll discern which of these flavors is best for you and your team.

To begin, you'll start up Microsoft Project and tour the windows, views, and modes where different features reside.

For this book, the procedures and examples are based on Microsoft Project Online Desktop Client as implemented in October 2021 as the Microsoft "Project Plan 3" for cloud-based project management solutions. This is largely the same as Microsoft Project Professional 2021, the perpetual (nonsubscription) version. You can learn about changes since then with help and tips located within the app, online, and in user forums.

How Microsoft Project Helps

Project management is a fascinating confluence of skills, knowledge, and intuition. It fully engages experience of the industry in which the project lives, while employing the soft skills and emotional intelligence associated with working with human beings.

All of this becomes clearer when you survey the list of the 10 *project management knowledge areas*: integration management, scope management, schedule management, cost management, quality management, resource management, communications management, risk management, procurement management, and stakeholder management.

Although you, the project manager, are responsible for orchestrating the disciplines of all these knowledge areas in a single project, Microsoft Project does the heavy lifting when it comes to managing the schedule, costs, and resources. Project also helps you communicate progress and formulate what-if scenarios for responding to risks and changes.

Manage the Schedule

With its powerful scheduling engine, Project shines brightest in helping you estimate, manage, and adjust your project schedule. At the start of project planning, you use Project to determine the timeframe for the project start and finish dates, along with the phases and milestones along the way.

When you specify how long each task will take to accomplish and link together tasks that depend on each other, Project calculates the schedule of linked task paths. If the project sponsor needs the project finish date to come in sooner, or when an unexpected change occurs in the middle of the project, you can adjust the timing of one task and all related tasks change with it (see Figure 2.1).

FIGURE 2.1   A Project schedule recalculation

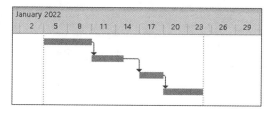

When the duration of one task changes...

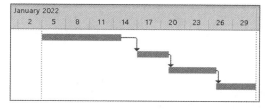

...any linked tasks are automatically rescheduled.

This automatic scheduling and rescheduling saves you a huge amount of time as you create, track, and adjust the project.

Project can also factor in other scheduling information you might provide, such as specific deadlines or "drop-dead dates," or the availability of assigned team members.

As you work through the project life cycle, you enter actual progress in Project, such as the percentage of specific tasks completed. Project updates the schedule accordingly, so you continue to see the projected schedule based on work already done. Then if necessary, you can adjust the timing of upcoming tasks to ensure that the schedule stays on track.

You'll start learning about scheduling tasks in Project in Lesson 4, "Set Up the Project and Tasks."

Calculate Costs

Project helps you determine your budget. The majority of most project costs come from team members, with additional costs from equipment, materials, and travel expenses. In Project, you enter the resources required to carry out the tasks, the resources' cost per hour or per unit, and when and how much they will be needed (see Figure 2.2).

Then when you assign the resources to tasks, Project calculates the cost for the task based on the cost for the assigned resources. As shown in Figure 2.3, these costs roll up in your project plan to show overall project costs.

FIGURE 2.2   The Resource Sheet in Project

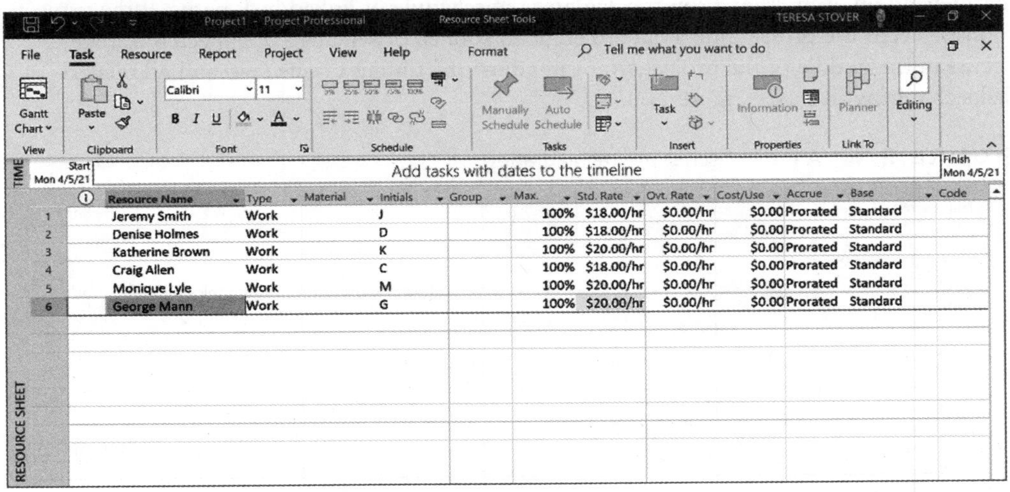

FIGURE 2.3   Task and project costs

Task Name	Duration	Start	Finish	Cost	Resource Names
▲ Lesson2 TrainingPlan	96 days	Wed 1/5/22	Wed 5/18/22	$10,064.00	
▲ Create Plan	20 days	Wed 1/5/22	Tue 2/1/22	$2,960.00	
Determine training needs	8 days	Wed 1/5/22	Fri 1/14/22	$1,152.00	Jeremy Smith
Analyze audience	4 days	Mon 1/17/22	Thu 1/20/22	$640.00	George Mann
Brainstorm training topics	4 days	Fri 1/21/22	Wed 1/26/22	$576.00	Denise Holmes
Organize training topics	2 days	Thu 1/27/22	Fri 1/28/22	$288.00	Denise Holmes
Determine training modules	1 day	Mon 1/31/22	Mon 1/31/22	$160.00	Katherine Brown
Present training proposal	1 day	Tue 2/1/22	Tue 2/1/22	$144.00	Jeremy Smith
▲ Develop Module 1	46 days	Wed 2/2/22	Wed 4/6/22	$7,104.00	
Research Module 1 topics	1 wk	Wed 2/2/22	Tue 2/8/22	$800.00	George Mann
Write Module 1 topics	2 wks	Wed 2/9/22	Tue 2/22/22	$1,600.00	George Mann
Test Module 1 topics	2 days	Wed 2/23/22	Thu 2/24/22	$288.00	Denise Holmes

As you enter actual progress on tasks, Project updates the costs so you can see actual costs so far and projected costs through to the end of the project. If the project is veering beyond the original project budget, you can adjust the plan to bring the project back under budget.

You'll learn about setting up costs in Lesson 6, "Set Up Resources," in the section titled "Enter Resource Costs."

Balance Resources

Project helps you keep a close eye on how your resources are used over the span of the project. After you assign resources to tasks, you can see when specific resources are overloaded or underused. You can then adjust the project plan to change resource assignments, adjust the schedule, or change the project scope to even out resource usage.

When you're first planning the project, seeing this overall resource picture can help you develop the resource plan, including the types of team members needed, how many team members with specific skills should be recruited, when they're needed, and who might have ramp-up and ramp-down periods. Your plan might also include equipment and materials needed to carry out tasks.

When the project is under way, being able to see and adjust your resource needs and allocations over time can help you use your resources—and therefore your budget—most effectively, avoiding downtime at one extreme and burnout at the other.

You'll start learning about resource planning and optimizing in Lesson 7, "Assign Resources to Tasks."

Communicate Progress

From sharing expectations with team members to updating status with stakeholders, clear and steady communication is essential to successful project management. You can use the built-in Project views, reports, and dashboards as is, or customize them as needed to share the most relevant information with your different audiences. For example, see the built-in Project Overview dashboard in Figure 2.4.

FIGURE 2.4   The Project Overview dashboard

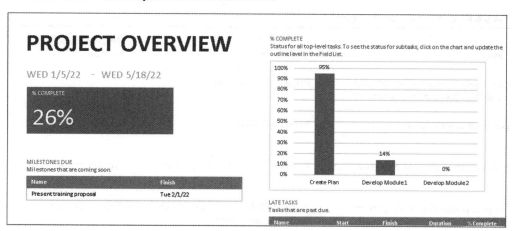

You'll learn about views and reports in Lesson 10, "View Project Information," and Lesson 11, "Report Project Information."

Respond to Changes

Some say that project management is essentially change management. When you create your project plan with the task schedule, assigned resources, and costs in place, it's only that—a plan. All the pieces are in exactly the right place, and the plan shows how you'll accomplish the project scope by the desired finish date and within the allotted budget. The plan reflects the perfect ideal. After you start executing the project in real life, however, things begin changing, and the project plan is no longer perfect.

For example, say a team member you were told would be available in May is not free until July. Materials that were estimated at $940 now cost $1,500. The project sponsor who originally agreed to a finish date of December 15 now insists on October 15.

These types of changes are inevitable, and they challenge your best efforts as a project manager. With Project, you can adjust various aspects of the project to compensate for these changes. If you have several choices to respond to a change, you might even run what-if scenarios in Project. You can then present the pros and cons of the scenarios to the team or other stakeholders to decide on the best course of action.

You'll learn techniques for responding to project changes in Lesson 8, "Check and Adjust the Project."

Microsoft Project Solutions

Microsoft Project is available in online cloud-based *subscription editions* and on-premises desktop *perpetual (nonsubscription) editions*. Table 2.1 lays out these choices.

TABLE 2.1 Microsoft Project Editions

Level	Online Editions	On-premises Editions
Basic work management and simple project management	Project for the web	
Basic project management	Project Online	Project Standard 2021
Professional project management	Project Online Desktop Client	Project Professional 2021
Project portfolio management (PPM)	Project Online with portfolio management features	Project Server

Project for the Web   Includes basic work management and project management features. With its intuitive design and rich collaboration features, it's meant for people who need to get their project up and running quickly and share project information easily with team members. Experience as a professional project manager or with Microsoft Project is not necessary. Built on the Microsoft Power Platform, work is done in a web browser (see Figure 2.5). Project for the web is an online subscription product.

FIGURE 2.5   Project for the web

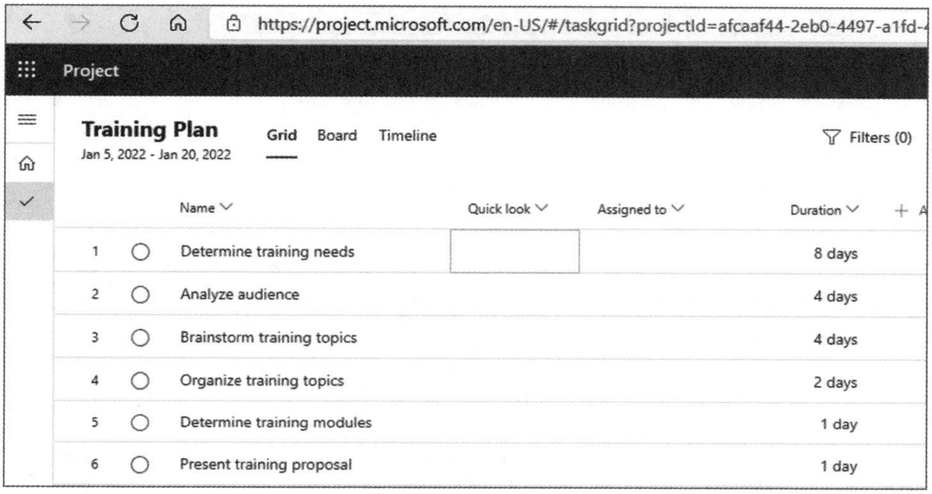

Project Online   A more robust edition of Project designed for online collaboration. Built on SharePoint, in previous versions it was known as Project Web App. Work is done in a web browser. Project Online is an online subscription product.

Project Online Desktop Client   A professional, full-featured edition of Project. This edition (see Figure 2.6) is similar to the Project Professional desktop app. Project Online Desktop Client is an online subscription product.

Project Online with Portfolio Management Features   Is scalable from regular work and project management up to enterprise-level *project portfolio management (PPM)*. This solution includes demand management, enterprise resource management, and portfolio analysis and optimization. This edition is best suited for organizations that use a centralized *project management office (PMO)* and prefer an online subscription product.

Project Standard 2021   The basic project management application installed on the project manager's desktop on the organization's premises; it is a one-time purchase rather than a subscription.

Project Professional 2021   The full-featured, comprehensive application for professional project managers who prefer an on-premises desktop nonsubscription solution.

Project Server   Is scalable from regular work and project management up to enterprise-level PPM. Features include demand management, enterprise resource management, and portfolio analysis and optimization. This edition is best suited for organizations that use a centralized PMO and prefer an on-premises desktop nonsubscription solution.

FIGURE 2.6 Project Online Desktop Client

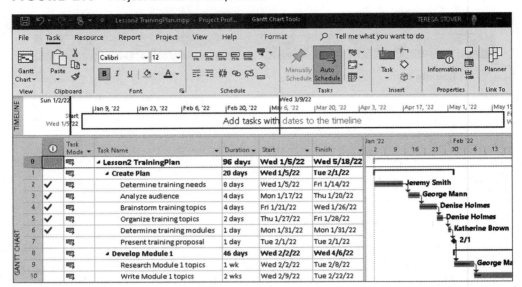

For more information about the features and prices of the various Microsoft Project editions, go to https://www.microsoft.com/en-us/microsoft-365/project/compare-microsoft-project-management-software.

Touring the Microsoft Project App

Now that you've learned how Project can help you manage projects and the different Microsoft Project solutions, it's time to actually open it up and take a look.

To start up Microsoft Project:

1. Start Project.

For example, if you're working with a Windows 10 system, click the **Start** button and then click **Project**.

2. In the opening Project screen that appears, click **Blank Project**.

A new, blank Gantt Chart view appears, as shown in Figure 2.7. Take a look at the columns in the sheet on the left and the timeline on the right side of the view.

Throughout this book, the procedures and examples are based on Microsoft Project Online Desktop Client as implemented in October 2021, running on Windows 10. If you're using this or the Microsoft Project Professional desktop app, your experience will be similar to what's shown and described in this book.

FIGURE 2.7   Gantt Chart

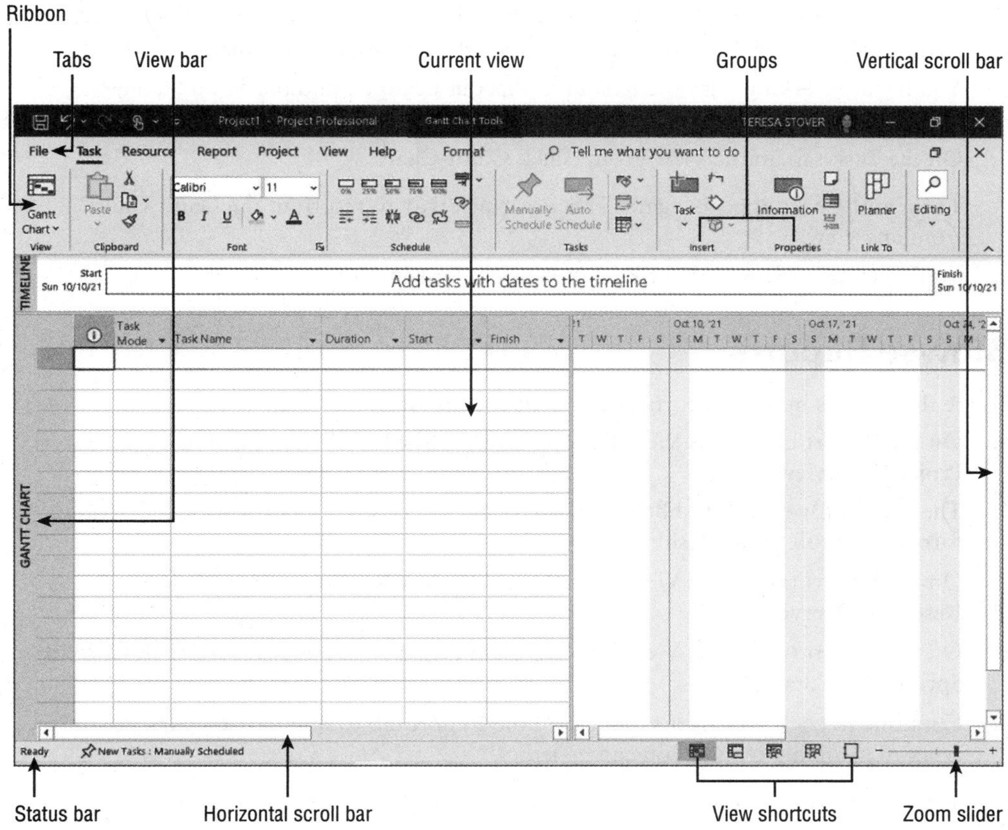

Browse Task and Resource Views

To see the list of Project views and switch between them:

1.   On the Task tab, in the View group, click the arrow under Gantt Chart. It's in the upper-left corner of the Project window.

2.   From the drop-down menu of project views, choose **Task Sheet**.

     The Task Sheet replaces the Gantt Chart and is similar to the sheet side of the Gantt Chart.

3.   On the Task tab, in the View group, click the arrow under Gantt Chart, then select **Task Board** from the list of project views.

     The Task Board view replaces the Task Sheet view. This is a task board, also known as a Kanban board, often used in agile project management.

     You'll start working with the Gantt Chart, Task Sheet, and Task Board in Lesson 4.

4. On the left side of the Project window, right-click the vertical **Task Board** label.

5. In the list of views that appears, click **Resource Sheet**.

6. Right-click the vertical **Resource Sheet label**, then click **Team Planner**.

   You'll start working with the Resource Sheet in Lesson 6 and the Team Planner in Lesson 8.

7. On the Task tab, in the View group, click **Gantt Chart**.

   The Gantt Chart appears again. This is a quick way to return to the Gantt Chart from any view.

   You'll get more details about Project views in Lesson 10.

Browse Reports

To see the various built-in reports and formatting options:

1. On the Report tab, in the View Reports group, click **Dashboards,** then click **Project Overview.**

   The Project Overview dashboard appears, and the Design ribbon appears for you to format the look of the dashboard.

2. On the Report tab, in the View Reports group, click **Resources,** then click **Resource Overview.**

3. On the Report tab, in the View Reports group, click **Task Boards,** then click **Current Sprint - Task Status.**

4. Continue to click on various reports on the Report tab to familiarize yourself with the types of available reports you can generate.

   You'll learn more about running built-in and custom reports in Lesson 11.

Click Through the Ribbons

To orient yourself to the location of feature categories, click through the ribbons as suggested here:

1. Click the **Task** tab and review the ribbon.

   The Task ribbon holds features and functions that you can use to work with tasks selected in the current view.

2. Click the **Resource** tab and review the ribbon.

   The Resource ribbon holds features and functions that you can use to work with resources selected in the current view.

3. Click the **Project** tab and review the ribbon.

   The **Project** ribbon holds functions that you can use to manage information about the project as a whole.

4. Click the **View** tab and review the ribbon.

    You can use the View ribbon to switch to a different view or manipulate data in the view.

5. Click the **Help** tab and review the ribbon.

    The Help ribbon includes the Help button, training resources, and information about new features.

6. Click the **Format** tab and review the ribbon.

    The content of the Format ribbon changes, depending on the current view showing.

    If a report is showing, the Design tab appears instead of the Format tab. The content of the Design ribbon changes depending on the current report showing.

Go Backstage

As with other Microsoft Office applications, you use the Backstage view to manage your Project files, your account, and your application options.

To familiarize yourself with the Project Backstage:

1. Click the **File** tab and review the Project Backstage (see Figure 2.8).

FIGURE 2.8   Project Backstage

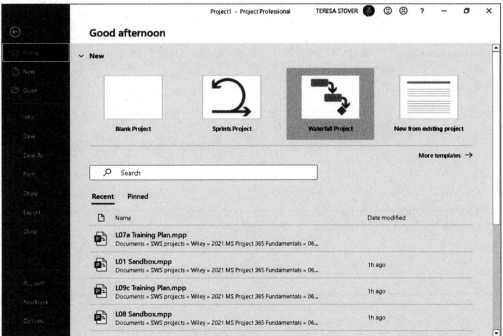

The left pane shows the standard Backstage commands, including Open, Save, and Print.

The Home page shows templates for a new project and a list of recent projects that you've worked with.

2. Near the bottom of the Project Backstage command pane, click **Account**.

The Account window shows your user information, your Project subscription information (if applicable), and information about updates and your license.

3. At the bottom of the Backstage command pane, click **Options**.

The Project Options dialog box appears, as shown in Figure 2.9. This is where you set your preferences for the appearance and behavior of various features throughout Project. Some options apply to the current Project file; others apply to any Project file globally.

FIGURE 2.9 Project Options

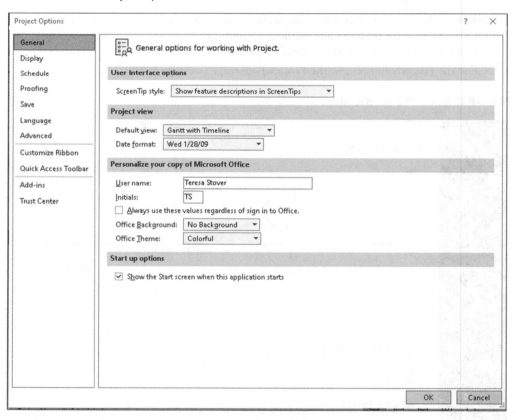

4. Click through the commands on the left side of the dialog box to get an idea of the types of preferences you can set.

You'll learn about many of these options in context throughout this book's lessons.

Get Help with Project

After you've learned Project fundamentals highlighted in this book, you can continue to broaden and deepen your knowledge of Project.

Help Within Project

When you're working in your project plan and you have a quick question or get stuck on something, you can get assistance without leaving Project.

Help   On the Help tab, click **Help**. A pane appears on the right side of your Project window (see Figure 2.10). Enter a search phrase in the Search Help box or click through the list of categories to find the Help topic you need to complete a task with your plan.

FIGURE 2.10   The Help pane

Tell Me What You Want To Do   To the right of the ribbon tabs is the Tell Me What You Want To Do control (see Figure 2.11).

FIGURE 2.11   The Tell Me What You Want To Do control

Type a phrase in that box, and you'll get a list of actions to do what you're asking, or a Help topic to tell you more, as shown in Figure 2.12. Click the action to do it right away, or click the **Help** topic to learn the steps. Finding the action is most helpful when you know the function is there somewhere, but you can't remember how to get there.

FIGURE 2.12   Actions and help offered

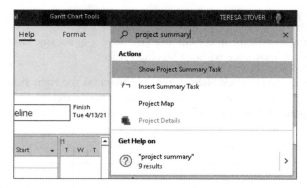

ScreenTips   Hold your mouse pointer over a ribbon command, a column heading, or other element on the Project window, and a ScreenTip will briefly tell you what that element does.

What's New   If you're using the Microsoft Project Online Desktop Client, your subscription brings you periodic updates to the software. To see what has changed and how you might use those changes, on the Help tab, click **What's New**. Information about the latest feature update will appear in the Help pane.

If you're using the nonsubscription version of Project, the What's New command will list the features new and changed since the previous version.

Account Information   You can review your Project product information, manage your account, change your license, and review your account profile. Click the **File** tab, and then click **Account**.

Feedback   On the Help tab, click **Feedback** to communicate with the folks at Microsoft. Click **I Like Something** or **I Don't Like Something** to enter a comment. You can optionally add a screenshot or your email address if you want as well. When you click **Submit,** your comment goes to the Microsoft Project team for consideration in a future enhancement.

To make a suggestion, on the Help tab, click **Feedback,** and then click **I Have a Suggestion.** Type your idea in the box, and add a screenshot or email address if you want (see Figure 2.13).

FIGURE 2.13   Feedback to Microsoft pane

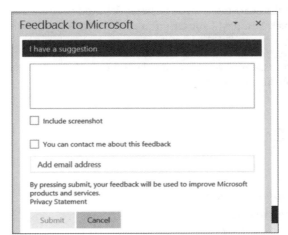

Help Outside Project

Here are some good sources of Project information beyond the boundaries of the application.

Project Help & Learning   This Microsoft support site includes articles, visuals, videos, and training for the various Microsoft Project editions. Categories include Get Started, Collaborate, Projects & Tasks, Resources, Reporting, Troubleshoot, and more. Check out https://support.microsoft.com/en-us/project.

Microsoft Project Blog   The Project Blog posts best practices, news, and trends from the Microsoft Project team. Check out https://techcommunity.microsoft.com/t5/project-blog/bg-p/ProjectBlog.

Microsoft Project Support Community   The Project Support blog includes articles, tips, and tricks about working with Project from the Microsoft Project user community. Review existing questions and answers, or post a new question to the group. Many questions are answered by Most Valuable Professionals (MVPs) who are Project experts who do not work for Microsoft. Check out https://techcommunity.microsoft.com/t5/project-support-blog/bg-p/ProjectSupport.

Microsoft Project User Group (MPUG)   This is a non-Microsoft community of project managers and Microsoft Project users. The organization provides member benefits including webinars, newsletters, events, and opportunities to earn professional development units (PDUs) toward your certifications. Check out www.mpug.com.

Video Learning Programs   Find Microsoft Project video training programs on platforms like LinkedIn Learning (`https://www.linkedin.com/learning`) and Udemy (`www.udemy.com`). You pay a subscription to the learning platform and/or a charge per course.

With learning and assistance resources inside and outside the Project app, you'll continue to learn how to use Project to effectively manage your projects.

Key Terms

editions

perpetual (nonsubscription) edition

project management knowledge areas

project management office (PMO)

project portfolio management (PPM)

subscription edition

Review Questions

1. How does Microsoft Project help with project scheduling?

    A. By helping you clearly define project scope and requirements, Project ensures that the project will finish on time.

    B. You can use Project to create the plan with tasks, durations, and linked dependencies.

    C. When a task starts or finishes late, or its duration changes, you can adjust that task and the schedule of the other linked tasks adjusts automatically.

    D. B and C

    E. A and C

2. Besides scheduling, what are two other ways in which Microsoft Project can help you manage projects?

    A. Balancing resources and mitigating risk

    B. Tracking costs and communicating progress

    C. Managing project procurements and responding to changes

    D. Setting quality specifications and tracking issues

3. Your team is geographically diverse, energetic, and highly collaborative, working on several small but fast-paced projects and other tasks at a time. You need a web-based solution that's quick and easy to learn and use to assign, manage, and track tasks. Which is the best Microsoft Project edition for your needs?

    A. Project Standard

    B. Project Online with portfolio management features

    C. Project for the web

    D. Project Server

4. You'll be managing a three-year project that will have hundreds of tasks, dozens of resources from different sources, and substantial cost-reporting requirements. You want a professional project management app that's always up to date. Which is the best Project edition for you?

    A. Project for the web

    B. Project Standard

    C. Project Professional

    D. Project Online Desktop Client

5. The main screen of the Project window is the:

    A. Current ribbon with features and functions that operate on the selected tasks or resources.

    B. Current view showing some aspect of project information, like tasks or resources.

    C. Current report showing the project overview dashboard.

    D. Kanban board showing task cards categorized by current status.

6. What appears when you type a phrase in the Tell Me What You Want To Do box located next to the ribbon tabs?

    A. The action you want to do in Project or a Help topic about how to do it

    B. A short tip about the screen element that's currently selected

    C. A comment box for submitting your issue to the Microsoft Project team

    D. A discussion post from the Project Support community where you can find answers to your question

Plan Your Project

Lesson 3

Establish a Strong Foundation

LESSON OBJECTIVES

✓ List the components of the initiating process of a project.

✓ Identify at least three types of project stakeholders.

✓ Name at least three elements of the project charter.

✓ Name at least three methods for learning potential project requirements.

✓ Identify at least three elements of the project scope statement.

✓ Explain the differences between the project charter and the scope statement.

✓ Decide on the best way to organize project plan documents and make them accessible to the stakeholders.

When you're assigned a new project, you might feel the enthusiasm or the pressure from others to immediately jump straight in and lay out tasks and responsibilities.

It can certainly be more fun—at least at first—to "plan first and ask questions later." It's all fun and games until you find out you're heading in the wrong direction or that the higher-ups weren't seriously committing to this project after all.

To prevent wasting precious time and money caused by having to double back and rework, when you take on a new project (or even inherit an existing one) one of your first jobs as a project manager is to get the powers that be to take a deep breath and think carefully about what this project is all about.

What's the source of this idea? What problem is it expected to solve? What will the project do and not do? How will you know if the project is successful? Who's paying for it?

In this lesson, you'll learn the important steps of initiating the project through preplanning. This entails identifying the stakeholders, including the project sponsor; writing the project charter and having it approved; collecting the project requirements; and defining the project scope.

You'll also determine the best approach for organizing your important project-planning documents, which can live within or beyond the boundaries of Microsoft Project. The key is to keep your project documents accessible for ready reference as you move through the processes and phases of your project.

Initiate the Project

The *initiating process* is the first of the six project life-cycle stages, or *project processes*. In this process, an initial idea grows into a project, in which the project charter is written and authorized, the stakeholders and project sponsor are identified, and you are assigned as project manager.

The steps in the initiating process can be formal or informal, depending on your organization's practices, the size of the project, and whether it's an agile or a waterfall project. However they're implemented, make no assumptions. Rather, be sure to define, document, and get approval for all these steps.

Identify the Stakeholders and Project Sponsor

Project *stakeholders* are the people who will be involved with the project or who hold some kind of "stake" in the successful outcomes of the project.

Project Sponsor　　This is the organizational executive or external customer who is funding the project costs. The *project sponsor* is often the person who conceived the project idea and is most interested in the project progress, deliverables, and outcomes. The sponsor will sign off on the project charter, clarify the scope, review progress, and influence others in support of the project.

Project Manager　　That's you—the person who is assigned the overall responsibility for planning, executing, monitoring, controlling, and closing the project. You set up and execute the project plan, secure and manage the project team and other resources carrying out the project tasks, track and report on progress toward deliverables and milestones, monitor costs, and adjust the project for changing conditions, all while moving toward a successful completion by the established finish date.

Managing Stakeholders　　These are leaders who have a management responsibility associated with the project. The project sponsor and project manager are two *managing stakeholders*, but there might be others. Examples might include department heads who are affected by the use of their team members on the project or who will review specific project deliverables.

Team Members　　Team members are those who will be assigned to project task responsibilities. You might not have a complete list at this stage, but you can identify names and job functions or titles, or just job functions or skill sets that will be required by the project. This information can help with high-level project and cost estimating.

Customers and End Users　　These are the people who stand to benefit from the results of the project. End users might (or might not) be directly consulted throughout the project. Either way, name them as a stakeholder category and consider developing customer profiles or user stories to keep their wants and needs in mind as you and the team work through the project.

Authorize the Project Charter

The *project charter* is like the project's mission statement. It's typically a two-page project overview document that concisely defines the project goal and other high-level parameters of the project.

The project charter formalizes the project, even in an informal organization. It can be invaluable to clarify when an organization executive or customer might have just been "thinking out loud" versus giving a real directive about a true commitment to a project.

Rather like an internal contract, the project charter names and authorizes the project manager and is signed by the project sponsor. The project charter can serve as the "North Star" when matters get murky.

Because the project charter is probably the first document generated for the new project, many unknowns are likely. Between this fact and the conciseness of the document, the more high level and broad the charter, the better it will serve everyone in the long run.

The project charter should include the following:

Project Goal   States the purpose or business case justification of the project and characteristics of the product or service being produced.

Objectives   List measurable objectives to meet the goal, along with a summary milestone schedule, including the overall project finish date.

High-Level Requirements   Describe the characteristics of the end product or service and summarize the project requirements in terms of time, quality, and scope. This or a separate section might also list known project risks, constraints, or issues.

Project Outcomes   Identify measurable success criteria to know when and whether the project has achieved its intended goal.

Overview Budget   Can be a single overall expected budget total or identify high-level budget categories for the project.

Stakeholders   Include the name, title, and responsibilities of the project sponsor and project manager, including their level of authority; managing stakeholders; project team members; and customers or end users.

Project Approval Requirements   Identify any interim review and approval points during the project and final project acceptance and sign-off upon project close.

Project Charter Authorization   Includes the signatures of responsible project stakeholders, especially the project sponsor and project manager. When the project charter is completed and signed, the project manager can move forward with budget and other resource authorization to start project planning and execution.

Drafting the project charter ensures that the project is not left to assumption or chance. As the project springboard, it's the first step in communicating expectations with your boss, the customer, or other project sponsor.

Start Planning

With authorization in hand, you can now take the time to drill down and detail the project requirements and scope that are broadly outlined in the project charter.

If you haven't done so already, this is the right time to decide whether the project will follow the agile or the waterfall project management methodology (refer back to Lesson 1, "Project Management Basics"). Which one you choose will determine how detailed your requirements and scope must be.

Then, after you finish the initiating process, your chosen methodology will determine how you'll build the project and how you'll use Microsoft Project beginning in Lesson 4, "Set Up the Project and Tasks."

Collect Requirements

Your project typically develops a new product, service, or other result. Requirements specify the condition or capability that a product or service must achieve in terms of function, features, technical specifications, quality standards, performance, or other characteristics.

In addition to *product requirements*, you have *project requirements* like the all-important total cost and finish date. By defining both types of requirements, you are managing customer expectations as well as gathering the information you'll need to develop the project's *work breakdown structure (WBS)* as the list of requirements become the focus of the project work.

Developing detailed requirements before starting the project is essential in a waterfall project. However, because of the agile project's nature of exploration and discovery, requirements can be broader and loosely defined, more as a starting point. Requirements are defined and reprioritized throughout the course of multiple project sprints, deliverables, and feedback loops.

In either case, identifying requirements is key to project success, because the final outcomes of the project are measured against the defined requirements. In the majority of projects that exceed budget or schedule, that are canceled, or that otherwise fail to meet their goals, the reason tracks back to issues relating to requirements.

The first step is to gather a list of potential requirements. Consider the following to tease out requirements with users and other stakeholders:

- Brainstorming
- Interviews
- Questionnaires
- Reviewing existing documentation
- Observing end users in their relevant tasks
- Mapping the as-is state for the existing product or service
- Prototyping

You might find prototyping an especially valuable deliverable in either an agile or a waterfall project. Whether it's a small-scale product, mockup, or simulation, you can present prototypes to your stakeholders at strategic points of a project to validate the requirements and make decisions and adjustments accordingly.

After you develop the list of requirements, work with your stakeholders to review and prioritize the requirements. A good method is to work with the group to reach consensus on the highest-value requirements. Then together rank those requirements in their priority order. This way, you and your stakeholders can finalize the requirements that will drive this project.

Define the Scope

Whereas the project charter is a high-level project overview that authorizes project implementation, the *project scope* is a more detailed version of much of the same information, laying out the parameters of the project.

In a waterfall project, the scope defines the boundaries of a project, not only saying what the project will accomplish but also indicating what the project will *not* do. Articulating these boundaries is essential to preventing *scope creep*, a common problem for waterfall projects. Throughout a project, team members and managing stakeholders often see opportunities for innovations or enhancements related to the work being done. The temptation is great to include these changes, which often seem inconsequential and easy to manage. These small changes beyond the specified scope can gradually creep up and have a cumulative effect, which results in project delays and cost overruns. Defining the scope well and keeping a close eye on its boundaries throughout the project is a key to project management success.

In an agile project, on the other hand, scope is continually refined throughout the life of the project with its iterative sprints. Because scope is expected to change and adjust throughout an agile project, scope creep is not an issue.

While the project charter is finished and "locked in" as soon as it's signed and therefore authorized, the project scope is a living document. Expect to update the project scope as conditions change and decisions are made throughout the project life cycle.

The project scope should include the following:

Project Scope   Specifies what is and is not included in the project. In this way, this section indicates the boundaries of the project.

Requirements   Define the conditions that must be met for the project sponsor to accept the project's deliverables.

Deliverables   List and describe all tangible or intangible goods or services produced for the project.

Project Constraints   Indicate any limitations on the project such as time, money, or resources.

Assumptions   Enumerate anything assumed but not definitely known about the project parameters.

The project scope statement defines the project's goals, requirements, and boundaries. It's typically presented to not only the project sponsor but also to the team leads and other project stakeholders as the "what" of the project. The "how" of the project is presented in the next step as the project plan and schedule.

Because the project scope defines the requirements and deliverables, it helps stakeholders determine where the project is in the process and whether the project is complete and has satisfied its objective.

Organize Project Plan Documents

You'll draft the project charter, stakeholders list, requirements, and project scope statement in a word processing document or other document outside of Microsoft Project. Determine who needs access to these key project planning documents and how best to organize and provide access. Here are some options:

- Using a network drive that managing stakeholders have access to

- Using a cloud drive (such as OneDrive or Google Drive) and giving stakeholders access

- Creating a SharePoint site that contains all key project documents

- Storing project documents as attachments to your project plan in Microsoft Project

To attach a document to a Project plan:

1. Open the Project plan.

2. If necessary, add the project summary task. On the Format tab, in the Show/Hide group, click **Project Summary Task**.

   The project summary task appears as the first task in the plan, as shown in Figure 3.1.

FIGURE 3.1   The Project summary task

Task Name	Duration	Start	Finish
03 TrainingPlan	**96 days**	**Wed 1/5/22**	**Wed 5/18/22**
⁴ **Create Plan**	**20 days**	**Wed 1/5/22**	**Tue 2/1/22**
Determine training needs	8 days	Wed 1/5/22	Fri 1/14/22
Analyze audience	4 days	Mon 1/17/22	Thu 1/20/22
Brainstorm training topics	4 days	Fri 1/21/22	Wed 1/26/22
Organize training topics	2 days	Thu 1/27/22	Fri 1/28/22
Determine training modules	1 day	Mon 1/31/22	Mon 1/31/22
Present training proposal	1 day	Tue 2/1/22	Tue 2/1/22
⁴ **Develop Module 1**	**46 days**	**Wed 2/2/22**	**Wed 4/6/22**
Research Module 1 topics	1 wk	Wed 2/2/22	Tue 2/8/22
Write Module 1 topics	2 wks	Wed 2/9/22	Tue 2/22/22

Project summary task → points to 03 TrainingPlan row

3. Double-click the project summary task to open the Summary Task Information dialog box.

4. Click the **Notes** tab.

5. In the toolbar under Notes, click **Insert Object**.

6. Click **Create from File**, then click **Browse**.

7. Navigate to the location of the file you want to attach to the project plan, then click **Insert**.

8. In the Insert Object dialog box, select the **Display As Icon** check box, then click **OK**.

   The document is attached as an icon in the Summary Task Information dialog box, as shown in Figure 3.2.

FIGURE 3.2   The Project document is attached to the project file.

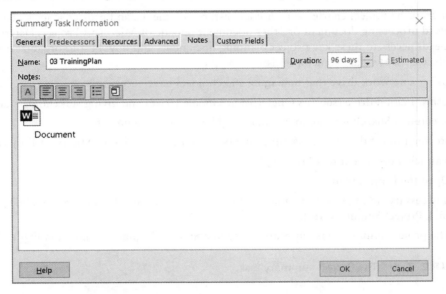

9. Click **OK** again.

   A note icon appears in the Indicator field next to the project summary task (see Figure 3.3). Double-click the note icon whenever you want to open the attached document.

FIGURE 3.3   The note icon indicating the attached project file.

	①	Task Mode ▾	Task Name ▾	Duration ▾	Start ▾	Finish ▾
0	📄	🖥	◢ **03 TrainingPlan**	**96 days**	**Wed 1/5/22**	**Wed 5/18/22**
1		🖥	◢ **Create Plan**	**20 days**	**Wed 1/5/22**	**Tue 2/1/22**
2		🖥	Determine training needs	8 days	Wed 1/5/22	Fri 1/14/22
3		🖥	Analyze audience	4 days	Mon 1/17/22	Thu 1/20/22

Note icon on project summary task

Whether you attach the project charter or scope document to the Microsoft Project plan file or store it separately on a network drive, cloud drive, or elsewhere, make sure it's available for ready reference by you and other stakeholders who might need access to the document.

Key Terms

initiating process

managing stakeholders

product requirements

project charter

project processes

project requirements

project scope

project sponsor

scope creep

stakeholders

work breakdown structure (WBS)

Review Questions

1. What are the components of the project initiating process?

   A. The stakeholder list, including the project manager and project sponsor, and the project charter

   B. The project plan, including the schedule and resource plan, and work and material resources

   C. The first progress report and team member timesheet, including titles and hourly rates

   D. The project dashboard showing the overview, and the cost analysis report listing the task and overall project costs

2. Which type of project stakeholder authorizes the project charter, including project funding?

   A. Project manager

   B. Department manager

   C. Project sponsor

   D. Resource manager

3. What are three characteristics of the project charter?

   A. Details the project and product requirements, is signed by the project manager, and is stored on the organization's SharePoint site

   B. States the project goal and objectives, is signed by one of the principal managing stakeholders, and is a permanent document

   C. Includes end-user interviews, details the work breakdown structure, and is signed by the project sponsor

   D. Includes the work breakdown structure, details the project resource plan, and is signed by the relevant department head

4. What are three characteristics of the project scope statement?

   A. Includes documentation about the existing product or service, and involves the schedule of sprints and the project organization chart

   B. Includes the prototype specification, contract with the project sponsor, and stakeholder list

   C. Ranks potential team members by preference and recruitment priority, defines project and product requirements, and describes potential risks

   D. Specifies what is and is not included in the project, defines the project and product requirements, and lists all project deliverables

5. What are good methods for organizing project documents?

   A. Attach them to your Microsoft Project plan.

   B. Upload them to a SharePoint site.

   C. Upload them to a network drive or cloud drive.

   D. All of the above

Lesson

4

Set Up the Project and Tasks

LESSON OBJECTIVES

✓ Create and save a project plan, including a project start date.

✓ Describe three types of task views in Project.

✓ Demonstrate switching from one task view to another.

✓ Enter and edit tasks in the Task Sheet.

✓ Insert and delete tasks in the Task Sheet.

✓ Enter, edit, and delete tasks on the Task Board.

✓ Identify at least three Project views designed for agile projects.

✓ Rearrange tasks in the Task Sheet and Task Board.

✓ Structure a task outline with summary tasks and subtasks.

With your project charter, requirements, and scope established, you're now ready to lay out your project plan. This lesson sees you starting a new project plan in Microsoft Project, entering and sequencing the project tasks, and establishing the outline structure of your task list.

Start a New Project Plan

You can choose from one of three good ways to start a new project plan:

- Create a new blank project. Starting from scratch gives you a clean slate and control for building the project to reflect your vision.

- Copy an existing similar project. This can give you a head start in brainstorming the tasks needed and how they relate to one another, especially if the other project was done within your organization.

- Use a template that reflects your project type. This can help you determine which tasks and task relationships apply to your project and also can highlight industry best practices.

Create a New Blank Project

To start a new project plan from a blank project:

1. Start Microsoft Project.

   The Project Home page appears as shown in Figure 4.1.

2. Click **Blank Project**.

   A new blank project plan appears (see Figure 4.2).

To save the new blank project plan:

1. On the File tab, click **Save As**.

2. Click **Browse**, then navigate to the drive and folder where you want to save your new project.

3. In the File Name box, change the filename to something more descriptive that works with your organization's file-naming conventions as applicable.

4. Click the **Save** button.

FIGURE 4.1   The Project Home page

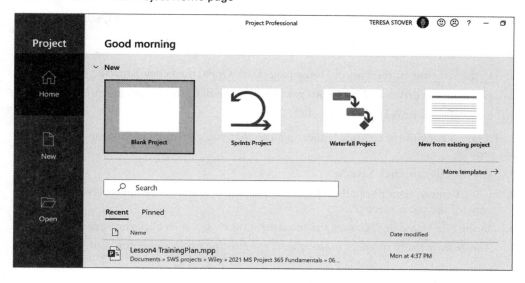

FIGURE 4.2   A new blank project plan

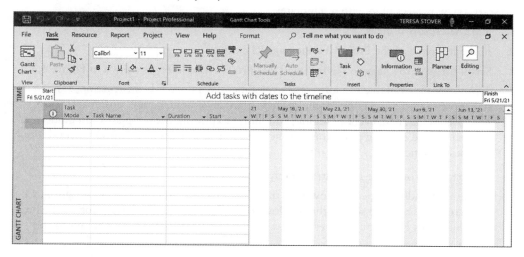

Copy an Existing Similar Project

Maybe someone else has used Project to create a project plan similar to the one you're starting. This project plan might include tasks and other structures that you can use as a starting point to save you some time in creating your new project.

To start a new project plan from an existing similar project:

1. Make sure the old project plan is accessible to you, either on your computer's hard drive or on your organization's network drive.

2. Start Microsoft Project.

3. In the left pane of the Project Home page, click **Open**, then click **Browse**.

4. Navigate the drives and folders to get to where the old project plan is stored.

5. Select the old project plan, then click **Open**.

To save a copy of the existing project plan so that you can adapt it without changing the old project:

1. On the File tab, click **Save As**.

2. Click **Browse**, then navigate to the drive and folder where you want to save your new copy of the old project.

3. In the File Name box, change the filename if necessary, then click the **Save** button.

You're now ready to adapt your copy of the existing project plan for your new project.

Adapt a Project Template

To start a new project plan with a template:

1. Start Microsoft Project.

2. In the left pane of the Project Home page, click **New**.

3. Scroll through the page to see the available Project templates, as shown in Figure 4.3.

   Templates are available for software development, commercial construction, residential construction, market research, business plan development, new business startup, new product launch, event planning, and more. Exploring the templates can guide you toward a good starting point for your new project or at least give you some good ideas and best practices.

4. To browse through the templates, simply click on one.

   A pop-up window appears, showing a thumbnail picture and template description. Click the arrow on the right side of the window to see the picture and description of the next template. This gives you a closer look at several templates before you commit to the one you want.

5. When you find the template you want, in the template window click the **Create** button.

   The template opens.

FIGURE 4.3   Project templates

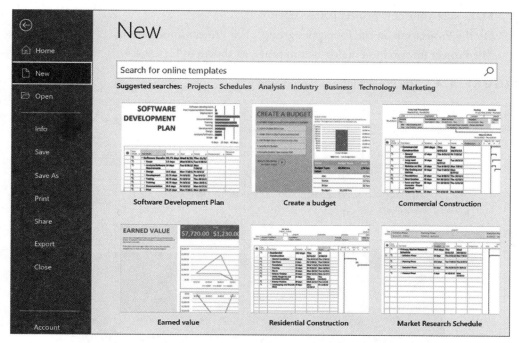

To save the template as your new project plan:

1. On the File tab, click **Save As**.

2. Click **Browse**, then navigate to the drive and folder where you want to save your new project.

3. In the File Name box, enter the filename.

4. Click the **Save** button.

Set the Project Start Date

With your new project plan created and saved, you're ready to start entering information about your project. The first bit of information your new project plan needs is the project start date. This date engages the Project scheduling engine, and the dates of the individual tasks you'll soon enter will be based on this project start date.

To set the project start date:

1. Make sure your new project plan is open.

2. On the Project tab, in the Properties group, click **Project Information**.

   The Project Information dialog box appears, as shown in Figure 4.4.

FIGURE 4.4   The Project Information dialog box

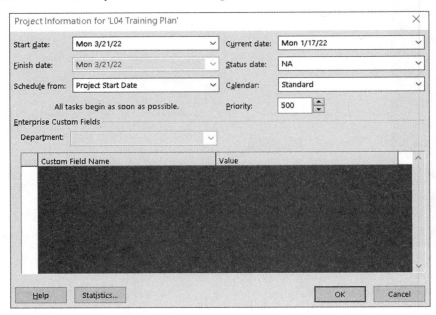

3. Be sure that the Schedule From box is set to Project Start Date.

> The other option is to schedule from the Project Finish Date. Using Project to schedule from the finish date is a more complex feature, and therefore you'll focus on scheduling from the Project Start Date here. It's true that you might often have the project finish date on your mind throughout a project, and especially when planning, there's often talk about "scheduling backwards from the finish date." You can use the finish date as a target you move toward and make sure you hit in your project planning as well as in project execution.

4. In the Start Date box, enter your project's start date. You can type the date or click the arrow in the box and select the date from the calendar.

   You can make the project start date earlier or later than today. The default start date is today's date.

5. Click **OK**.

The dialog box closes. Your project start date shows on the left edge of the Timeline view just below the ribbon. The project start date also shows in the timesheet portion of the Gantt Chart.

Enter Task Names

Now that you've created your Project file and entered the project start date, the next step is to enter the task names. Task names are the fundamental building blocks to your project, describing what exactly is being done in the project.

Project Building Blocks

Microsoft Project is a database that operates on and calculates your project schedule, costs, and resource allocation based on three major pieces of information, or records: *tasks*, *resources*, and *assignments*.

Tasks   Tasks are the units of work to be done to accomplish the project scope. Information you'll enter about each task will include the task name, whether it's a *summary task* or a *subtask* in a structured hierarchy of tasks, the task duration, how different tasks are related to each other, and the start and finish dates of the task. You'll learn how to enter and sequence tasks in this lesson, and you'll also structure tasks as summary tasks and subtasks. This lesson starts to answer the question, "What will be done?" In Lesson 5, "Build the Schedule," you'll enter task durations and link-related tasks together. You'll enter other time-related information that influences the task schedule, and therefore, the overall project schedule. This answers the question, "How long will it take?"

Resources   Resources are the people, equipment, and materials assigned to carry out the tasks. Information you'll enter about each resource will include the resource name, the cost of the resource, and the dates the resource is available. In Lesson 6, "Set Up Resources," you'll add resources to your project plan. This answers the question, "Who will do it?"

Assignments   Assignments are the intersection of resources assigned to tasks. When you assign a resource to a task, you create this intersection: the assignment. Information associated with the assignment includes the start and finish dates and the cost of the assignment itself. You'll start doing this in Lesson 7, "Assign Resources to Tasks." This answers the question, "Who's responsible for which tasks?"

Where Do Task Names Come From?

Task names start with the initiating process you carried out in Lesson 3, "Establish a Strong Foundation." That's where you collected requirements and defined the scope of the project. To develop your project tasks, start with your project scope and the ultimate outcome or deliverable that your project will produce. The components or phases you and your team will work through to produce that outcome become summary tasks in your project plan. The activities needed to accomplish those components or phases become your tasks or subtasks. You will continue to subdivide tasks into their bite-sized pieces in a hierarchy of tasks, which will all work together to achieve the project scope.

For example, suppose your project scope is the development of an online training program consisting of multiple self-paced modules. You can break that scope down into the following components:

- Plan the training.

- Develop the modules.

- Compile the modules in the learning management system.

- Release the training program online.

You continue to break each component down into tasks and subtasks until you get to a point where you have tasks at a manageable size that you, as the project manager, will be able to track and manage. In the online training program example, you could further break down the "Plan the training" task into the following subtasks:

- Analyze the audience.

- Assess the audience training needs.

- Identify the training topics.

- Evaluate and select the learning management system tools.

- Organize the content for the modules.

Another way to develop your tasks is to take a "bottom-up" approach, where you and your team brainstorm all the tasks at any level in the hierarchy. You collect all the tasks and enter them into Project. Then you sequence them and arrange them into their hierarchy.

Whether you take the top-down or the bottom-up approach to developing project tasks, remember to:

- Gather input from team members, stakeholders, and other experts for this type of project.

- Arrange the sequence and hierarchy to reflect your organization's phases and process for this project type.

- If you're reusing an existing project plan or template, add tasks and remove extraneous tasks to be sure the tasks fulfill your scope, which is your project's "North Star."

- Consider how detailed you want your tasks to be. A good rule of thumb is that a single task should take about 8–10 hours of effort. Any more than that and you might be missing other component tasks that should be tracked. Any less than that and it might take more of your management time than it's worth.

Work Breakdown Structure

The task list in your project plan is related, but not necessarily identical, to the *work breakdown structure (WBS)*, which is defined by the Project Management Body of Knowledge (PMBOK®) as a "deliverable-oriented hierarchical decomposition of the work to be executed by the project team."

Many organizations produce the WBS as part of the initiating process, because it helps the stakeholders understand all the components involved in the project scope and, therefore, helps estimate costs, including resource requirements. In this way, the WBS becomes essential to the project getting the green light to move forward to planning and scheduling.

If you developed a WBS as part of your initiating process, it will be easy to translate that to your project task list. If you have not yet developed a WBS, you can accomplish both at the same time when you develop your hierarchical task list in Project.

A WBS is often laid out as a flowchart, a table, or an outline, and these formats are all available as different Project views.

Name Your Tasks

When first entering your tasks, consider keeping your focus on the task name, sequence, and hierarchy. You can get hung up in extraneous details if you try to enter durations, dependencies, and resources while you're just beginning to develop the task list. If these bits of information suggest themselves to you easily, or if they're notes you don't want to forget later, then go ahead and enter them. But don't put the brakes on your work by researching those details. You'll fill those details in after the task list is refined.

When entering your task names, do your best to make them:

Descriptive   Make the task names descriptive enough to be meaningful, especially if the task names are seen out of context from the rest of the plan. Some views list tasks assigned to certain resources, or tasks that are due in the next week.

Unique   Having multiple tasks with the same name can become confusing, especially if you switch to a view that doesn't show the summary task. For example, if five training modules are being developed, you could have five instances of "Test topics." To make each instance unique while still being concise, you could add the module number to the task name, like "Test Module 1 topics."

Concise   Balance descriptive and unique task names with as much brevity as possible. The shorter your task names, the easier they will be to work with throughout the project.

Consistent   Develop a model for how you phrase your tasks. Consider imperative verb phrases ("Conduct needs assessment") or simple noun phrases ("Needs assessment"). Some project managers like to have one kind of phrase for summary tasks and another one for subtasks to indicate this is where the work is actually happening.

Explore Task Views

When you enter your tasks in Project, you can choose the view that reflects how you prefer to see your task list. When you first open a new Project file, the default view is the Gantt Chart, which combines a task list with a timescale. But with 29 *task views* in Project, you don't have to stay in the Gantt Chart. This is especially true when at first you're focusing on just the names and structure of the tasks, and not the scheduling, which is a major feature of the Gantt Chart.

Types of Task Views

While 29 task views can sound daunting, they're really variations of the following four types of views:

Gantt Views   These are a combination of a sheet view on the left side and a corresponding timescale/bar chart view on the right. Examples include the Gantt Chart and the Tracking Gantt.

Sheet Views   These show task information in a table or spreadsheet. Examples of *sheet views* include the Task Sheet and Sprint Planning Sheet.

Board Views   These show task information in boxes on a board, analogous to sticky notes on a whiteboard. Examples of *board views* include the Task Board and Sprint Board.

Specialized Task Views   These present different task layouts, for example, the Calendar, Network Diagram, Task Form, Task Entry combination view, and Task Usage view.

To see the list of all available views and switch to a different view:

1. On the View tab, in the Task Views group, click **Other Views**, and then click **More Views**.

   The More Views dialog box appears, as shown in Figure 4.5. Except for the Team Planner and the views whose names start with "Resource," all the views listed are task views.

2. Select a view, then click **Apply**.

   The selected view appears. Although different views show different types or layouts of task information, any tasks you've entered in Project will appear in any other task view. You never have to reenter task information just because you switch to a different view.

FIGURE 4.5   The More Views dialog box

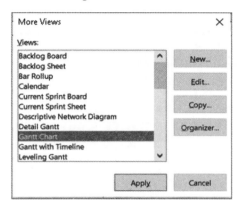

Work with Tasks in the Task Sheet

You can enter and work with tasks in the default Gantt Chart view, but you might find it easier and less distracting to enter them in the Task Sheet. The Task Sheet is like a spreadsheet of basic task information. You won't need the timescale view in the Gantt Chart until you start entering scheduling information.

After you have done your first pass in entering tasks, it's never set in stone. You can add, edit, or remove tasks as needed.

These procedures apply not only to the Task Sheet, but to any task view that has a table format—for example, any Gantt view, Task Usage view, and Backlog Sheet.

Enter Tasks in the Task Sheet

To switch to the Task Sheet and enter tasks:

1.   On the View tab, in the Task Views group, click **Other Views**, then click **Task Sheet**.

    The Task Sheet replaces the current view, as shown in Figure 4.6.

2.   Click in the first cell in the Task Name column, type your first task name, then press Enter.

    Don't worry about the exact sequence or hierarchy of tasks just yet. You'll adjust sequence and hierarchy in the next sections of this lesson. The priority now is to just enter your task names, in whatever order, and at the same *outline level* for now.

3.   To give yourself more room, widen the Task Name column. Position your mouse pointer at the right edge of the Task Name column heading until your pointer changes to a double-arrow icon. Drag the column edge to the right to make it the size you want.

    Because you're not entering anything in the other fields just yet, give yourself as much room as you like. Also note that longer task names will wrap to multiple lines if necessary.

FIGURE 4.6   The Task Sheet view

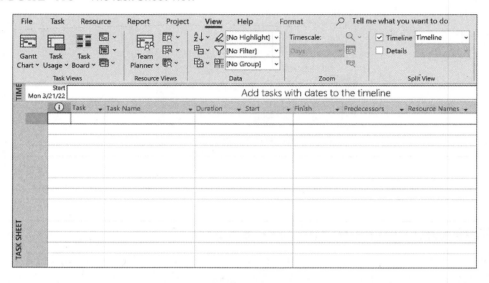

Enter a Column Width Value and Control Wrapping

You can enter rather than drag the column width, if you prefer. Click in any part of the Task Name column. On the Format tab, in the Columns group, click **Column Settings**, then click **Field Settings**. The dialog box shown in the following graphic will appear.

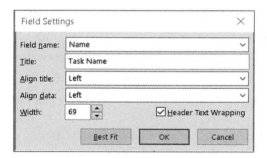

In the Width box, type a number to specify the width you want.

If you want the column to automatically stretch as wide as the longest text in the column, select the Best Fit check box.

By default, text wrapping is turned on. You can turn text wrapping off if you prefer that all your task names stay on one line, even if they're longer than the column width. To do this, click in any part of the Task Name column. On the Format tab, in the Columns group, click **Column Settings**, then click **Wrap Text**, which turns it off. Follow the same steps if you want to toggle it back on.

4. Continue entering your tasks.

   Remember that your task list doesn't need to be perfect or complete just yet. You'll review the list with your team and other stakeholders, and there will be time for refinement later.

Add New Tasks to a Task Sheet

To add a new task at the end of the list in any task sheet, simply click in the next empty Task Name cell, type the new task name, then press Enter.

To insert a new task between existing tasks:

1. Click in the row below where you want the new task to be inserted.

   For example, if you want to insert a new task between rows 3 and 4, click in row 4.

2. On the Task tab, in the Insert group, click **Task**.

   A new row labeled <New Task> appears at your selected location, and the Task Name field is already selected and ready for entry.

3. Type the new task name, then press Enter.

Edit a Task Name in a Task Sheet

To edit an existing task name in any task sheet:

1. Double-click the task name you want to edit.

   The Task Information dialog box appears (see Figure 4.7).

FIGURE 4.7 The Task Information dialog box

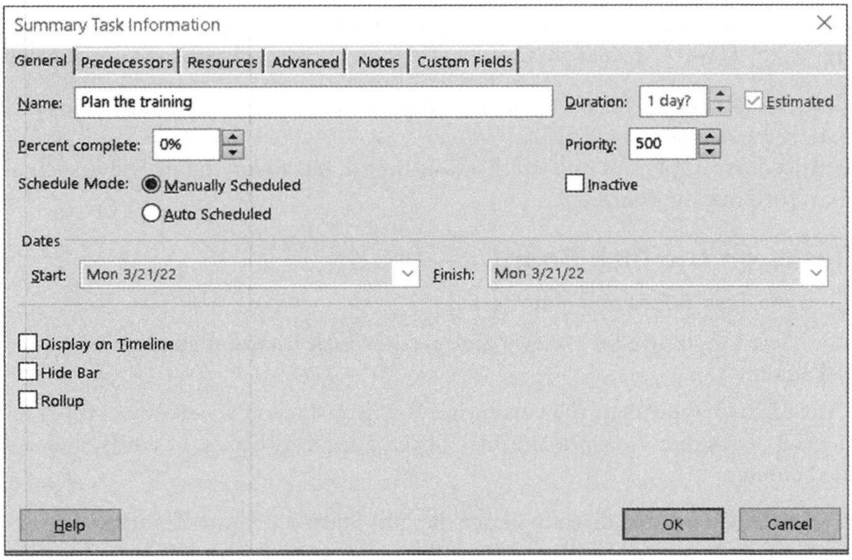

2. Make sure the General tab is active.

3. Click in the **Name** box and revise the name as you wish.

4. Click **OK** or press Enter.

You can also edit the task name directly in the Task Name cell. Click the name to select it. Then click it a second time. The text is now selected and editable.

Delete a Task from a Task Sheet

To delete a task from any task sheet:

1. Right-click anywhere in the row containing the task you want to delete.

2. On the menu that appears, click **Delete Task**.

You can also clear the contents of a row but keep the blank row. Right-click anywhere in the row, and then on the menu that appears, click **Clear Contents**.

If you delete a task and realize it was a mistake, you can quickly undo it. In the Quick Access Toolbar in the upper-left corner of the Project window, simply click **Undo** or press Ctrl+Z.

Work with Tasks on the Task Board

You might prefer to enter tasks on the Task Board, which mimics sticky notes on a whiteboard, a popular technique in agile project management. In this step, you focus on entering the task names on those virtual sticky notes or *task cards*.

You'll learn how to set up your *sprints*, for example, two-week increments of work, in Lesson 5. You'll also learn how to add tasks to your sprints.

Just as with the Task Sheet, after you've entered tasks on the Task Board, you can always add, edit, or remove tasks as needed.

These procedures apply not only to the Task Board, but to any board view, such as the Sprint Board or Backlog Board.

Enter Tasks on the Task Board

To switch to the Task Board and enter tasks:

1. On the View tab, in the Task Views group, click **Task Board**, then click **Task Board** again.

    The Task Board appears as the current view. Any tasks you've already entered in this plan, even in another view like the Task Sheet, appear as boxes, or cards, under the Not Started column.

2. Click **New Task**, located directly under the Not Started column heading.

3. In the card that appears, type a new task name, then click **Add**.

The new task name appears in a card under the New Task control, as shown in Figure 4.8.

FIGURE 4.8   New tasks in the Task Board

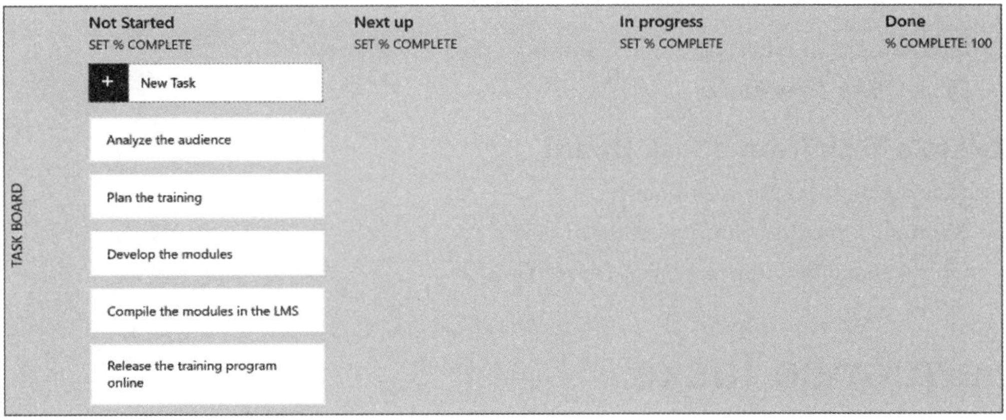

4. Click **New Task** again, type another task name, then click **Add** or simply press Enter.

Each new task you enter appears at the top of the Not Started column. As before, don't worry about the sequence or scheduling of tasks just yet. Just enter the task names you've identified. You'll arrange the order later.

Agile Task Views

The following Project task views are designed especially for agile projects:

- Backlog Board
- Backlog Sheet
- Current Sprint Board
- Current Sprint Sheet
- Sprint Board
- Sprint Planning Board
- Sprint Planning Sheet
- Task Board
- Task Board Sheet

You'll learn about many of these in Lesson 5 and later lessons. However, feel free to experiment with them on your own.

Edit a Task Name on a Task Board

To edit an existing task name in any Task Board:

1. Double-click the card containing the task name you want to edit.

   The Task Information dialog box then appears.

2. On the General tab, click in the **Name** box, then edit the task name.

3. Click **OK** or press Enter.

Delete a Task from a Task Board

To delete a task from any task board:

1. Right-click the task card you want to delete.

2. On the menu that appears, click **Delete Task**.

Sequence Tasks

After you have entered your tasks into the Project view, you can rearrange them into a logical sequence.

Reorder Tasks in the Task Sheet

To rearrange tasks in the Task Sheet:

1. In the Task Sheet, click the numbered row heading of the task you want to move.

   The entire row is then selected.

2. Right-click in the row and then in the menu that appears, click **Cut**.

3. Right-click anywhere in the row that is below where you want the cut task to be inserted.

   For example, if you want to insert the cut task between rows 3 and 4, click in row 4.

4. In the menu that appears, click **Paste**.

   The cut row is moved to the new location.

   You can also drag the task row to the new location. As you drag, a gray line appears. When the gray line is between the rows where you want the task to be moved, release the mouse button.

   Use these techniques to rearrange tasks in any task sheet.

Reorder Tasks on the Task Board

To rearrange tasks among others on the Task Board in the Not Started column:

1. On the Task Board, drag the task card to the new location.
2. Release the mouse button.

    The dragged task card is then inserted between the existing cards.

Use these techniques to rearrange tasks on any task board.

Later, when you're tracking task status, you'll also drag task cards horizontally to move them to the Next Up, In Progress, and Done columns. You'll learn more about this in Lesson 9, "Track Project Information."

Rearranging Tasks in Agile-Oriented Views

Rearranging tasks on any task board view or even an agile-oriented task sheet has a different effect from rearranging the same tasks in a task sheet. In any agile-oriented view, moving tasks is considered a temporary arrangement in that the tasks' ID numbers (that is, the numbers shown in the task row headings) stay as they were when they were first entered.

By contrast, when you rearrange tasks in the Task Sheet or Gantt Chart, it's considered a permanent arrangement. The tasks' ID numbers change to reflect their new order.

Project assumes that when you rearrange tasks in an agile-oriented board or sheet, you want to preserve a visual layout of the tasks as you move from view to view. Project also assumes that this layout will change over time, and so it retains the original order.

If you want to permanently change the order of tasks, you can do so from the Task Sheet.

Organize the Task Outline

With your tasks entered and in a logical sequence, you're now ready to set up your task hierarchy with summary tasks and subtasks. This structure helps you group your tasks into manageable and related chunks of activity, which will in turn help you set the schedule, assign resources, and track and manage progress (see Figure 4.9).

FIGURE 4.9   A task outline structure

	ⓘ	Task ▾	Task Name
1			⊿**Plan the training**
2			Analyze the audience
3			Assess audience training needs
4			⊿**Identify the training topics**
5			Brainstorm training topics
6			Select and oganize training topics
7			Evaluate and select the learning management system tools
8			Organize module content
9			Present training proposal
10			Develop the modules
11			⊿**Develop Module 1**
12			Research Module 1 topics
13			Write Module 1 topics
14			Have Module 1 topics reviewed
15			Revise Module 1 topics
16			Test Module 1 topics
17			⊿**Develop Module 2**
18			Research Module 2 topics

Whether your project is using the waterfall or the agile methodology, be sure to outline your tasks in a non-agile view like the Task Sheet or Gantt Chart. There are two reasons for this:

- Your non-agile view shows the permanent arrangement of your tasks, so you can see and continue to adjust their logical sequence. The agile views show the temporary arrangement of your tasks, so if you indent a task in an agile view, you might see unexpected results.

- Your non-agile view shows all summary tasks and subtasks by default, whereas the agile views only show subtasks.

When creating your task outline structure, keep the following in mind:

- When you *indent* a task, it becomes a subtask to the task immediately above it, which becomes the summary task. Therefore, summary task names must be above the subtasks.

- You can have as many levels of summary tasks and subtasks as your project requires.

- As you indent tasks to create subtasks, you will probably continue to rearrange tasks.

- You will probably add new summary task names as you work.

- Summarized information about all the subtasks rolls up and appears in the summary task row. For example, the latest finish date of all the subtasks shows as the finish date in the summary task, and the cost of all subtasks are totaled in the summary task row.

To create a subtask:

1. Click the task to select it.

2. On the Task tab, in the Schedule group, click **Indent Task**.

The selected task is indented under the task above it, which in turn becomes a summary task displayed in bold type.

To create multiple levels of subtasks:

1. Select a summary task that's under another task at the same outline level.

2. On the Task tab, in the Schedule group, click **Indent Task**.

    The selected summary task, along with all of its subtasks, are indented under the task above it, which in turn becomes a summary task to another summary task.

    To insert a summary task:

1. Click the task that's below where you want the new summary task to be inserted.

    For example, if you want to insert a blank summary task above row 4, click in row 4.

2. On the Task tab, in the Insert group, click **Summary**.

    Project inserts a task labeled <New Summary Task> above your selected task. The new task is *outdented* one outline level from the selected task.

    To raise a subtask in the outline hierarchy:

1. Select a subtask you want to move to a higher level in the structure.

2. On the Task tab, in the Schedule group, click **Outdent Task**.

    Note that Outdent Task will not work on any tasks that are already at the highest outline level.

If your project is large and has several outline levels, you might find it useful to filter your view by certain outline levels. On the View tab, in the Data group, click **Outline**. Use the Outline menu, shown in Figure 4.10, to filter your project to see only the higher summary tasks, to see only subtasks, or to see all tasks.

FIGURE 4.10   The Outline menu

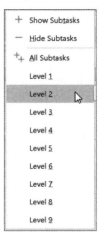

All levels of summary tasks show the rolled-up information of their subtasks. This means each summary task shows the total duration and total cost of all its subtasks. In addition, each summary task shows the earliest start date of its subtasks as well as the latest finish date. In the same way, if you show the Project Summary Task, you can also see rolled-up information of the entire project, including full project duration, start and finish dates, and total project cost.

To show the Project Summary Task:

1. On the Format tab, in the Show/Hide group, select the **Project Summary Task** check box.

   The Project Summary Task appears as row 0 in the task sheet and uses your project file-name as the project summary task name (see Figure 4.11).

FIGURE 4.11   The Project Summary Task

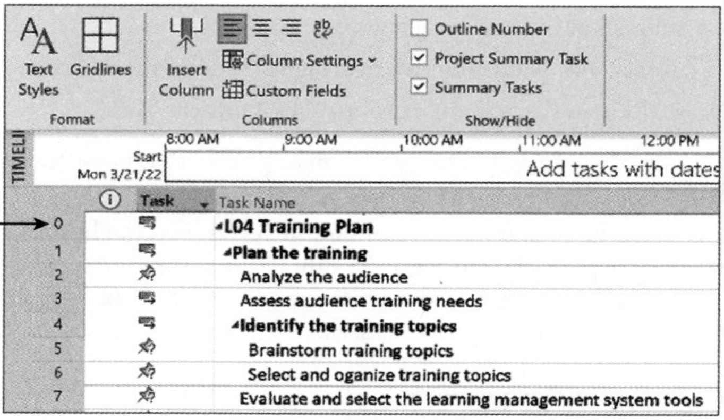

2. If you want, click in the project summary task name to change it.

Continue using these techniques to solidify the outline structure of your task list. Have your team members and other project stakeholders review the task list and its sequence and structure for completeness and accuracy. Soon you'll be ready to start scheduling these tasks.

Key Terms

assignments

board views

indent

outdent

outline level

resources

sheet views

sprints

subtask

summary task

task cards

task views

tasks

work breakdown structure (WBS)

Review Questions

1. List the steps for starting a new Microsoft Project plan from a blank project and setting the project start date.

2. List the steps for switching from the current Project view to the Task Sheet view.

3. Name three Project views designed for agile projects.

4. What's the difference between rearranging tasks in the Task Sheet or Gantt Chart and rearranging tasks in the Task Board or other agile-oriented view?

   A. When you rearrange tasks in a non-agile view like the Task Sheet or Gantt Chart, the new task order is considered permanent. When you rearrange tasks in an agile-oriented view, the new task order is considered temporary.

   B. When you rearrange tasks in a non-agile view like the Task Sheet or Task Usage view, the new task order is considered temporary. When you rearrange tasks in an agile-oriented view, the new task order is considered permanent.

   C. You can only filter an agile view by the Task ID, whereas you can filter a non-agile view by any field name.

   D. The Task ID, which reflects the task sequence, is only visible in non-agile views.

5. Why is it useful to arrange your project tasks into an outline structure of summary tasks and subtasks?

   A. It's visually easier to read and report on to team members and management.

   B. It creates the work breakdown structure, which is part of the closing processes.

   C. It groups your tasks into manageable and related activities so that they're easier to schedule, assign, and track.

   D. You can review rolled-up information about the summary tasks in each of the subtasks.

Lesson

5

Build the Schedule

LESSON OBJECTIVES

✓ Demonstrate how to switch a project and tasks between automatic and manual scheduling.

✓ List the three key pieces of information you see quickly on the Gantt Chart bars.

✓ Name three of the four major schedule drivers for your project.

✓ Identify the significance of a task with a duration of 0.

✓ Demonstrate how to link and unlink dependent tasks.

✓ Set up a series of sprints in an agile project.

✓ Name the default constraint type in Project.

✓ Apply a date constraint on a task.

✓ Specify the difference between a deadline marker and a date constraint.

✓ Describe the use of base calendars, project calendar, and task calendars.

You've detailed your work breakdown structure and started your project plan with tasks developed, sequenced, and outlined. Now you can dive in to scheduling those tasks, and this work will help you estimate the finish date for the overall project. Along with the project start date, the major drivers of your schedule are the task durations, task dependencies, and any hard dates a task might require.

In this lesson, you'll decide whether you want to use Microsoft Project's automatic or manual scheduling feature, and you'll learn about the Gantt Chart view in which you can work with a visual representation of your project schedule.

In your practice with the major schedule drivers, which are used in automatic scheduling, you'll learn how to set task durations, link related tasks, and enter date constraints. You'll see how to mark milestones and deadline reminders. You'll finesse your scheduling accuracy through the use of project and task calendars.

Task scheduling is relevant whether you're working with an agile or a waterfall project. If you're working with an agile project, you'll learn how to set up the dates and durations of your sprints and add tasks to each sprint.

Decide on Automatic Scheduling

Project has two scheduling modes from which you can select for your project: manual or automatic.

In the *manual scheduling mode*, you can use Project like a static spreadsheet or task board in which you can enter your tasks and their start and finish dates that you figure yourself. This gives you more control and flexibility, especially in the beginning of a project when you might not yet have all the information you need about durations, dates, and dependencies.

In the *automatic scheduling mode*, you can use the full capabilities of the *Project scheduling engine*. Taking your project start date, task durations, linked tasks, and any hard constraint dates into consideration, Project calculates the task schedule and ultimately the full project schedule. The automatic scheduling mode uses the full power of the Project scheduling engine, which in turn frees you up from calculating dates to focus on other important project management responsibilities.

Change All Tasks to Automatic Scheduling

When you first start a new file in Project, tasks are set by default to manual scheduling. However, you'll get better results if you switch to automatic scheduling.

To change existing tasks from manual to automatic scheduling:

1. With your project plan open in Project, switch to the Gantt Chart if necessary. On the View tab, in the Task Views group, click **Gantt Chart**.

2. Click in the upper-left corner of the sheet view to select all rows, as shown in Figure 5.1.

FIGURE 5.1   The Select All cell

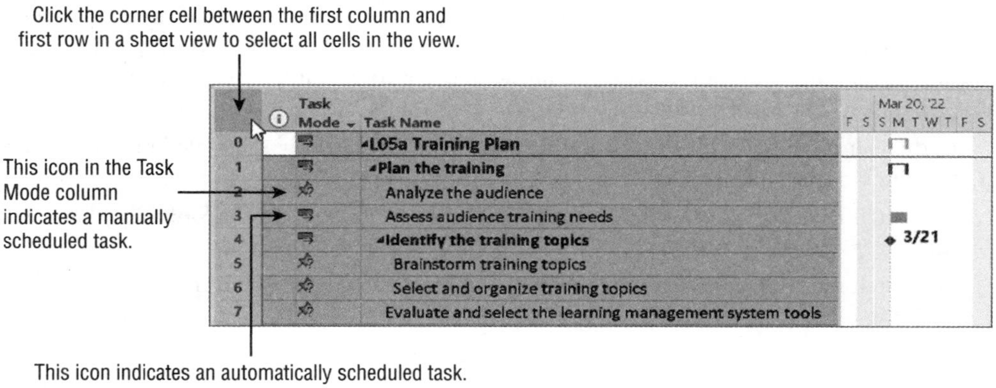

Click the corner cell between the first column and first row in a sheet view to select all cells in the view.

This icon in the Task Mode column indicates a manually scheduled task.

This icon indicates an automatically scheduled task.

The Select All cell is available in any sheet view (like the Task Sheet) or any combination view (like the Gantt Chart or Task Usage view).

3. On the Task tab, in the Tasks group, click **Auto Schedule**.

All existing tasks in the project plan will now be automatically scheduled. In the Task Mode column, the icons change from Manually Scheduled to Auto Scheduled (see Figure 5.2).

FIGURE 5.2   All tasks to be automatically scheduled

This icon indicates that the task will be automatically scheduled.

The bars in the timescale side of the Gantt Chart will show how the tasks will be scheduled based on the information you enter.

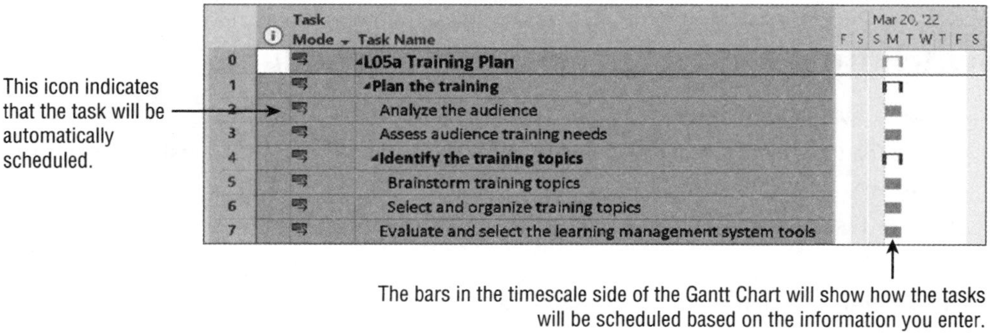

Set Any New Tasks to Automatic Scheduling

Although you've changed your existing tasks from manual to automatic scheduling, by default any new tasks will still be set to be manually scheduled.

To change the entire project to automatically schedule all newly added tasks, on the Task tab, in the Tasks group, click **Mode**, then click **Auto Schedule**.

Now whenever you enter a new task, its default task mode will be Auto Scheduled.

Switch from Automatic to Manual Scheduling

The procedures in the previous two sections changed all existing tasks and any new tasks to be automatically scheduled. However, you can change individual tasks to be manually scheduled. You might want to do this if you want more control over specific tasks, or if you're waiting for more information before you allow the task to be automatically scheduled.

To change a task from automatic to manual scheduling:

1.   In the Gantt Chart or other task sheet, select the automatically scheduled task you want to switch to manual scheduling.

To switch multiple adjacent tasks, click the first task, hold down the Shift key, then click the last task in the grouping.

To switch multiple nonadjacent tasks, click the first task, hold down the Ctrl key, then click the other tasks you want to change.

2.   On the Task tab, in the Tasks group, click **Manually Schedule**.

The selected task changes to the manually scheduled task mode. The icon in the Task Mode cell changes and the color of the Gantt bars change from blue to green.

As you make changes to the manually scheduled task's duration, start and finish dates, and linking, you'll start to see the differences in manually scheduled versus your automatically scheduled tasks.

With manually scheduled tasks, you're not restricted to entering a duration and time unit in the Duration field or a date in the Start or Finish field. You can enter text like "about a week" or "before year-end."

If you do enter durations or dates, however, Project still calculates a manually scheduled task. For example, if you enter a duration and a start date, Project figures the finish date for you. If you enter a duration and a finish date, Project calculates the duration.

Switch from Manual to Automatic Scheduling

To change a task from manual to automatic scheduling:

1.   In the Gantt Chart or other task sheet, select the manually scheduled task you want to switch to automatic scheduling.

2.   On the Task tab, in the Tasks group, click **Auto Schedule**.

The selected task changes to the automatically scheduled task mode. The icon in the Task Mode cell changes, and the Gantt bar colors change from green to blue.

Get to Know the Gantt Chart

Because this lesson is all about scheduling, it's best to work in a view that visually shows your schedule and the changes you'll be making.

In Project, the *Gantt Chart* shows your task schedule visually (see Figure 5.3). The left side of the view is a table listing your task names. The right side of the view is a timescaled bar chart that shows how those tasks are scheduled over time. This bar chart gives you a quick glance at the start, duration, and finish dates of each task. You can also see graphically how the tasks relate to each other, including whether there's any overlap or lag between related tasks.

FIGURE 5.3   Gantt Chart view

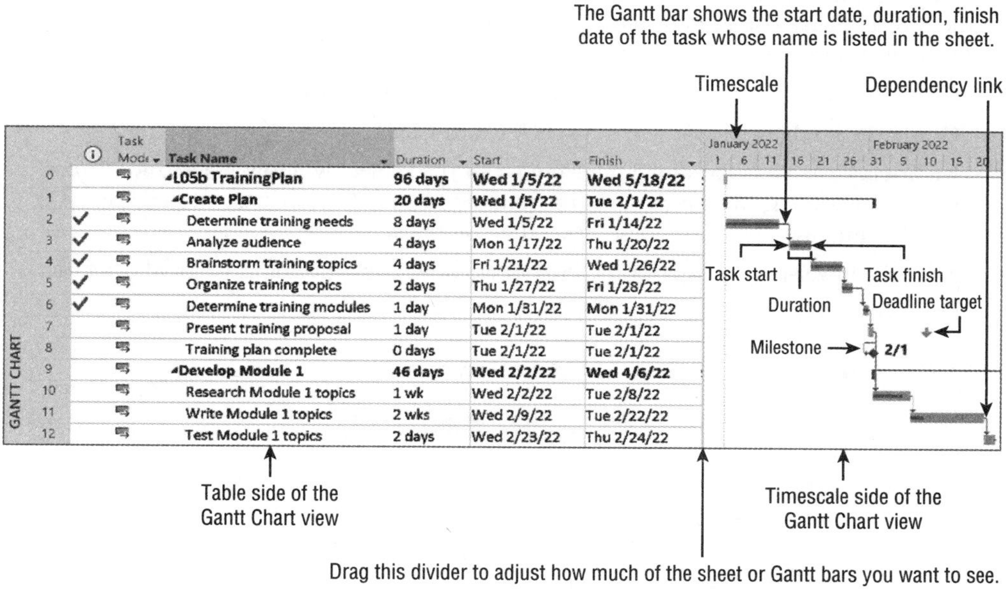

The Gantt bar shows the start date, duration, finish date of the task whose name is listed in the sheet.

Timescale

Dependency link

Task start

Task finish

Duration

Deadline target

Milestone → 2/1

Table side of the Gantt Chart view

Timescale side of the Gantt Chart view

Drag this divider to adjust how much of the sheet or Gantt bars you want to see.

Because the Gantt Chart consists of two views put together, it's considered a *combination view*. Here are more details about the Gantt Chart elements:

Table Side   The left side of the Gantt Chart contains a table whose main column contains the task names. By default, the Task Entry table is shown in the default Gantt Chart. This table contains the same columns as the Task Sheet view you worked with in Lesson 4, "Set Up the Project and Tasks," to enter your tasks. You can switch to a different table—like the Cost table or Tracking table—to see different sets of columns. In any table, you can add or remove columns to reflect the information you want to see. For example, you can add the Sprint column to a table to see which sprint each task belongs to. You'll learn more about switching tables and adding and removing columns in Lesson 10, "View Project Information."

Timescale Side   The right side of the Gantt Chart contains the timescale and the bars showing the scheduling of each task. Under the timescale, each Gantt bar shows the task's start date, duration, and finish date. The timescale side can also show if a task is a milestone as well as any deadlines set.

Timescale   By default, the Gantt Chart timescale shows days within weeks. You can change that timescale to show different time units—for example, weeks within months or months within quarters. Learn more about the timescale in Lesson 10.

Divider   You can adjust the divider between the table and timescale sides of the Gantt Chart to see more of one and less of the other. Position your mouse pointer on the divider until the icon changes to a double arrow, then drag the divider to the position you want.

You'll typically use several different views when working in your project plan, depending on the project phase you're in or what you're focusing on at the time. You can quickly return to the Gantt Chart from other views in these ways:

- On the View tab, in the Task Views group, click **Gantt Chart**.

- On the Task tab, in the View group, click **Gantt Chart**.

- Right-click the view bar along the left edge of the Project window where the current view name shows; then in the menu that appears, click **Gantt Chart** (see Figure 5.4). Your menu might look different, depending on the views you have visited.

- Near the lower-right corner of the Project window, click the **Gantt Chart** shortcut icon (see Figure 5.5).

FIGURE 5.4   The shortcut menu from the view bar

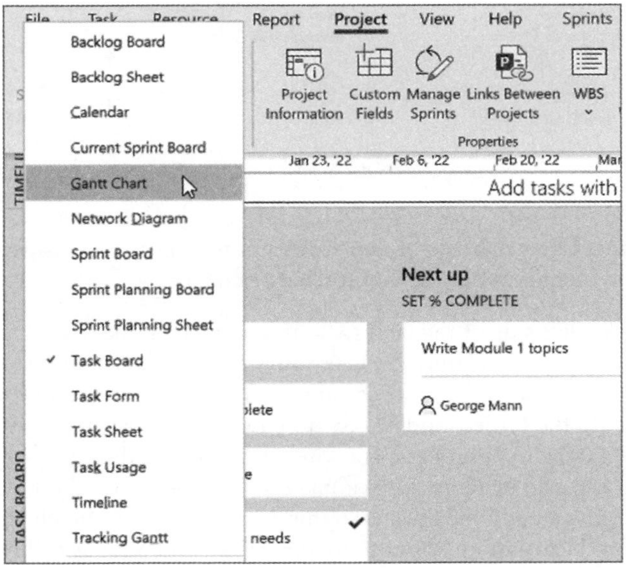

FIGURE 5.5   The view shortcut icons

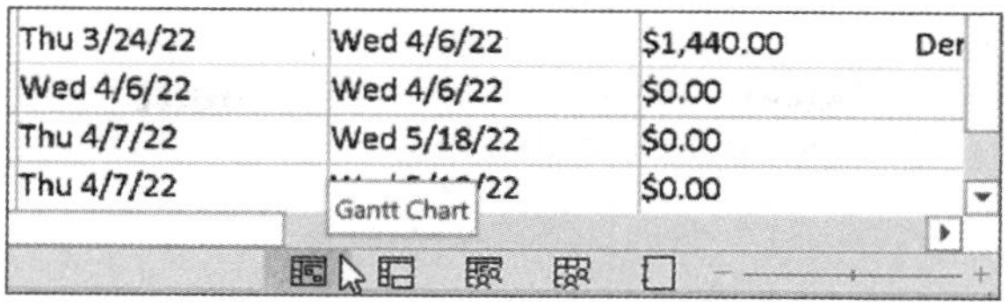

Thu 3/24/22	Wed 4/6/22	$1,440.00	Der
Wed 4/6/22	Wed 4/6/22	$0.00	
Thu 4/7/22	Wed 5/18/22	$0.00	
Thu 4/7/22	Gantt Chart /22	$0.00	

Enter Task Durations

After the project start date, which you set in Lesson 4, the next major schedule driver you establish are durations for the tasks you've entered. The *duration* indicates how much time you think it'll take to complete the task.

Here are some points to remember about entering task durations:

- When you enter the name of a task that's automatically scheduled, Project sets an estimated duration of one day, and this estimate is shown as *1 day?*. You can change the duration to what you think it will be.

- You enter the duration in the Duration field of the Gantt Chart. The Gantt bar for the task changes to reflect the duration you enter.

- Use the appropriate abbreviation to indicate the unit of time for your duration, for example, *3d* or *2w*:

  - d = days (This is the default unit of time; if you enter a number without the abbreviation, Project will assume you mean days and will fill that in for you.)

  - w = weeks

  - mo = months (while m = minutes, which is rarely used)

- If you add a question mark after a duration entry, for example—*6d?*—Project flags it as an *estimated duration*. The "?" doesn't affect how the task is scheduled, or even how its Gantt bar appears. It's just a reminder to you that you want to refine this duration later, perhaps after you gather more information.

- Only add durations to the lowest level of subtasks in your project. Never add a duration to a summary task at any outline level. Even though it's an editable field, you want the duration of the summary task to represent the collective or rolled-up duration of the subtasks. Summary tasks at any level are always in boldface type in a sheet.

How to Estimate Durations

The best way to estimate accurate task durations is by asking your team members who will be carrying out the tasks for this project. If your team isn't assembled just yet, try to get estimates from people who are experienced with the work. You can always adjust the durations later when your team is in place. Consulting your team is a great way to get solid commitments and buy-in from your resources on the tasks to which they're assigned.

You can also find good duration estimates from previous similar projects, a project template for your type of project, or a professional organization's best practices.

Enter Durations in the Gantt Chart

To enter durations for your tasks:

1. In the Gantt Chart, click in the Duration field for the task.

2. Type the duration, remembering to include the number and the time unit, such as *2w* or *1mo*.

3. Press Enter.

   The duration is set for the task, and the Gantt bar changes accordingly.

4. Repeat these steps for all your tasks.

   Notice that while the length of the Gantt bar changes with the duration you enter, the start date does not. At this point, all tasks look like they're starting on the project start date you previously set (see Figure 5.6). This will change when you start linking related tasks in the next section.

5. If you need to change a duration, simply click in the field, type it in, and press Enter.

FIGURE 5.6   Task durations entered

	Task Name	Duration	Start	Finish	Mar 20, '22 / Mar 27, '22
0	▪L05 Training Plan	10 days?	Mon 3/21/22	Fri 4/1/22	
1	▪Plan the training	10 days	Mon 3/21/22	Fri 4/1/22	
2	Analyze the audience	1 wk	Mon 3/21/22	Fri 3/25/22	
3	Assess audience training needs	2 wks	Mon 3/21/22	Fri 4/1/22	
4	▪Identify the training topics	4 days	Mon 3/21/22	Thu 3/24/22	
5	Brainstorm training topics	4 days	Mon 3/21/22	Thu 3/24/22	
6	Select and organize training topics	3 days	Mon 3/21/22	Wed 3/23/22	
7	Evaluate and select the learning management system tools	2 wks	Mon 3/21/22	Fri 4/1/22	
8	Organize module content	3 days	Mon 3/21/22	Wed 3/23/22	
9	Present training proposal	1 day	Mon 3/21/22	Mon 3/21/22	
10	▪Develop the modules	10 days?	Mon 3/21/22	Fri 4/1/22	
11	▪Develop Module 1	10 days?	Mon 3/21/22	Fri 4/1/22	

What About the Start and Finish Dates?

With the Start and Finish fields next to the Duration fields in the Gantt Chart and other task sheets, it seems intuitive to fill those in. And you can certainly do that, especially if you're working with manually scheduled tasks.

However, if you're working with automatically scheduled tasks, it's best to leave the Start and Finish fields as they are for now. Project will calculate those dates for you when you set up task relationships in the section titled "Link Dependent Tasks" later in this lesson.

Also, if you enter start and finish dates for automatically scheduled tasks, you are inadvertently setting date constraints that will significantly limit your schedule's flexibility. You'll learn more about date constraints in the "Identify Any Hardwired Dates" section later in this lesson.

View Durations on the Task Board

You can add the Duration field to your Task Board cards. However, on the Task Board, Duration is a read-only field; you can't change it there.

To add the Duration field to a Task Board card:

1. Switch to the Task Board; on the View tab, in the Task Views group, click **Task Board**.

2. On the Format tab, in the Customize group, click **Customize Cards**.

3. In the Customize Task Board Cards dialog box, under Additional Fields, click in the first empty Select Field box, then either type **Duration** or select it from the list of fields.

4. Click **OK**.

The Duration field is added to all Task Board cards, as shown in Figure 5.7. The Duration amount stems from the entries in the Gantt Chart.

FIGURE 5.7   Duration is added to Task Board cards.

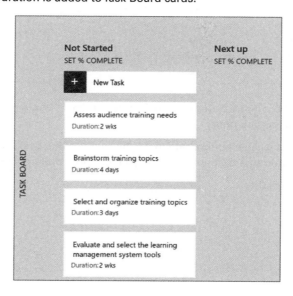

Define a Day, Week, and Month

For the purposes of your project, you can define the length of a day, week, or month. By default, Project says a day is 8 hours long, a week is 40 hours long, and a month consists of 20 days.

A good reason to change these time unit definitions is to ensure a more realistic project schedule, allowing time for administrative tasks, department or company meetings, regular training, and other non-project-related work.

To set your calendar options:

1. On the File tab, click **Options** at the bottom of the left pane.

2. In the left pane of the Project Options dialog box, click **Schedule**.

3. Review the controls in the section labeled "Calendar options for this project," as shown in the following graphic.

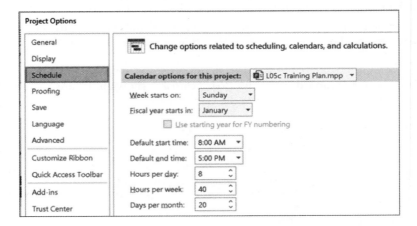

4. Change the numbers in the boxes labeled "Hours per day," "Hours per week," and "Days per month" as you prefer.

5. Review the other available options and make the changes that best reflect the scheduling reality for your organization as well as your calendar preferences.

6. When finished, click **OK**.

Set Milestones

A *milestone* is any event in your project that you see as a noteworthy achievement. It might be the completion of a deliverable, a sprint, or a phase.

In Project, you can identify tasks as milestones and have them show as such in your Gantt Chart. It's easiest and clearest to identify a milestone as a task that has a duration of 0.

To identify a milestone task with a 0 duration:

1. In the Gantt Chart (or other task view), enter the name of the milestone task—for example, Test Phase Complete, End of Sprint 4, or Prototype Delivered to Customer.

2. In the Duration field, type 0, then press Enter.

   A 0 duration signals to Project that this is a milestone task.

   In the timescale side of the Gantt Chart, notice that the milestone is marked with a black diamond on the scheduled date (see Figure 5.8).

FIGURE 5.8   A milestone task in the Gantt Chart

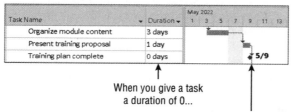

To mark a task with a nonzero duration as a milestone:

1. In the Gantt Chart (or other task view), enter the name of the milestone.

2. In the Duration field, enter the amount of time you expect the task to take.

3. On the Task tab, in the Properties group, click **Information**, or just double-click the task.

4. In the Task Information dialog box, click the **Advanced** tab.

5. Near the bottom of the dialog box, select the **Mark Task As Milestone** check box, then click **OK**.

   In the timescale side of the Gantt Chart, the black diamond milestone marker shows at the end of the task's duration.

   The downside of this method is that the Gantt bar does not show the task's start date or duration; it only shows the milestone marker at the end date. Because of this, the Gantt bar can look misleading (see Figure 5.9).

FIGURE 5.9   A task with a nonzero duration in the Gantt Chart.

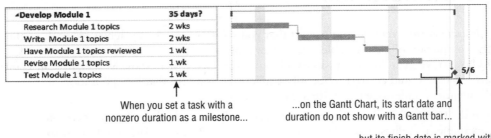

When you set a task with a
nonzero duration as a milestone...

...on the Gantt Chart, its start date and
duration do not show with a Gantt bar...

...but its finish date is marked with a
black diamond milestone marker.

Link Dependent Tasks

Many tasks in your project are related to other tasks—that is, one task can start or finish only after an earlier task finishes or starts. Such a relationship between two tasks is called a *task dependency* or *task link*. The earlier task in the pair is called the *predecessor task*, and the later task is called the *successor task*.

The *Finish-to-Start task relationship* is the most common dependency. The earlier task (predecessor) must finish before the later task (successor) can start. In our training program example, the "Brainstorm training topics" task is the predecessor to the "Select and organize training topics" successor.

Task dependencies are another major schedule driver, in addition to the project start date and the task durations. When you link dependent tasks, you start to see a more realistic representation of your schedule in Project.

Different Task Dependency Types

While the Finish-to-Start dependency is the most common and therefore the default task link type in Project, you can also identify dependencies as Finish-to-Finish, Start-to-Start, or the unusual but available Start-to-Finish.

To change to a different link type:

1. Double-click the successor task to open the Task Information dialog box, then click the **Predecessors** tab.

   The table shows the name of the selected task's predecessor along with the current link type between the predecessor and successor.

2. Click the arrow in the **Type** field, then click the link type you want between the selected task and its predecessor. Click **OK**.

Set Up Task Dependencies

To link dependent tasks in a Finish-to-Start task relationship:

1. In the Gantt Chart (or other task sheet), click the task that will be the predecessor, or the first one in the pair.

2. Hold down the Ctrl key and then click the task that will be the successor, or the second task in the pair.

3. On the Task tab, in the Schedule group, click **Link the Selected Tasks**.

    The tasks are linked with the default Finish-to-Start relationship, and this link shows in the timescale side of the Gantt Chart.

As soon as you link tasks, your tasks no longer all start on the project start date. Any linked tasks are scheduled after their predecessor's start date, duration, and finish date are taken into consideration.

 Never link summary tasks; only link the lowest levels of subtasks. The schedule and sequence of all summary tasks follow the schedule and sequence of their subtasks. Linking summary tasks can cause scheduling conflicts and error messages.

You can link subtasks under different summary tasks as necessary.

You can have a string of dependent tasks in a phase or sprint of your project, and it's easy to link that string quickly in Project. Be careful to link only those tasks that are truly dependent on each other; otherwise you can make your project longer and more complex than it needs to be.

To link several dependent tasks at once:

1. In the Gantt Chart, click the task that will be the earliest predecessor in the group of dependent tasks.

2. Hold down the Ctrl key and then click the tasks in the order in which you want them to be linked, from the earliest predecessor to the latest successor.

3. On the Task tab, in the Schedule group, click **Link the Selected Tasks**.

    All the selected tasks in the group are linked with the Finish-to-Start relationship, as shown in Figure 5.10.

4. Continue linking tasks in this manner throughout your project. Remember that tasks need not be in consecutive rows to be properly linked.

    In the Gantt Chart or Task Sheet, you can see the task numbers of predecessors in the Predecessors column.

FIGURE 5.10   Tasks linked with a Finish-to-Start dependency

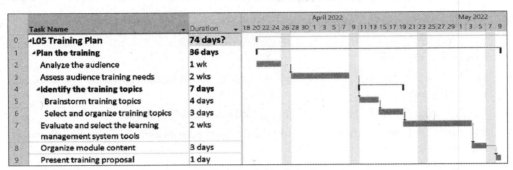

As you link tasks, you create multiple *task paths* throughout your project, and you start to see a clearer picture of how the project will be scheduled. The longest task path is considered the *critical path*, because this longest task path determines the finish date of the entire project. You'll learn more about the critical path in Lesson 8, "Check and Adjust the Project."

To remove a link:

1. In the Gantt Chart, use the Ctrl or Shift key to select the pair of tasks whose links you want to remove.

   Use Shift to select an additional task that's adjacent to the selected task. Use Ctrl to select an additional task that's not adjacent to the selected task. You can select as many tasks as you want to remove their links.

2. On the Task tab, in the Schedule group, click **Unlink Tasks**.

   The links connecting the selected tasks are removed.

View Dependencies on a Task Board

There's no way to visually show dependencies on the Task Board. However, you can add the Predecessor field to your task cards. This field will show on the cards on any board view, like the Backlog Board or Sprint Planning Board.

To add the Predecessor field to a Task Board card:

1. Switch to the Task Board view.

2. On the Format tab, in the Customize group, click **Customize Cards**.

3. In the Customize Task Board Cards dialog box, under Base Fields, select the **Show Task ID** check box.

4. Under Additional Fields, click in the next empty Select Field box, and then either type *Predecessors* or select it from the list of fields.

5. Click **OK**.

   The Task ID and Predecessors fields are added to all cards on the Task Board and any other board view, as shown in Figure 5.11.

FIGURE 5.11   The Task ID and Predecessor fields on the task cards

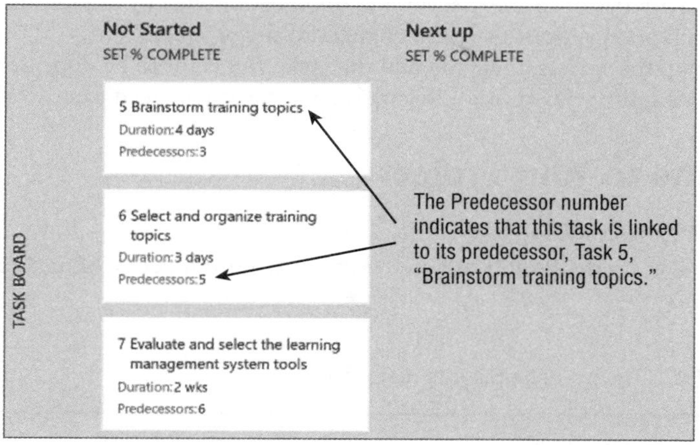

The Predecessor field on a task card is not directly editable. You generally set up your predecessors by linking tasks on the Gantt Chart. However, you can use the Task Information dialog box to add, edit, or remove a predecessor.

To change the predecessor in the Task Information dialog box:

1. On the Task Board view, double-click the task card whose predecessor you want to change.

    The Task Information dialog box appears. You can also open the dialog box by selecting the task and then, on the Task tab, in the Properties group, click **Information**.

2. In the Task Information dialog box, click the **Predecessors** tab.

3. Change the task's predecessor by using the Predecessors table.

    To add a predecessor, click the arrow in a blank cell under Task Name, then select the task name from the list of tasks that appears.

    To change an existing predecessor, click the arrow in the predecessor's Task Name cell, then select the task name from the list of tasks.

    To remove a predecessor, click anywhere in its row, then press the Delete key.

4. Click **OK**.

    The changed predecessor shows in the task card. If you don't see the change right away, refresh the Task Board. The easiest way is to right-click the view bar on the left side of the Project window, then click Task Board.

Schedule Sprints for an Agile Project

If yours is an agile project, you can set up your sprints in Project, then add tasks to the sprints. *Sprints* are regularly spaced periods of time in your project, usually between two and four weeks. The end of each sprint typically results in an increment of the project completed—that is, a distinct deliverable that can be presented to the customer and the team for review. The activities of the next sprint are often determined by the results of this iterative review, which often suggest or reveal changes to the product.

First you set up the sprints, then you add the tasks you want to be done during specific sprints. You can modify your sprint information whenever you need to.

Add Sprints to Your Project

To add sprints to your project:

1. From any view, on the Project tab, in the Properties group, click **Manage Sprints** (see Figure 5.12).

FIGURE 5.12   The Manage Sprints dialog box

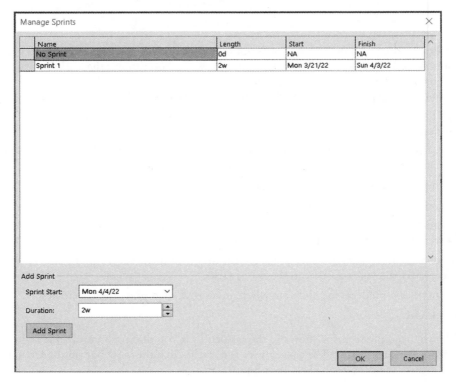

2. Under Add Sprint, in the Sprint Start field, enter the date of the first sprint.

    The default sprint start date is today's date. You might change this to match the project start date you've already entered in the Project Information dialog box. Or you might prefer to start your first sprint a short time after the project start date.

3. In the Duration box, enter the period of time you want for each sprint.

   Although a typical sprint ranges from two to four weeks, you can enter any duration you like.

4. Click the **Add Sprint** button.

   The first sprint is added to the sprints table in the dialog box. Each added sprint is sequentially numbered with the next available number, starting with Sprint 1. The Length column shows the length of the sprint as you specified in the Duration box, and the Start and Finish columns show the start and finish date of the sprint, based on the date you entered in the Sprint Start date field.

5. Click the **Add Sprint** button again.

   The second sprint, Sprint 2, is added to the sprints table, and the sprint start and finish dates follow the finish date of Sprint 1.

6. Click the **Add Sprint** button again, as needed, to add the proper number of sprints to your project. When you're done, click **OK**.

   As soon as you add sprints to your project, the Sprints tab appears on the Project ribbon.

Add Tasks to Your Sprints

With your sprints defined and scheduled, you can now add tasks to the sprints. You can add tasks you've already entered to a sprint, and you can create new tasks and add them to a sprint. To add tasks to sprints:

1. On the Sprints tab, in the Views group, click **Planning**, then click **Sprint Planning Board** (see Figure 5.13).

FIGURE 5.13   The Sprint Planning Board

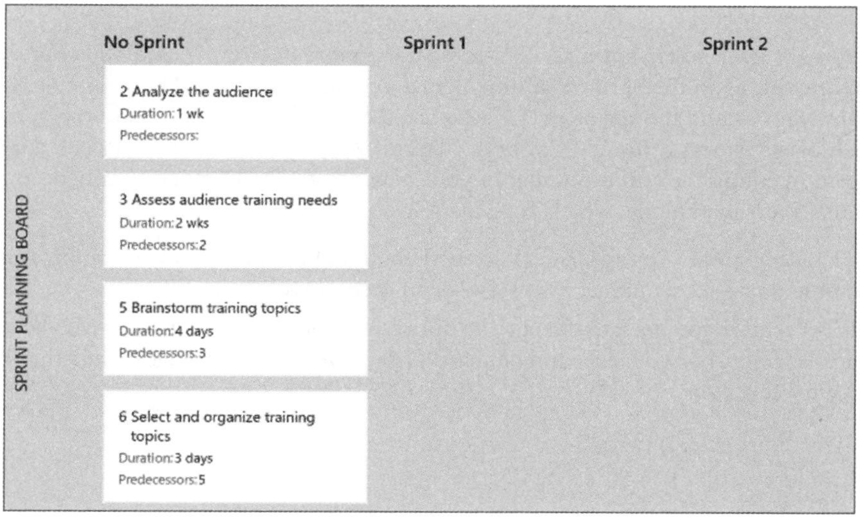

The sprints you've defined show as columns across the top of the Sprint Planning Board.

The cards for any tasks you've already entered appear under the No Sprint column on the far left.

2. Drag task cards from the No Sprint column to the column of the sprint when you want the tasks to be done.

    If a task does not belong to a specific sprint, leave it under the No Sprint column.

    You can drag the task cards to arrange them in the order you want under each sprint.

3. To create a new task, under the No Sprint column, click **New Task**, type the task name, then click **Add**. Drag it under the sprint where it belongs.

If you prefer, you can add tasks to sprints in a sheet view. To add tasks to sprints by using the Sprint Planning Sheet:

1. On the Sprints tab, in the Views group, click **Planning**, then click **Sprint Planning Sheet**.

    The Sprint column shows the sprint number for the task that appears in the Name column.

2. For the task you want to assign to a sprint, click the arrow in the Sprint column, then click the sprint number.

Modify Sprint Information

You don't have to keep the default sprint names or even the sprint durations and dates you previously established. You can also delete a sprint. Change sprint information in the Manage Sprints dialog box.

To modify sprint information:

1. From any view, on the Project tab, in the Properties group, click **Manage Sprints** to open the Manage Sprints dialog box.

2. To change a sprint's name, click in the Name field, type the new name over the old one, then press Enter.

    You might want to change a sprint's name to be more descriptive and add context when you're working in the Sprint Planning Board or other sprint view. For example, you might want to add the sprint's key phase or deliverable ("Sprint 2 Prototype"), add the finish date ("Sprint 2 Jun28"), or both ("Sprint 2 Prototype Jun28"). It's still a good idea to maintain the sprint number in your new name. The number usually becomes the sprint's shorthand name, which your team will use often.

3. To change a sprint's duration, click in the Length field, type the new duration amount and time unit—for example, 3w or 4w—and then press Enter.

    This is useful if you need to change the duration of one or more sprints. Maybe your typical sprints are two weeks long, but you have two more complex sprints that need to be four weeks long.

If you need to delete a sprint, any tasks assigned to that sprint are not deleted but rather moved to the "No Sprint" column on the Sprint Planning Board. Project also adjusts the dates for succeeding sprints to maintain the sprint duration (like 2w or 3w) you established so there are no time gaps.

To delete a sprint:

1. From any view, on the Project tab, in the Properties group, click **Manage Sprints** to open the Manage Sprints dialog box.

2. Select the sprint you want to delete.

3. Right-click anywhere in the dialog box, and then click **Delete Sprint**.

4. In the message that appears, click **OK**.

"Ew" or Elapsed Weeks

If you use the arrows in the Length field of the sprints table (or the Duration field under Add Sprint), the time unit might change to something like "ew," which means *elapsed weeks*. *Elapsed durations* refer to normal calendar time periods.

For example, your project might define one week as five business days, while one elapsed week is seven calendar days. In most cases, this has the same effect. However, if you define a week or month differently, your time period can have a different effect from the elapsed time period.

For more information, see the section "Define a Day, Week, and Month" earlier in this lesson.

Identify Any Hardwired Dates

Now that you've entered task durations and linked dependent tasks, your plan is shaping up like a real project schedule. Now it's time to look at the start and finish dates of key tasks and make sure they're falling where they need to be.

Up to this point, the Project scheduling engine has assumed that you want your tasks to happen as soon as possible, given your project start date, task durations, and the dependencies.

However, you might have a task that can't start as soon as possible, but instead must start on or finish no later than a particular date. A good example is when one of your project tasks are tied to the date of a particular event, like a kickoff assembly or a trade show. If the event is happening on May 25, it doesn't matter how quickly you complete the tasks leading up to the event; the event can't happen on any other day but May 25.

Or suppose your project relies on a piece of equipment or software app, and the supplier has informed you it will absolutely not be available until June 29. You will not be able to start on any of the tasks that depend on this item until after June 29.

You can reflect such a hard and fast date in your project plan by setting a *date constraint* on the task.

If you have no such dates in your project, then you can skip this step. If your overall project finish date needs to hit a certain target not tied to a hardwired date, you can handle that in better ways. You'll learn about adjusting the schedule to a targeted project finish date in Lesson 8.

You can set one of eight constraint types as described in Table 5.1. They're listed in order from least to most restrictive for your schedule.

TABLE 5.1 Constraint types

Constraint name	Abbreviation	How restrictive	Notes
As Soon As Possible	ASAP	Least	The default constraint for tasks in a project scheduled from the start date.
As Late As Possible	ALAP	Least	The default constraint for tasks in a project scheduled from the finish date.
Start No Earlier Than	SNET	Medium	This constraint is set when you enter a date in the Start field for a project scheduled from the start date.
Start No Later Than	SNLT	Medium	
Finish No Earlier Than	FNET	Medium	This constraint is set when you enter a date in the Finish field for a project scheduled from the finish date.
Finish No Later Than	FNLT	Medium	
Must Start On	MSO	Most	
Must Finish On	MFO	Most	

To change a constraint for a task:

1. In the Gantt Chart (or other task view), double-click the task whose constraint you want to change.
2. In the Task Information dialog box, click the **Advanced** tab.

3. Click in the Constraint Type box, then click the constraint type you want, such as Start No Earlier Than or Must Start On.

4. Click the arrow in the Constraint Date box, then click the date associated with the constraint type you just selected.

   You must enter a date for any constraint type except As Soon As Possible or As Late As Possible. These constraints with dates are referred to as date constraints.

5. Click **OK**.

   The Gantt bars change to reflect the new constraint. Tasks set with a date constraint are flagged with a constraint icon in the Indicator column of any task sheet view (see Figure 5.14).

FIGURE 5.14   The constraint icon in the Indicator column

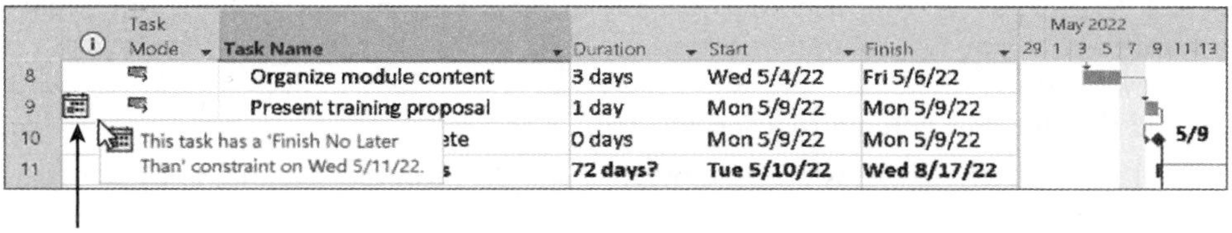

When you apply a date constraint to a task, the constraint indicator appears. Rest your mouse pointer over the indicator for more details.

Because all tasks are associated with a constraint, you can never actually delete a constraint. But if you want to remove a date constraint to allow more schedule flexibility, simply follow the steps above to change the constraint to the least-restrictive As Soon As Possible constraint.

Enter Deadline Reminders

Your project might have specific dates that are goals or markers, rather than date constraints that should and do affect your schedule. With the latter, you set a Start No Earlier Than or Must Finish On constraint that Project will figure into its schedule calculations. With the former, you can set a *deadline* that shows up on your Gantt Chart merely as a gentle reminder. Unlike date constraints, deadlines do not affect Project scheduling; it's just a helpful flag on the Gantt Chart.

To set a deadline:

1. In the Gantt Chart or other task view, double-click the task to which you'd like to add a deadline.

2. In the Task Information dialog box, click the **Advanced** tab.

3. In the Deadline box, click the arrow, then click the date for your deadline.

4. Click **OK**.

    An arrow appears on the timescale side of the Gantt Chart at the deadline date (see Figure 5.15).

FIGURE 5.15   A deadline in the Gantt Chart

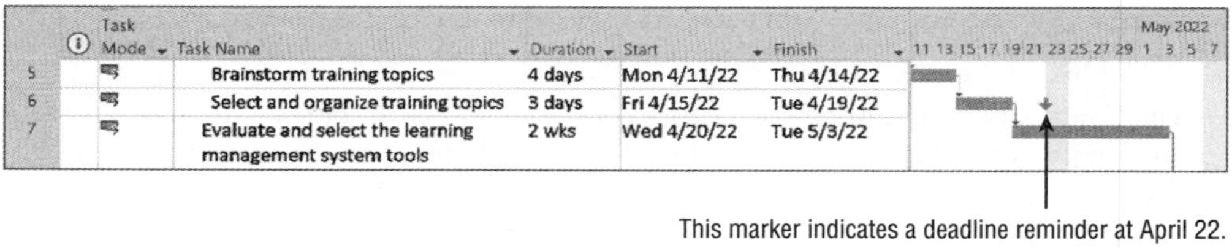

	Task Mode	Task Name	Duration	Start	Finish	May 2022
						11 13 15 17 19 21 23 25 27 29 1 3 5 7
5		Brainstorm training topics	4 days	Mon 4/11/22	Thu 4/14/22	
6		Select and organize training topics	3 days	Fri 4/15/22	Tue 4/19/22	
7		Evaluate and select the learning management system tools	2 wks	Wed 4/20/22	Tue 5/3/22	

This marker indicates a deadline reminder at April 22.

While it's great to see your deadlines visually displayed on the Gantt Chart, you might also want to see them as a column in other task sheet views like the Task Sheet or Task Usage view.

To add the Deadline column to a sheet view:

1. Display the sheet view to which you want to add the Deadline column. For example, on the View tab, in the Task Views groups, click **Task Sheet** or **Sprint Planning Sheet**.

2. At the right edge of the sheet, click the **Add New Column** heading to see the list of all available column headings or fields.

3. Type or click **Deadline**.

    The Deadline column is added to the sheet, and any deadlines you've entered appear with their tasks. You can enter deadlines on other tasks using this column.

To add the Deadline column to any task board view:

1. Switch to the Task Board view, or another board view like the Backlog Board or Sprint Planning Board.

2. On the Format tab, in the Customize group, click **Customize Cards**.

3. In the Customize Task Board Cards dialog box, under Additional Fields, click in the next empty Select Field box, then either type or click **Deadline**.

4. Click **OK**.

    The Deadline field is added to all cards on this and any other board view.

Use Project and Task Calendars

You can use calendars in Project to more accurately indicate when work on your project should be scheduled. In some cases, you might also apply a calendar to one or more tasks that are done according to a different set of *working times* and *nonworking times*. Project comes with three *base calendars* that you can use or adapt to your organization's working times:

- Standard calendar
- Night Shift calendar
- 24-Hours calendar

Review and Change the Project Calendar

By default, all projects have the Standard base calendar applied as the *project calendar*. The Standard calendar reflects working times of Monday to Friday, 8 a.m. to 12 p.m. and 1 to 5 p.m. Project only schedules work on tasks during these working times.

Use this or another base calendar as your starting point to add company holidays, retreats, and other regular days and times when project work should not be scheduled.

To see and change the base calendar applied as your project calendar:

1. Have your project plan open in any view.

2. On the Project tab, in the Properties group, click **Change Working Time**.

   The **Change Working Time** dialog box appears. At the top of the dialog box, the "For calendar" box indicates the name of the project calendar, which by default is the Standard (Project Calendar).

3. To change your project calendar to a different base calendar, click in the **For calendar** box, then click the name of the base calendar you want to use for your project.

   The calendar in the dialog box changes to show the working time (in white) and non-working times (in gray) for that base calendar.

4. Click **OK**.

If necessary, use the Change Working Time dialog box to modify the applied base calendar to reflect your organization's working times. The calendar you set for your project then becomes the basis for scheduling resources and tasks. To learn more about modifying a base calendar, including changes to the standard work week, see "Customize Resource Calendars" in Lesson 6, "Set Up Resources."

Apply a Task Calendar

Tasks are generally scheduled according to the working times on the project calendar. But sometimes a task or set of tasks needs a different schedule of its own. For example, perhaps a set of tasks involved with manufacturing components are scheduled to be done on a night shift or across a 24/7 production schedule. You can make sure these tasks are scheduled accurately by applying a *task calendar* independent of the project calendar.

To apply a task calendar:

1. With your project plan open in any task view, double-click the task to which you want to apply a task calendar.

2. In the Task Information dialog box, click the **Advanced** tab.

3. Click in the **Calendar** box, and then click the name of the base calendar you want to apply to this task—for example, **Night Shift** or **24 Hours**.

4. Click **OK**.

   This task will now be scheduled according to the applied task calendar, rather than the project calendar.

You can apply the same task calendar to multiple tasks at one time. Select the tasks by using the Shift or Ctrl keys. On the Task tab, in the Properties group, click **Information**. The Multiple Task Information dialog box appears. It's similar to the Task Information dialog box, but it only shows those controls that can work with several tasks at once. On the Advanced tab, click in the **Calendar** box, then click the name of the base calendar you want to apply to all selected tasks. Click **OK**.

Project and task calendars add another dimension to Project's scheduling controls for your project. Together with task durations, dependencies, sprint scheduling, and date constraints, project and task calendars can help you accurately schedule your tasks, which in turn will help you complete the project on time.

Key Terms

automatic scheduling mode

base calendars

combination view

critical path

date constraint

deadline

duration

elapsed duration

elapsed weeks

estimated duration

Finish-to-Start task relationship

Gantt chart

manual scheduling mode

milestone

nonworking times

predecessor task

project calendar

Project scheduling engine

sprints

successor task

task calendar

task dependency

task link

task paths

working times

Review Questions

1. You started your project by adding tasks using the default manual scheduling mode. You have since received more information about task durations, how tasks relate to each other, and some hard dates. You now want to use the Project scheduling engine to calculate the schedule for you based on this information. How do you switch the scheduling mode of existing tasks *and* any future tasks from manual to automatic?

    A. In a task view like the Gantt Chart, select all tasks, then on the Task tab, in the Tasks group, click **Auto Schedule**. Then, on the Task tab, in the Tasks group, click **Mode**, then click **Auto Schedule**.

    B. On the File tab, click **Options**, then click **Schedule**. Under Scheduling Options, change the entry in the New Tasks Created field from Manually Scheduled to Auto Scheduled.

    C. In the Gantt Chart, select all tasks, then on the Task tab, in the Tasks group, click **Auto Schedule**.

    D. On the Task tab, in the Tasks group, click **Mode**, then click **Auto Schedule**.

2. What are the three key pieces of scheduling information you see quickly with the Gantt Chart bars on the timescale side of the view?

    A. Durations, milestones, and task names

    B. Assigned resources, task links, and durations

    C. Start date, durations, and finish dates for each task

    D. Start dates, date constraints, and deadlines

3. For an automatically scheduled project, what are three of the four scheduled drivers—that is, task information you enter that controls how the task is scheduled?

    A. Any three of the following: project start date, task duration, sprint duration, and deadline

    B. Any three of the following: project start date, task duration, task links or dependencies, and date constraints

    C. Any three of the following: timescale, task duration, task links or dependencies, and milestone

    D. Any three of the following: sprint start date, sprint length, task duration, and date constraints

4. What happens if you create a task with a duration of 0?

    A. The task is represented with a deadline marker in the timescale side of the Gantt Chart.

    B. The task is represented with a milestone marker in the timescale side of the Gantt Chart.

    C. The task has an estimated duration and is a reminder for you to obtain more specific information.

    D. The task has a Start No Later Than date constraint at the date of the marker.

5. You're using Project to schedule your office remodel, and you want to show that the "Prepare walls" predecessor task must be finished before the "Paint walls" successor task can begin. How do you link the two tasks with a Finish-to-Start dependency in Project?

   A. In the Task Board, click the "Prepare walls" task card, hold down the Ctrl key, then click the "Paint walls" task card. On the Task tab, in the Schedule group, click **Link the Selected Tasks**.

   B. On the Timeline view above the Gantt Chart, drag from the "Prepare walls" task to the "Paint walls" task.

   C. Double-click the "Prepare walls" task, then in the Task Information dialog box, click the **Advanced** tab, then select the "Paint walls" task and the type of constraint you want.

   D. In the Gantt Chart or other task sheet, click the "Prepare walls" task, hold down the Ctrl key, then click the "Paint walls" task. On the Task tab, in the Schedule group, click **Link the Selected Tasks**.

6. How would you set up a series of five three-week sprints starting on May 24 in the next year?

   A. On the Project tab, in the Properties group, click **Manage Sprints**. In the Sprint Start field, enter **May 24** and the year. In the Duration box, enter **3w**. Click **Add Sprint** five times.

   B. In any view, double-click a task, then in the Task Information dialog box, enter the sprint start date, the sprint duration, and the number of sprints in the appropriate fields.

   C. On the Sprint Planning Board, enter the sprint start date, sprint duration, and the number of sprints in the appropriate columns.

   D. In the Sprint Planning Sheet, type the sprint name, start date, and duration for the first sprint in the appropriate columns. Repeat this process to define the other four sprints.

7. What is the default constraint type for all tasks in Project?

   A. Start No Earlier Than

   B. Finish No Later Than

   C. Must Finish On

   D. As Soon As Possible

8. How would you apply a Must Finish On date constraint of July 16 to an automatically scheduled task?

   A. In the Gantt Chart or other task sheet, enter **July 16** in the Finish column for the task.

   B. In the Gantt Chart or other task sheet, double-click the task to open the Task Information dialog box and make sure the General tab is active. Under Dates, enter **July 16** in the Finish box.

   C. In the Gantt Chart or other task sheet, double-click the task to open the Task Information dialog box, then click the Advanced tab. Click in the Constraint Type field, then click **Must Finish On**. Click the arrow in the Constraint Date box, then click July 16 on the calendar.

   D. The methods described in options A and B both set a Must Finish On date constraint on the task.

9. What's the difference between a deadline and a Finish No Later Than date constraint?

   A. A deadline is a marker that serves as a simple reminder on the timescale side of your Gantt Chart, whereas a Finish No Later Than constraint updates the schedule to ensure that the task is scheduled to finish before the specified date.

   B. A deadline updates the schedule to ensure that the task is scheduled to finish before the specified date, whereas a Finish No Later Than constraint is a reminder on the sheet side of your Gantt Chart that does not affect the schedule itself.

   C. The deadline and constraint are both simple reminders of a target date that do not affect the task schedule. The constraint shows as an icon on the sheet side of the Gantt Chart, whereas the deadline shows as an arrow on the timescale side of the Gantt Chart.

   D. The deadline and constraint both update the schedule to ensure that the task is scheduled to finish before the specified date. The constraint shows as an icon on the sheet side of the Gantt Chart, whereas the deadline shows as an arrow on the timescale side of the Gantt Chart.

Lesson 6

Set Up Resources

LESSON OBJECTIVES

✓ Explain the three types of resources in Project and add them to your plan.

✓ Enter cost information for the three types of resources.

✓ Define cost per use and the cost accrual choices.

✓ Describe resource units or max units.

✓ Change the max units for a resource.

✓ Describe how availability affects the project schedule and resource allocation.

✓ Customize a normal work week for a resource calendar.

✓ Specify an exception to a resource calendar.

✓ Explain how Project calculates a resource's availability using max units and the resource calendar.

With your schedule now built, your project is looking like a solid guide toward achieving your deliverables and milestones on time. Your project is mapped out based on your project start date, project working times calendar, task durations, linked task dependencies, and any hard date constraints. With this information, Microsoft Project is able to calculate your task start and finish dates.

You don't necessarily have to add information to your project plan about the people responsible for carrying out the tasks. If you do, though, you'll be able to create a more realistic and accurate schedule. This is because the Project scheduling engine can figure in information about the people's working hours and days, in addition to whether they're working part time or full time on this effort. Project can also show how well resources are being used, and whether you have resource gaps that will hold up progress.

In this lesson, you'll learn how to add information about the people who will carry out the project tasks—that is, your project team members who will transform the project vision into a tangible reality. You'll also see how to add equipment and material resources that are instrumental to the completion of tasks.

You'll enter the costs for these resources so that when you assign the resources to tasks you'll be able to see the cost for those tasks and, by extension, the cost for a phase or the entire project.

Finally, you'll learn how to enter information about a resource's availability on this project, which goes a long way toward creating a realistic schedule and seeing reliable cost projections.

Add Resources to the Plan

In Project, you can add work resources, material resources, and cost resources to your plan and assign those resources to tasks.

Although you can add resources "on the fly" in the Gantt Chart or other task view, it's more efficient to set up your resources and their basic information on the Resource Sheet. You'll save yourself backtracking by defining your resources in the Resource Sheet first, and then assigning them to tasks next. You'll learn more in Lesson 7, "Assign Resources to Tasks."

To switch to the Resource Sheet:

1. Open your project plan in Project.

2. On the View tab, in the Resource Views group, click **Resource Sheet**.

You can also right-click the view bar on the left edge of the Project window, and then click **Resource Sheet**.

The blank Resource Sheet appears, as shown in Figure 6.1.

FIGURE 6.1   The Resource Sheet

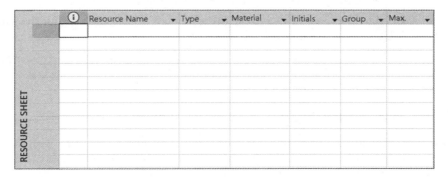

Define Human and Equipment Resources

In Project, your team members assigned to tasks are considered *work resources*, as their effort on an assigned task is based on the amount of work, usually the number of hours, that a person can spend on the task.

Work resources can also be equipment or machinery, whose resource unit is based on the amount of work for which the equipment is available for assigned tasks. Examples include a 3D printer needed to produce a certain number of parts per hour or a cargo van needed for four days as part of an office relocation project.

To add a work resource in the Resource Sheet:

1. In the Resource Sheet, click in the Resource Name field in the first blank row, and type the work resource name—for example, **Monique** or **3D Printer**.

2. Press Enter.

3. Leave the Type field at Work for the default resource type.

   When you define this resource as a work resource, you activate the Max, Std Rate, Ovt Rate, and other fields, and they are filled in with default values. You'll learn more about these fields later in this lesson.

Define Material Resources

Material resources are tangible consumable supplies needed to complete a task. Examples include a quantity of board-feet of lumber in a building project or gallons of paint for a remodeling project.

To add a material resource:

1. In the Resource Sheet, click in the Resource Name field in the next available blank row, and then type the material resource name—for example, **Lumber** or **Paint**.

2. Press Enter.

3. Click the arrow in the **Type** field, and then click **Material**.

4. Click in the Material Label field, and then type the unit of measurement for the material (for example, board-feet, gallons, cubic yards, or boxes).

When you define this as a material resource, you activate the Std Rate and Cost/Use fields. You'll learn more in the section "Enter Resource Costs" later in this lesson.

Define Cost Resources

Cost resources are expenses other than work or material resources associated with the task. Examples include travel costs to qualify a manufacturing process or conference room rental for a training program. Create a cost resource for any such expenses that you want to track with your project costs.

To add a cost resource:

1. In the Resource Sheet, click in the Resource Name field in the next available blank row, and type the cost resource name—for example, **Airfare** or **Room Rental**.

2. Press Enter.

3. Click the arrow in the **Type** field, and then click **Cost**.

With your new cost resource entered, along with the work and material resources, your Resource Sheet might look similar to the one in Figure 6.2.

FIGURE 6.2 Work, material, and cost resources in the Resource Sheet

		Resource Name	Type	Material Label	Initials	Group	Max. Units	Std. Rate
	1	Monique	Work		M		100%	$0.00/hr
	2	Daunte	Work		D		100%	$0.00/hr
	3	Soon Hee	Work		S		100%	$0.00/hr
	4	Color Printer	Work		C		100%	$0.00/hr
	5	Binders	Material	each	B			$0.00
	6	Scratchpads	Material	each	S			$0.00
	7	Pens	Material	package	P			$0.00
	8	Airfare	Cost		A			
	9	Hotel	Cost		H			
	10	Conference Room	Cost		C			
	11	Leo	Work		L		100%	$0.00/hr

Enter Resource Costs

Just as entering resources themselves is optional yet highly recommended for your project plan, entering resource costs is also optional and recommended.

When you enter resource costs and then assign the resources to tasks, Project instantly calculates the cost of carrying out the task. Those costs roll up to any summary tasks and in turn roll up to the project as a whole.

These cost calculations in your plan are a great way to estimate project expenses when you're setting the budget in the initiating and planning processes. After you start executing the project, having costs readily visible helps you monitor expenses against the budget and make any necessary adjustments to control costs.

Group or Highlight Your Resources by Type

If you have many resources of different types, like 20 work resources and 10 material resources, you might find it convenient to group or highlight the list of resources by type as you enter their cost information.

To group your resources by type:

1. Open the Resource Sheet, and then on the **View** tab, in the **Data** group, click the arrow in the **Group By** box, and then click **Resource Type**.

    Your resources are grouped by type, as shown in the following graphic.

Resource Name ▾	Type ▾	Material Label ▾	Initials ▾	Group ▾	Max. Units ▾	Std. Rate ▾	Ovt. Rate ▾
◢ **Type: Work**	**Work**				**800%**		
Monique	Work		M		100%	$0.00/hr	$0.00/hr
Daunte	Work		D		100%	$0.00/hr	$0.00/hr
Soon Hee	Work		S		100%	$0.00/hr	$0.00/hr
Color Printer	Work		C		100%	$0.00/hr	$0.00/hr
Leo	Work		L		100%	$0.00/hr	$0.00/hr
Xavier	Work		X		100%	$0.00/hr	$0.00/hr
Neveah	Work		N		100%	$0.00/hr	$0.00/hr
Nicole	Work		N		100%	$0.00/hr	$0.00/hr
◢ **Type: Material**	**Material**						
Binders	Material	each	B			$0.00	
Scratchpads	Material	each	S			$0.00	
Pens	Material	package	P			$0.00	
◢ **Type: Cost**	**Cost**						
Airfare	Cost		A				
Hotel	Cost		H				
Conference Room	Cost		C				

2. To remove the grouping, on the View tab, in the Data group, click the arrow in the **Group By** box, and then click **No Group**.

To highlight your resources by type:

1. On the View tab, in the Data group, click the arrow in the **Highlight** box, and then click **Resources - Work**, **Resources - Material**, or **Resources - Cost**.

    The selected resource type is highlighted, as shown in the following graphic.

Resource Name	Type	Material Label	Initials	Group	Max. Units	Std. Rate	Ovt. Rate
Monique	Work		M		100%	$0.00/hr	$0.00/hr
Daunte	Work		D		100%	$0.00/hr	$0.00/hr
Soon Hee	Work		S		100%	$0.00/hr	$0.00/hr
Color Printer	Work		C		100%	$0.00/hr	$0.00/hr
Binders	Material	each	B			$0.00	
Scratchpads	Material	each	S			$0.00	
Pens	Material	package	P			$0.00	
Airfare	Cost		A				
Hotel	Cost		H				
Conference Room	Cost		C				
Leo	Work		L		100%	$0.00/hr	$0.00/hr
Xavier	Work		X		100%	$0.00/hr	$0.00/hr
Neveah	Work		N		100%	$0.00/hr	$0.00/hr
Nicole	Work		N		100%	$0.00/hr	$0.00/hr

2. To remove the highlight, on the View tab, in the Data group, click the arrow in the **Highlight** box, and then click **No Highlight**.

Specify Work Resource Costs

To enter costs for a work resource:

1. In the Resource Sheet, go to the first work resource for which you want to enter costs.

2. Enter information in one or more of the following cost fields, as appropriate for the selected work resource:

    - **Std Rate.** If the work resource has a cost per period of time, enter it here. The default is a cost per hour, but you can enter a cost per day, week, or month.

    - **Ovt Rate.** If the work resource has an overtime rate, enter it here.

- **Cost/Use.** If the work resource incurs a cost each time the resource is used, enter that *cost per use* here.

- **Accrue.** Specify how the standard rate and overtime rate you just entered should *accrue*. Choices are to *prorate* the cost throughout the duration of the assigned task, incur at the start of the task, or incur at the end of the task. The default is for costs to be prorated.

3. Repeat this for all your work resources.

Specify Material Resource Costs

To enter costs for a material resource:

1. In the Resource Sheet, go to the first material resource for which you want to enter costs.

2. Enter information in one or more of the following cost fields, as appropriate for the selected material resource:

- **Std Rate.** For material resources, the standard rate refers to the cost per unit of measurement you entered in the Material field (for example, gallons, board-feet, or cubic yards). Enter the cost per unit here. When you assign the material resource to a task, you'll enter the quantity needed for that task, and that's how Project will calculate the materials cost for that task.

- **Cost/Use.** If the material resource incurs a cost each time the resource is used, enter that cost here.

- **Accrue.** Specify whether the standard rate you entered should be prorated throughout the duration of the assigned task, should incur at the start of the task, or incur at the end of the task. The default is for costs to be prorated.

3. Repeat this for all your material resources.

Specify Cost Resource Costs

The Accrue field is the only cost field available for cost resources. This is because the costs for a cost resource is likely to be different depending on which task you assign it to.

For example, suppose you know you need an "Airfare" cost resource because of all the travel your project will require. You then assign "Airfare" to the "Conduct training in Seattle" task and also to the "Meet with vendor in Chicago" task. The airfare cost for the two tasks are probably different, so after you assign the "Airfare" cost resource to the tasks in the Gantt Chart or other task sheet, you enter the specific costs for each.

You'll learn more in the section "Assign Cost Resources to Tasks" in Lesson 7.

With cost information entered for your work, material, and cost resources, your Resource Sheet might look similar to the one in Figure 6.3.

FIGURE 6.3 Cost information in the resource sheet

Resource Name	Type	Material Label	Initials	Group	Max. Units	Std. Rate	Ovt. Rate
Monique	Work		M		100%	$20.00/hr	$30.00/hr
Daunte	Work		D		50%	$22.00/hr	$0.00/hr
Soon Hee	Work		S		100%	$25.00/hr	$0.00/hr
Color Printer	Work		C		100%	$10.00/hr	$0.00/hr
Binders	Material	each	B			$4.00	
Scratchpads	Material	each	S			$1.00	
Pens	Material	package	P			$12.00	
Airfare	Cost		A				
Hotel	Cost		H				
Conference Room	Cost		C				
Leo	Work		L		100%	$25.00/hr	$0.00/hr
Xavier	Work		X		100%	$22.00/hr	$0.00/hr
Neveah	Work		N		100%	$28.00/hr	$0.00/hr
Nicole	Work		N		100%	$24.00/hr	$0.00/hr

Refine Resource Unit Availability

Many of your work resources will be 100 percent dedicated to your project. If you have exceptions to this, you can note that in the Resource Sheet to make sure your resources and tasks are scheduled properly.

For example, you might have a team member who is only available 50 percent of the time for your project. This might be because they are splitting their time with another project, or because they have additional supervisory responsibilities.

Another example is if you have access to a necessary equipment resource only 20 percent of the time.

To specify a work resource's *availability* on your project, you use the **Max Units** field on the Resource Sheet. *Max Units* indicates the availability a resource has for this project during the current period of time. You might also think of max units as *resource units*, or resource availability.

The default **Max Units** is 100 percent, meaning the work resource is available full time on your project. You can change this to another percentage like 50 percent or 25 percent as appropriate.

You can also use **Max Units** to indicate multiples of the same kind of resource. For example, maybe you have three graphic designers and four 3D printers available full time. Instead of entering the graphic designers separately in the Resource Sheet, you can enter them as a single work resource with max units of 300 percent. Likewise, you can specify the availability of the four 3D printers as 400 percent.

In another scenario, suppose you have three carpenters on a building project, and two of them are available full time and one of them is available one-third of the time. You can express these max units as 233 percent.

When you assign work resources that have max units different from 100 percent, it can affect how the task is scheduled or whether the resource shows as *overallocated* (that is, with more work assigned in a given time period than the resource has availability). You'll learn more about this in the section "Review Resource Assignments" in Lesson 7.

Change Resource Units

To change resource availability units for the duration of the project:

1. In the Resource Sheet, go to the work resource whose max units you want to change.
2. In the Max Units field, enter the percentage that reflects the resource's availability for this project (for example, 66% or 300%).

Specify Differing Availability Over Time

If a resource's availability changes to different levels over the duration of the project, you can specify the date of the change and the differing resource availability.

For example, you might have resources who start the project with 50 percent availability, and then three months later they are freed up to devote 100 percent of their time to the project. You can specify this by using the Resource Information dialog box.

To specify changing levels of resource availability:

1. In the Resource Sheet, double-click the name of the work resource who has varying levels of resource availability throughout the project.

   When you double-click a resource, the Resource Information dialog box appears. You can also open this dialog box by going to the Resource tab, in the Properties group, and clicking **Information**.

2. If necessary, click the **General** tab.

   The first row of the Resource Availability table shows the current max units of the selected resource. The Available From field shows "NA," or not applicable. This indicates that the resource is available from the project start date. Likewise, the Available To field shows "NA," or not applicable, meaning the resource's availability continues through the project finish date.

3. In the first row of the Resource Availability table, click the arrow in the **Available To** field, then click the date when the first level of availability ends.

   For example, if the resource is 50 percent available from the project start until April 30, click April 30 in the Available To field.

4. Make sure the Units field shows the correct resource availability for the first time period.

5. In the second row, click the arrow in the **Available From** field, and then click the date when the second level of availability begins.

6. In the second row, click the arrow in the **Available To** field, and then click the date when the second level of availability ends.

7. In the second row, click in the Units field, and then type the units to indicate the level of availability—for example, **20%** or **100%**.

8. Continue adding rows with the start and finish dates to reflect the resource's changing levels of availability over the life of the project (see Figure 6.4).

FIGURE 6.4   The Resource Availability table in the Resource Information dialog box

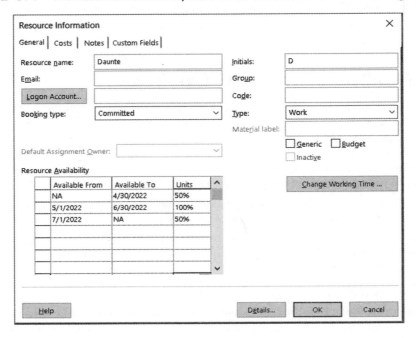

9. Click **OK**.

The Resource Information dialog box closes. As you work through the project, the value in the resource's Max Units field will change according to the dates you scheduled for the changing availability.

Customize Resource Calendars

The resources' max units specify the level a resource is available—like 50 percent or 100 percent—against the overall project working time specified in the *project calendar*. Project then schedules the resources according to that availability and also indicates whether they have more work than they can accomplish in a given time period.

Another way to specify resource availability is through *resource calendars*, which indicate a resource's individual working days and times.

By default, the resource calendar for each work resource is identical to the project calendar, which might reflect a calendar of working time like Monday to Friday, 8 a.m. to 5 p.m. Having your resource calendar the same as the project calendar is probably accurate for most of your resources.

If you have a part-time team member, or one who works three 12-hour days instead of five 8-hour days, or if you have an equipment resource that's available 24/7, you can specify this in the resource calendar. Doing so ensures a more accurate picture of availability for the resources and the tasks to which they're assigned.

Working Times Calendars in Microsoft Project

To help you more accurately specify when work on a project should be scheduled, you can use calendars in Project.

Base Calendar   Project comes with three *base calendars*, or templates, for a starting point you can use for your project and resource calendars. They show different configurations of working time and nonworking time. Project can schedule tasks during the *working times* but not during the *nonworking times*.

Standard Base Calendar   The Standard base calendar reflects a working time schedule of Monday to Friday, 8 a.m. to 12 p.m. and 1 p.m. to 5 p.m. The weekends and the weekday 12-1 p.m. hour are nonworking time.

Night Shift Base Calendar   The Night Shift base calendar reflects a working time schedule of Monday to Friday, 11 p.m. to 8 a.m. with 3 a.m. to 4 a.m. as nonworking time.

24 Hours Base Calendar   The 24 Hours base calendar reflects all working time and no nonworking time 12 a.m. to 12 a.m. daily from Sunday to Saturday.

Project Calendar   Your project calendar starts out identical to the Standard base calendar. You can choose a different base calendar as the template for your project calendar. Use the base calendar as your starting point to add company holidays, retreats, and other regular days and times when project work should not be scheduled. For more information, see the section "Use Project and Task Calendars" in Lesson 5, "Build the Schedule."

Resource Calendar   Each resource calendar starts out identical to the project calendar. If any resources work a schedule different from the days and times reflected in your project calendar, you can specify that schedule in the resource calendar. This is covered in more detail in this section.

Task Calendar   Like the resource calendar, each *task calendar* starts out identical to the project calendar. If a task requires scheduling different from the project calendar, you can specify that change. For more information, see the section "Use Project and Task Calendars" in Lesson 5.

Switch the Base Calendar

By default, the resource calendar is based on the project calendar, which in turn is often based on the Standard base calendar of Monday to Friday, 8 a.m. to 5 p.m. If a resource calendar is closer to the working times reflected in the Night Shift or 24 Hours calendar, you can change the base calendar for the resource calendar.

To change the base calendar for a resource calendar:

1. In the Resource Sheet, double-click the name of the work resource whose base calendar you want to change.

2. In the Resource Information dialog box, click **Change Working Time**.

    The Change Working Time dialog box appears. Another way to open this dialog box: On the Project tab, in the Properties group, click **Change Working Time**.

3. Make sure the top of the dialog box indicates that this is the resource calendar for the resource you selected.

4. Also near the top of the dialog box, click in the **Base Calendar** field and select the base calendar you want to change for this resource. The choices are **24 Hours**, **Night Shift**, and **Standard** (see Figure 6.5).

    When you select a different base calendar, the calendar in the dialog box changes to show the working time (in white) and nonworking times (in gray) for that base calendar.

5. Click **OK**.

If necessary, you can now go on to customize the individual days and times in the resource calendar, but you've probably saved yourself some time by changing the base calendar first.

Change the Work Week in a Resource Calendar

You can specify the normal work week for the selected resource by using the Work Weeks tab in the Change Working Time dialog box.

To change the normal working days and times for a resource calendar:

1. In the Resource Sheet, double-click the name of the work resource whose normal work week you want to change.

2. In the Resource Information dialog box, click **Change Working Time**.

3. In the table section of the dialog box, click the **Work Weeks** tab.

FIGURE 6.5   Base calendars in the Change Working Time dialog box

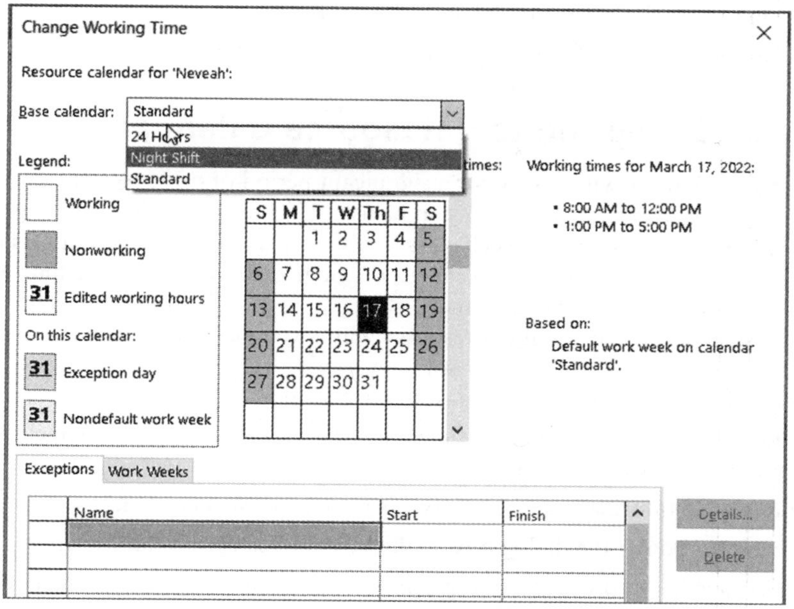

4. Make sure the "Default" row is selected, and then click the **Details** button.

5. In the Details dialog box, click the day(s) of the week you want to change from the state of the base calendar.

    Hold down the Shift or Ctrl key to select multiple days of the week.

6. To change a working day to a nonworking day, click **Set Days To Nonworking Time**.

7. To change the working times in a day, click **Set Day(s) To These Specific Working Times**. In the working time table, enter the working times in the From and To fields, as shown in Figure 6.6.

FIGURE 6.6   Customizing the default work week for a resource calendar

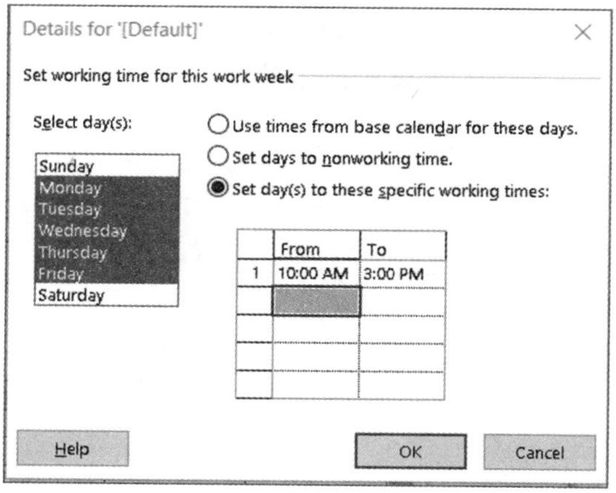

8. When you finish customizing the working and nonworking days and times, click **OK**.

9. In the Change Working Time dialog box, click **OK**.

10. In the Resource Information dialog box, click **OK**.

Specify an Exception to a Resource Calendar

If a resource's work week will change for a significant period of time, you can enter an exception in the resource's calendar. This can be useful if a team member is taking a two-week vacation or is going to a one-week class that's not part of project activities. For an equipment resource, you might want to enter a calendar exception if the machine will be down while awaiting parts for maintenance.

You can also enter an exception if a resource will have more availability than usual for a significant period of time, like a week or so.

To specify a temporary exception to a resource calendar:

1. In the Resource Sheet, double-click the name of the work resource for which you want to enter a work week exception.

2. In the Resource Information dialog box, click **Change Working Time**.

3. In the table section of the dialog box, make sure the Exceptions tab is active.

4. In the first available row in the Exceptions table, click in the Name field and then type a name for the exception, like **Vacation**, **Training**, or **Maintenance**.

5. In the Start field, enter the start date for the exception period.

6. In the Finish field, enter the finish date for the exception period (see Figure 6.7).

FIGURE 6.7   Dates for a resource calendar work week exception

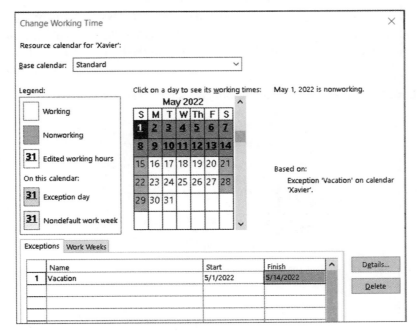

7. Click the **Details** button.

The Details button becomes available after you enter the dates for the exception period.

8. In the Details dialog box, click **Nonworking** if the exception period will be a nonworking period (see Figure 6.8).

FIGURE 6.8   Details for a resource calendar work week exception

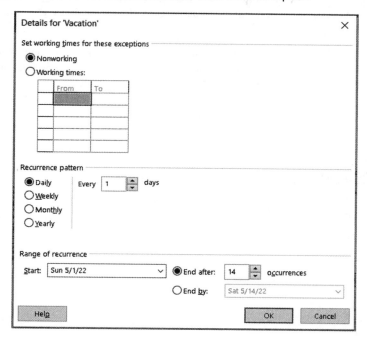

If the exception is to add working times, click **Working Times**, and then enter the working times in the From and To fields.

9. If this is a recurring exception, under Recurrence Pattern, specify the details of the recurrence.

10. Click OK, and then in the Change Working Time dialog box, click **OK**, then click **OK** again.

Resource Calendars and Max Units

The resource calendar and max units work together to determine resource availability. Project calculates resource availability by first looking at the resource calendar, and then figuring in the percentage of that availability as reflected in the max units. This means if a team member's resource calendar indicates that they work 20 hours per week, and then the max units says they are available at 50 percent, their availability will show as 10 hours per week.

Using one or the other, or both in tandem, will help you reflect your resources' true availability so that their assigned tasks will be scheduled appropriately, and you'll be able to monitor their *allocations*—and possible overallocations—accurately.

Key Terms

accrue

allocation

availability

base calendar

cost per use

cost resources

material resources

max units

nonworking times

overallocated

project calendar

prorated

resource calendar

resource units

work resources

working times

Review Questions

1. What are the three types of resources you can specify in Project?
   A. Work, human, and overallocated
   B. Material, airfare, and equipment
   C. Work, material, and cost
   D. Human, equipment, and travel

2. What are two examples of work resources, whose availability and scheduling depends on the number of hours (or days) an assigned task can take?
   A. People and equipment
   B. Cost and materials
   C. People and materials
   D. Machines and materials

3. Which Project view is best for efficiently adding resources to your plan, including entering the resource names, resource type, cost information, and max units?
   A. Gantt Chart
   B. Resource Sheet
   C. Task Board
   D. Resource Graph

4. What are the choices for cost accrual methods for resource costs?
   A. Start, Prorated, and End
   B. Standard Rate, Overtime Rate, and Cost Per Use
   C. Start, 100%, and End
   D. Cost Rate Table, Prorated, and Cost Per Use

5. What are other names for max units, which determine how much a resource is available during the project time period?
   A. Assignment units or resource units
   B. Resource calendar or accrual
   C. 100 percent working time or full time
   D. Resource units or percent availability

6. Which dialog box do you use to change the base calendar, normal work week, or work week exception for a resource calendar?
   A. **Details for '[Default]'** dialog box
   B. **Change Working Time** dialog box
   C. **Resource Availability** table on the **Resource Information** dialog box
   D. **Exceptions** tab on the **Change Working Time** dialog box

7.   How does Project calculate resource availability from the max units and resource calendar?

   A.   Project calculates the total days and hours of working time in the resource calendar and multiplies it by the max units percentage.

   B.   Project calculates the total days and hours of working time in the resource calendar and makes sure it matches the max units percentage against the project calendar.

   C.   Project compares the working time in the resource calendar with the max units and uses whichever availability is higher.

   D.   Project compares the working time in the resource calendar with the max units and uses which availability is lower.

Lesson

7

Assign Resources to Tasks

LESSON OBJECTIVES

✓ Assign work, material, and cost resources to tasks.

✓ Review assignments in different views including the Gantt Chart, Team Planner, Task Usage view, and Task Board.

✓ Explain how Project calculates costs for tasks with work, material, and cost resources assigned to them.

✓ View costs for tasks with assigned resources in a task sheet and an agile planning board.

✓ Replace one resource assigned to a task with a different resource.

✓ Add and remove work resources assigned to a task and choose how this change should affect the assignment.

✓ Change the duration on a task with work resources assigned and choose how this change should affect the assignments.

In Lesson 6, "Set Up Resources," you added resource information to your Microsoft Project plan. Your resources probably include people—your team members who will carry out the project tasks. You might have also added information about equipment resources, material resources, and cost resources—the other items that help accomplish your project goals.

In this lesson, you'll assign people, equipment, materials, and cost resources to tasks and see the impact this has on your project plan.

After you assign resources to tasks, you can use different views to look at your assignments from various angles, which enables you to see if any resources are overbooked or underutilized throughout the project. You'll be able to view better projections of your overall project costs based on the cost of resources and the tasks to which they're assigned. You can then change assignments as necessary, like replacing, adding, or removing resources assigned to tasks.

Assign Work Resources to Tasks

When you assign resources to tasks, you're identifying who's doing what. In Project, your team members are considered *work resources*, as their effort on an assigned task is based on the amount of *work*, usually the number of hours, that an assigned person can spend on the task.

A work resource can also be equipment of some kind, whose resource *unit* is based on the amount of time that the equipment is available for assigned tasks.

You can use the Assign Resources dialog box in any task view, including the Task Board. This dialog box is a convenient and quick way to view all resources because it stays open as you switch from task to task when making multiple assignments.

To assign a person or equipment work resource to a task:

1. Right-click the view bar on the left edge of the Project window, and then click the name of the task view you want to use as you make your assignments.

    The Gantt Chart is an ideal view for seeing the results of your assignments.

2. On the Resource tab, in the Assignments group, click **Assign Resources**.

    The Assign Resources dialog box appears, as shown in Figure 7.1. It lists all the work, material, and cost resources you have already entered in the Resource Sheet.

FIGURE 7.1   Assign Resources dialog box

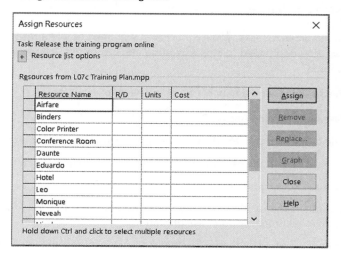

3. In the Gantt Chart or other task view, click the task to which you want to assign a work resource.

4. In the Assign Resources dialog box, click the name of the work resource you want to assign to the selected task.

5. Click **Assign**.

    The selected resource is assigned to the selected task. In the dialog box, the resource name is shown with a check mark and moves to the top of the list. If the view includes a Resource Names field, the assigned resource appears in that field. In the Gantt Chart, the resource name also appears next to the Gantt bar on the timescale (see Figure 7.2).

FIGURE 7.2   A work resource assigned to a task

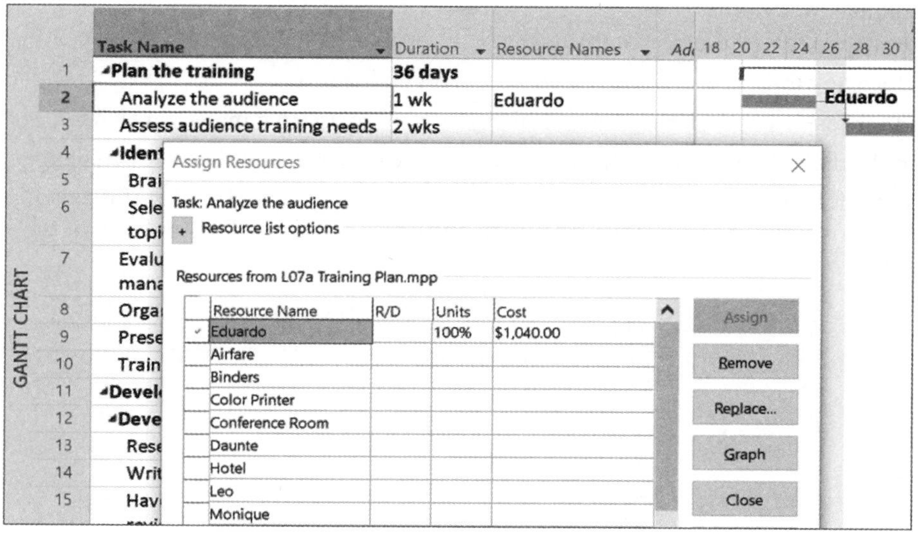

Create and Assign a New Resource on the Fly

While assigning resources to tasks, you might realize you need to add a resource to the list. However, to do so, you don't need to stop assigning and return to the Resource Sheet to add the new resource.

Instead, you can add and assign a new resource in one step:

1. Open any task view and the Assign Resources dialog box.

2. In the task view, click the task to which you want to assign a new resource.

3. In the dialog box, click in the next available blank Resource Name field.

4. Type the resource name, and then click **Assign**.

   The new resource is then assigned to the selected task. It is also added to the resource list for you to choose from for other assignments.

When you add a new resource on the fly like this, it takes on all resource defaults. This means that, until you change it, the resource is specified as a work resource at 100% *max units* (full time), with no cost information. When you're done assigning resources to tasks, simply return to the Resource Sheet to complete the necessary information such as resource type, max units, and cost.

Assign Material Resources to Tasks

A *material resource* is a quantity of tangible consumable supplies needed to complete a task. This might be a quantity of concrete or number of windows in a building project, for example.

To assign a material resource to a task:

1. Open any task view and the Assign Resources dialog box.

2. In the task view, click the task to which you want to assign a material resource.

3. In the dialog box, click the name of the material resource, and then click **Assign**.

   The selected material resource is assigned to the task. Its material label (for example, boxes or cubic yards) and the default quantity of 1 appear in the Units field of the dialog box.

4. If you need to change the quantity, click in the Units field for the assigned material resource and enter the number.

The Units field updates with the new quantity and label. If the task view includes a Resource Names field, the material resource's name, quantity, and label appear in that field. In the Gantt Chart, this information appears next to the Gantt bar (see Figure 7.3).

FIGURE 7.3   A material resource assigned to a task

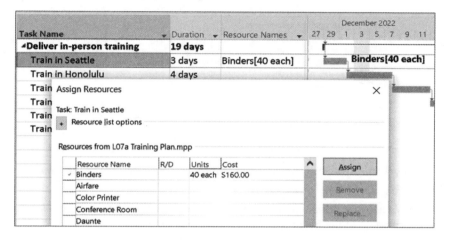

Assign Resources by Using the Resource Names Field

As an alternative to the Assign Resources dialog box, you can assign resources directly from the Gantt Chart, Task Sheet, or any other task sheet view that contains the Resource Names column.

To use the Resource Names field to assign a resource to a task:

1. Right-click the view bar on the far left edge of the Project window, and then click **Gantt Chart** or **Task Sheet**.

2. Go to the task to which you want to assign a resource.

3. Click the arrow in the **Resource Names** field for the selected task.

All the resources you entered in the Resource Sheet appear in a drop-down list, as shown here.

Task Name	Duration	Resource Names	27
0	◢L07a Training Plan	200 days		
1	◢Plan the training	36 days		
2	Analyze the audience	1 wk	Eduardo	
3	Assess audience training needs	2 wks	▾	
4	◢Identify the training topics	7 days	☐Airfare	▲
5	Brainstorm training topics	4 days	☐Binders	
6	Select and organize training topics	3 days	☐Color Printer ☐Conference Roo	
7	Evaluate and select the learning management system tools	2 wks	☐Daunte ☐Eduardo ☐Hotel	
8	Organize module content	3 days	☐Leo	
9	Present training proposal	1 day	☐Monique	
10	Training plan complete	0 days	☐Neveah	
11	◢Develop the modules	140 days	☐Nicole	
12	◢Develop Module 1	140 days	☐Pens	
13	Research Module 1 topics	2 wks	☐Scratchpads	
14	Write Module 1 topics	2 wks	☐Simone	
15	Have Module 1 topics	1 wk	☐Soon Hee	▼

4. Select the check box for the resource you want to assign to the selected task.

    Note that you can select more than one resource to assign several to the same task at once.

    If the resource is not listed, you can type the name directly in the Resource Names field, and then go to the Resource Sheet later to add details.

5. Press Enter.

    The selected resource is assigned to the task. The resource name appears in the Resource Names field and also alongside the Gantt bar on the timescale side of the Gantt Chart.

Assign Cost Resources to Tasks

A *cost resource* is a direct expense associated with the task beyond those costs associated with a work or material resource. Examples include travel costs to meet with a vendor or catering costs for a major planning conference. Distinguished from consumable material resources or work resources spending time to accomplish tasks, cost resources are additional costs incurred in carrying out a task. If you're using your project plan to track costs, you'll want to include cost resources to capture these additional expenses.

To assign a cost resource to a task:

1. Open your preferred task view and the Assign Resources dialog box.

2. In the task view, click the task to which you want to assign a cost resource.

3. In the dialog box, click the name of the cost resource, and then click **Assign**.

    The selected cost resource is assigned to the task. A value of $0.00 appears in the Cost field of the dialog box.

4. Click in the Cost field for the cost resource, and then enter the expense amount for this resource on this task.

    For example, if the cost resource is "Airfare," enter in the Cost field the amount of airfare associated with just this task.

    If the view includes a Resource Names field, the cost resource's name and amount appear in that field. In the Gantt Chart, this information appears next to the Gantt bar (see Figure 7.4).

FIGURE 7.4   Cost resources assigned to tasks

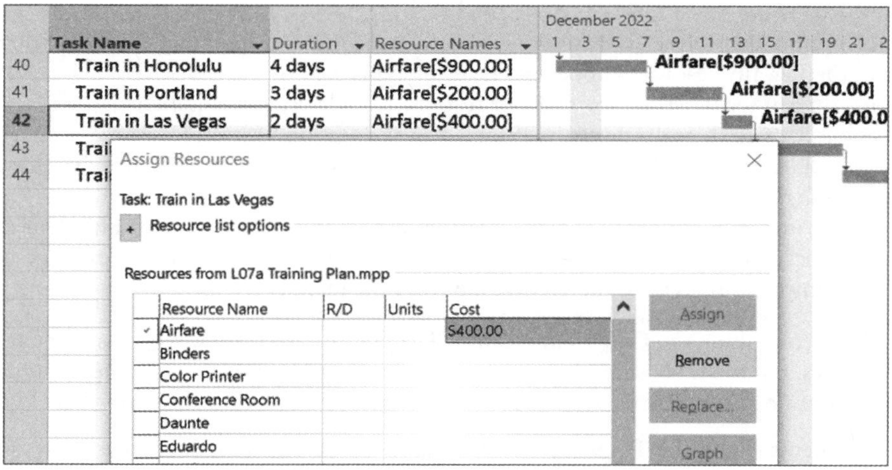

5. When you're done assigning resources, in the Assign Resources dialog box, click **Close**.

Assign Multiple Resources at Once

To assign multiple resources to a selected task at one time:

1. Open your preferred task view and the Assign Resources dialog box.

2. In the view, click the task to which you want to assign multiple resources.

3. In the dialog box, click the first resource you want to assign.

4. Hold down the Ctrl key, and then click the additional resources.

5. Click **Assign**.

    All the selected resources are assigned at once to the selected task. In the dialog box, they all show with a check mark and move to the top of the Resources table.

6. Enter any quantities for material resources in the Units field or amounts for cost resources in the Cost field.

Review Resource Assignments

When you assign a resource to a task, you are creating an *assignment*. In Project, an assignment is the intersection of a resource assigned to a task. After you've assigned resources to tasks, it's a good idea to review your assignments to ensure that it all makes sense. You can look for whether any resources appear to be double-booked or otherwise overallocated. In addition, you can see whether any tasks or resources are lacking assignments.

In Lesson 8, "Check and Adjust the Project," in the section "Check Resource Assignments," you'll learn more about how to optimize resource usage and minimize overallocations and underallocations.

The following list highlights the views you can use to review assignments and their effect on your project. To switch to a different view, right-click the view bar on the left edge of the Project window, and then click the view name from the menu.

Assignments Along the Gantt Timescale   The Gantt Chart shows you assignments in two ways. On the table side, assignments are shown in the Resource Names column. On the timescale side of the view, resource names are shown next to the Gantt bar.

Assignments Along the Team Planner Timescale   The Team Planner view shows tasks along a timescale by the resource assigned. This is a good way to see how much or how little a specific resource is being used throughout the life of the project. With this view, you can quickly see whether a resource is *overallocated* (that is, assigned to more work than the resource has availability to accomplish). You can also see if a resource has additional availability where they are not assigned to any tasks (see Figure 7.5).

All Tasks for a Resource   Similar to Team Planner, the Resource Usage view shows task assignments by resource. And similar to the Gantt Chart, the Resource Usage view is a combination view, with a table on the left and a timescale on the right. Each resource is listed in the table, and the assigned tasks are listed below the resource name. The timescale side of the view shows the number of hours assigned per time period (see Figure 7.6).

All Resources Assigned to Tasks   Similar to the Resource Usage view, the Task Usage view shows resource assignment by task. Each task is listed in the table side of the view, with the assigned resources listed below each task name. The timescale side of the view shows the number of hours assigned per time period (see Figure 7.7).

Resource Assignments on the Agile Task Board   Assigned resources appear by default on each task card on the Task Board (see Figure 7.8).

FIGURE 7.5 Assignments in Team Planner

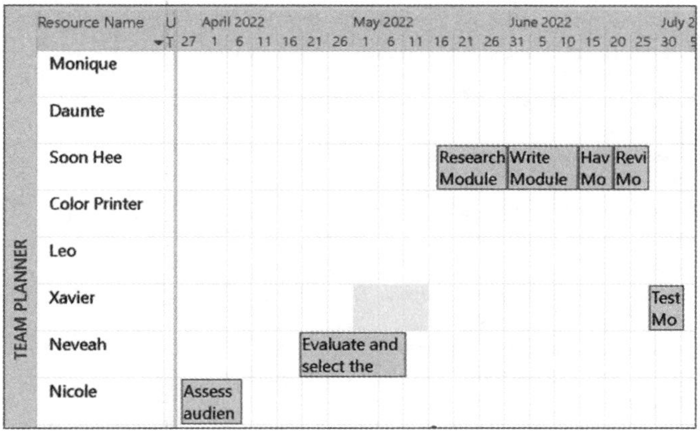

FIGURE 7.6 Resource Usage view

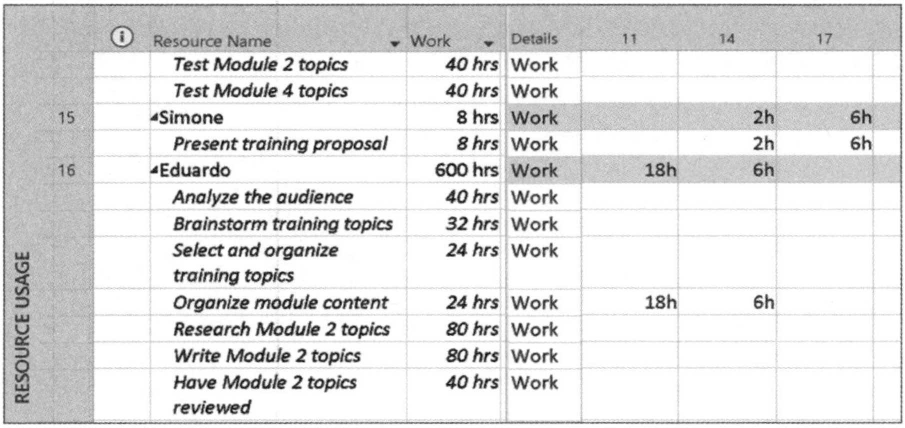

	Resource Name	Work	Details	11	14	17
	Test Module 2 topics	*40 hrs*	Work			
	Test Module 4 topics	*40 hrs*	Work			
15	◢Simone	8 hrs	Work		2h	6h
	Present training proposal	*8 hrs*	Work		2h	6h
16	◢Eduardo	600 hrs	Work	18h	6h	
	Analyze the audience	*40 hrs*	Work			
	Brainstorm training topics	*32 hrs*	Work			
	Select and organize training topics	*24 hrs*	Work			
	Organize module content	*24 hrs*	Work	18h	6h	
	Research Module 2 topics	*80 hrs*	Work			
	Write Module 2 topics	*80 hrs*	Work			
	Have Module 2 topics reviewed	*40 hrs*	Work			

Scroll to Tasks in a Timescale

When reviewing tasks in a Gantt Chart, Team Planner, Task Usage view, Resource Usage view, or other combination view, sometimes you don't see where a task or resource's information is located in the timescale. You could hunt for it by scrolling through the time-scale, but that can become tedious. Instead, on the Task tab, in the Editing group, click **Scroll to Task**. The view scrolls immediately to the information in the timesheet for the task, resource, or assignment selected in the table side of the view. You can also press Ctrl+Shift+F5.

FIGURE 7.7   Task Usage view

	Task Name	Details	11	14	17	20
1	**◢Plan the training**	Work	24h	16h	16h	15h
2	◢Analyze the audience	Work				
	Eduardo	Work				
3	◢Assess audience training needs	Work				
	Nicole	Work				
4	**◢Identify the training topics**	Work	24h	16h	16h	
5	◢Brainstorm training topics	Work	24h	8h		
	Eduardo	Work	24h	8h		
6	◢Select and organize training topics	Work		8h	16h	
	Eduardo	Work		8h	16h	
7	◢Evaluate and select the learning management system tools	Work				15h
	Neveah	Work				15h
8	◢Organize module content	Work				
	Eduardo	Work				
9	◢Present training proposal	Work				
	Simone	Work				

FIGURE 7.8   Resource assignments in Task Board cards

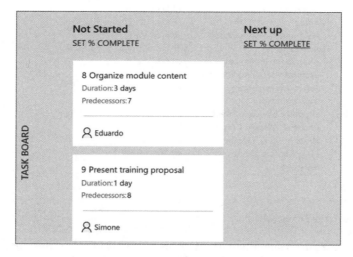

Resource and Assignment Reports

In addition to views that highlight assignments, you can run resource reports. On the Report tab, in the View Reports group, click **Resources**, and then click **Resource Overview** (see the following graphic) or **Overallocated Resources**.

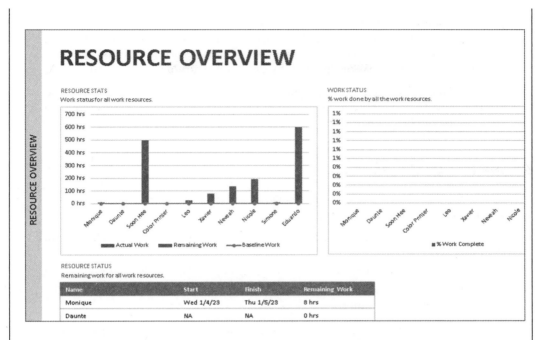

Learn more about reports in Lesson 11, "Report Project Information."

See Task Costs from Assignments

When you enter costs associated with your project resources, and then you assign those resources to tasks, you can see how much it will cost to complete a task. By extension, you can then see how much it will cost to complete a sprint or phase, and how much the entire project will cost.

This list details how Project calculates the cost for the three types of resources:

Work Resource Calculation   When you first set up your people and equipment resources in the Resource Sheet, you specify how much they cost per hour or per day. Then when you assign the work resource to a task, Project multiplies that cost by the number of hours or days of work the resource is assigned to on that task.

Material Resource Calculation   In the Resource Sheet, you specify the material resource cost per unit, such as the gallon or case. Then when you assign the material resource to a task, you also indicate the number of units needed for the task. Project then multiplies the material cost per unit by the quantity for the assigned task.

Cost Resource Calculation   You initially specify a cost resource in the Resource Sheet by name only. Then when you assign the cost resource to a task, you specify what the cost amount will be for that task.

Review Task Costs

To see task costs based on resource assignments:

1. Switch to the Task Sheet or Gantt Chart.

2. Right-click the column heading next to where you want to add the Cost field, and then click **Insert Column**.

   Project adds a new column to the left of the one you selected, and lists all available fields.

3. Type **cost** and then press Enter.

   The Cost column appears. Based on the cost of assigned resources, task costs appear in the field, as shown in Figure 7.9.

FIGURE 7.9   A Cost column added to the Task Sheet

		Task Name	Duration	Cost	Resource Names
	30	⁴Develop Module 4	35 days	$7,200.00	
	31	Research Module 4 topics	2 wks	$2,080.00	Eduardo
	32	Write Module 4 topics	2 wks	$2,080.00	Eduardo
	33	Have Module 4 topics reviewed	1 wk	$1,040.00	Eduardo
	34	Revise Module 4 topics	1 wk	$1,040.00	Eduardo
	35	Test Module 4 topics	1 wk	$960.00	Nicole
	36	Compile the modules in the LMS	3 days	$672.00	Neveah
TASK SHEET	37	Release the training program online	2 days	$0.00	
	38	⁴Deliver in-person training	19 days	$2,560.00	
	39	Train in Seattle	3 days	$160.00	Binders[40 each]
	40	Train in Honolulu	4 days	$900.00	Airfare[$900.00]
	41	Train in Portland	3 days	$200.00	Airfare[$200.00]

See Summary Task or Sprint Costs

When you add the Cost field to a task sheet, you see *rolled-up costs* on the summary tasks. Rolled-up costs add the costs of the subtasks so that you can see the cost of the summary task, which often can represent a phase or category of the project.

In the same way, you can add the Cost field to the Sprint Planning Sheet. This will show you the cost projection for each sprint, based on the cost of assigned resources.

Review Task Costs on an Agile Planning Board

To see task costs on the Task Board or Sprint Board:

1. Switch to the Task Board or Sprint Board.
2. On the Format tab, in the Customize group, click **Customize Cards**.
3. In the Customize Task Board Cards dialog box, under Additional Fields, click in the first empty **Select Field** box, and then either type **cost** or select it from the list of fields.
4. Click **OK**.

   The Cost field is added to all Task Board cards and any other board view like the Sprint Planning Board or Current Sprint Board.

Review the Overall Project Cost Estimate

All levels of summary tasks show the rolled-up information of their subtasks. If you show the Project Summary Task in a task sheet that shows the Cost field, you can see the rolled-up cost for the entire project.

   To see overall project costs:

1. Switch to the Task Sheet or Gantt Chart, and make sure the Cost field is showing in the table.
2. On the Format tab, in the Show/Hide group, select the **Project Summary Task** check box.

   The project summary task appears as row 0 in the task sheet and uses your project filename as the project summary task name.
3. If you want, click in the project summary task name to change it.
4. Review the rolled-up cost in the project summary task.

   This is the overall cost estimate for the entire project, based on the costs of resources assigned to tasks (see Figure 7.10).

FIGURE 7.10   Cost field in the Project Summary Task

		Task Mode	Task Name	Duration	Cost	Resource Names
0			⊿L07b Training Plan	207.63 days	$38,896.00	
1			⊿Plan the training	41.75 days	$7,504.00	
2			Analyze the audience	1 wk	$1,040.00	Eduardo
3			Assess audience training needs	2 wks	$1,920.00	Nicole
4			⊿Identify the training topics	7 days	$1,456.00	
5			Brainstorm training topics	4 days	$832.00	Eduardo
6			Select and organize training topics	3 days	$624.00	Eduardo

In the section "Reduce Costs" in Lesson 8, you'll learn how to adjust your project so that your cost projections meet your budget target.

Show, Hide, and Move Columns on a Sheet View

You work with various Project fields in columns in a sheet view like the Task Sheet, Gantt Chart, or Resource Sheet. In these views, you can show other columns, hide columns you don't need, or move columns to a layout that better suits your needs.

Show a Column   Right-click the column heading next to where you want to add the new column, and then click **Insert Column**. Alternatively, on the Format tab, in the Columns group, click **Insert Column**. Project adds a new column to the left of the one you selected and lists all available fields. Type the name of the field you want and press Enter. Or, scroll through the list and click the field name. The new column appears, with information filled in as appropriate.

Hide a Column   Right-click the column heading you want to hide, and then click **Hide Column**. Or, on the Format tab, in the Columns group, click **Column Settings**, and then click **Hide Column**.

When you hide a column, you're not deleting the information. The information is always there in the database that is your Microsoft Project plan. When you show a column again as described above, all the information stored in your project database reappears.

Move a Column   Click the column heading and drag it to the location you want. As you drag, a vertical gray bar appears to show where the column will be placed when you release the mouse.

Change Assignments

After you've assigned resources to tasks, you can still change the assignments. For example, you might need to replace one resource with another on a task, or you might want to add or remove resource assignments. While some changes are simple, others need you to make a choice to ensure the change has the effect on the schedule that you expect. These changes can influence task duration or how much the assigned resources work on a task. Even changing the duration on tasks with assigned work resources can affect those resources.

Replace a Resource Assignment

It's easy to replace one assigned resource with another, and it typically has little to no impact on the schedule.

To replace a resource assigned to a task:

1. Switch to any task view.

2. On the Resource tab, in the Assignments group, click **Assign Resources**.

3. In the task view, click the task with the resource assignment you want to replace.

4. In the dialog box, click the name of the resource you want to replace.

   The resources assigned to the selected task appear at the top of the Resources table with a check mark next to their names.

5. Click **Replace**.

6. In the Replace Resource dialog box that appears, click the name of the resource you want to assign to this task instead.

7. Click **OK**.

   The old resource is removed and the new resource is added as a resource assigned to this task.

8. If you've replaced a material resource, enter the quantity in the Units field.

   If you've replaced a cost resource, enter the amount in the Cost field.

9. In the dialog box, click **Close**.

Add or Remove a Resource Assignment

Unlike replacing a resource, it takes a bit more thought to add or remove a work resource (person or equipment) assigned to a task. For tasks to which you've already assigned work resources, when you add or remove a work resource assignment, or even change the duration, Project confirms your intentions.

This is because you might want to add another resource to shorten the *duration* and bring in the finish date. You might remove a team member to prevent overallocation. Or, you might need to add a resource because an existing resource can only work part time on this task.

These examples speak to the following three aspects of a resource assignment that can flex when you add or remove resources or change the duration:

Duration   The length of time you expect the task to take from start to finish

Work   The number of hours (or days) you expect the assigned work resources to spend on the task

Units   The level or percent of effort the assigned work resources are to spend on the task—for example, 100% (full time) or 50% (part time) of the working time available in the resource calendar

---

Understand the Relationship between Duration and Work

Adding or removing work resources can change the task duration or change the amount of work (number of hours) the assigned resources are expected to devote to this task to accomplish it within the specified duration. The work value becomes available as soon as you assign work resources to a task.

To see how the Duration and Work fields are related, add the Work column to the Task Sheet or Gantt Chart:

1.   With the Task Sheet or Gantt Chart open, right-click the **Start** column heading, and then click **Insert Column**.

2.   In the Type Column Name field that appears, type **work**, and then press Enter.

The Work column appears in the sheet between the Duration and Start columns, as shown in the following graphic.

	Task Name	Duration	Work	Start
1	◢**Plan the training**	**41.75 days**	**288 hrs**	**Mon 3/21/22**
2	Analyze the audience	1 wk	40 hrs	Mon 3/21/22
3	Assess audience training needs	2 wks	80 hrs	Mon 3/28/22
4	◢**Identify the training topics**	**7 days**	**56 hrs**	**Mon 4/11/22**
5	Brainstorm training topics	4 days	32 hrs	Mon 4/11/22
6	Select and organize training topics	3 days	24 hrs	Fri 4/15/22
7	Evaluate and select the learning management system tools	2 wks	80 hrs	Wed 4/20/22

Now, assume that all assigned resources are working full time according to their resource calendars, and that one day is defined as 8 hours, which is the Project default.

You see that a task with a duration of two days and one full-time resource shows 16 hours of work. The following graphic shows more examples of the relationship between duration and work under these assumptions.

Task Name	Duration	Work	Resource Names
Train in Tacoma	1 day	8 hrs	Monique
Train in Eugene	2 days	16 hrs	Leo
Train in South Bend	2 days	32 hrs	Soon Hee,Eduardo
Train in Monterey	4 days	32 hrs	Nicole

Assign Another Work Resource to a Task

To add a work resource to a task that already has a work resource assigned:

1. Switch to the Task Sheet, Gantt Chart, or other task sheet view.

2. Click the task to which you want to add a work resource.

3. On the Resource tab, in the Assignments group, click **Assign Resources**.

4. In the Assign Resources dialog box, click the name of the resource you want to add to this task.

5. Click **Assign**.

 The new resource is assigned to the task, joining the other existing assignments. Next to the Task Name field, a temporary alert flag appears with the label **Click to set how the task is rescheduled as a result of this assignment**.

6. Click the flag to see your choices, as shown in Figure 7.11.

FIGURE 7.11   Choices for adding a work resource

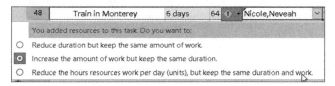

7. If your intended result is to add work within the existing duration, you don't need to do anything, because this is the default.

 If you want the added work resource to reduce the duration, click the first option labeled **Reduce duration but keep the same amount of work**.

 If you want the added work resource to reduce the units for all assigned work resources, click the third option labeled **Reduce the hours resources work per day (units) but keep the same duration and work**.

 The alert icon stays next to the Task Name field until you either make a choice or move on to your next change.

Remove a Work Resource from a Task

To remove one of several work resources from a task assignment:

1. In the Task Sheet, Gantt Chart, or other task sheet view, click the task from which you want to remove one of several assigned work resources.

2. On the Resource tab, in the Assignments group, click **Assign Resources**.

3. In the Assign Resources dialog box, click the name of the assigned resource you want to remove from this task.

4. Click **Remove**.

The resource is removed from the task. Next to the Task Name field, a temporary alert flag appears with the label **Click to set how the task is rescheduled as a result of removing this assignment.**

5. Click the flag to see your choices, as shown in Figure 7.12.

FIGURE 7.12   Choices after removing a work resource

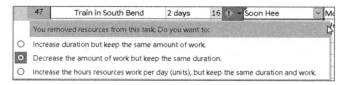

If you remove the only work resource from a task, the message does not appear, because there are no choices to make about the change.

6. If your intended result is to decrease work within the same duration, you don't need to do anything, because this is the default.

If you expect to increase the duration, click the option labeled **Increase duration but keep the same amount of work.**

If you want to increase the units for the remaining assigned work resources, click the third option labeled **Increase the hours resources work per day (units), but keep the same duration and work.**

7. When you're finished changing resource assignments, click **Close** in the Assign Resources dialog box.

Change Duration on Tasks with Assignments

Similar to adding or removing work resources on tasks with existing assigned work resources, if you change duration after you have assigned one or more work resources, Project wants to know your expectation regarding the effect of the duration change on assigned resources' work and units (see Figure 7.13).

FIGURE 7.13   Choices after changing a duration

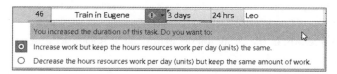

> ### Calculated Changes Are Temporarily Highlighted
>
> When you add resources, update duration, or make any other edit to your project plan that causes Project to calculate a schedule change, blue shading appears in the cells that have changed. This blue shading signals to you the nature of the schedule change.
>
> The shading disappears when you make your next change or when you save the plan.
>
> If you see there's been an unwanted change, you can reverse it. Immediately click the **Undo** button in the Quick Access Toolbar, or press Ctrl+Z.

With your team identified and assigned to your project tasks, and any equipment, material, and cost resources also specified, you now have all the pieces in place. You're ready to take a clear-eyed look at your project scope, schedule, and costs, and see what adjustments should be made before the project launches.

Key Terms

assignment

cost resource

duration

material resource

max units

overallocated

rolled-up costs

units

work

work resources

Review Questions

1. What are two methods for assigning resources to tasks?

   A. The Assign Resources dialog box and the Resource Sheet

   B. The Customize Task Board Cards dialog box and the Task Information dialog box

   C. The Assign Resources dialog box and the Resource Names field in a task sheet like the Gantt Chart

   D. The Resource Names field in a task sheet like the Gantt Chart and the Resource Information dialog box

2. When you assign a material resource to a task, what additional information besides the resource name should you include with the assignment?

   A. The cost amount for this assignment

   B. The quantity of material needed for this assignment

   C. The work, or number of hours, for this assignment

   D. The material label, like boxes or gallons

3. When you assign a cost resource to a task, what additional information besides the resource name should you include with the assignment?

   A. The cost amount for this assignment

   B. The quantity of material needed for this assignment

   C. The work, or number of hours, for this assignment

   D. The cost resource label, like boxes or gallons

4. What is an assignment in Project?

   A. A resource, like a team member, equipment, material, or cost

   B. An incremental task or activity that helps achieve the project goal

   C. The percentage of time, or units, that a team member is scheduled to work on a task

   D. A resource assigned to a task and therefore responsible for helping complete the task

5. How do you switch to another view, like the Team Planner, Task Usage view, Task Board, or Resource Usage view, to review assignments in different ways?

   A. On the Resource tab, in the View group, click the arrow under Team Planner, and then click the view you want.

   B. On the View tab, in the Task Views or Resource Views group, find and click the view you want.

   C. Right-click the view bar on the left edge of the Project window, and then click the name of the view you want.

   D. All of the above.

6. How does Project calculate costs for a task with a work resource assigned to it?

   A. Project multiplies the hourly (or daily) cost for the assigned work resource by the number of hours (or days) the resource is assigned to work on that task.

   B. Project multiplies the hourly (or daily) cost of the material resource by the amount of time represented in the task duration.

   C. Project multiplies the hourly (or daily) cost of the assigned work resource by the max units percentage.

   D. Project rolls up the cost of the summary task to extrapolate the costs of the individual subtasks beneath it.

7. How do you see costs for tasks with assigned resources in a task sheet like the Gantt Chart?

   A. Double-click the task to open the Task Information dialog box and see the task costs on the Advanced tab.

   B. Insert the Cost column in the task sheet.

   C. In the Customize Task Board Cards dialog box, add the Cost field.

   D. Run the Task Cost Overview report.

8. How is work defined in the context of assignments in Project?

   A. The length of time the task will take from start to finish

   B. The level or percent of effort that assigned work resources are to spend on the task—for example, 100 percent (full time) or 50 percent (half time) of the available working time

   C. The amount of time that the assigned work resources are scheduled to spend on the assigned task

   D. The hours and days specified as working time in the assigned resource calendar

Lesson 8

Check and Adjust the Project

LESSON OBJECTIVES

✓ View the project finish and cost in the project summary task.

✓ Explain critical path and how it affects the project finish.

✓ Show the critical path on a Gantt view.

✓ List two of the three methods for bringing in the finish date.

✓ List two of the three methods for cutting project scope.

✓ Reduce costs in a task sheet and in the Resource Sheet.

✓ Explain the problem with overallocation and under-allocation.

✓ Reschedule resources in Team Planner.

✓ Set a baseline and describe how you might use the data.

At this point, you have built your plan in Microsoft Project with all the essential pieces. You've confirmed the requirements with the project sponsor or customer, researched and entered the necessary tasks and their durations, and built the team and assigned people and other resources to tasks.

But before you and your team take off on your project implementation, you must work through one more important task: checking the plan and making final adjustments. If you consider your project plan to be the roadmap along your project's journey, you must be sure that the roadmap will get you where you plan to go and not overshoot, leave you stranded, or veer off in the wrong direction. It's essential you do this *before* your team starts work on their project tasks. If a project starts with faulty assumptions, it'll be all the harder—and probably more expensive—to fix things mid-project.

In this lesson, you examine and refine three key elements to your project: overall finish date, project cost, and resource allocation. You confirm whether your plan predicts that your project will, indeed, hit the agreed-upon finish date and cost, and that resources are efficiently used.

If you find your project plan predicts an outcome with the finish date, costs, or resources that conflict with your intended goal, this lesson demonstrates adjustments for bringing your plan into alignment. In many cases, these techniques take care of the problems.

However, sometimes the problem is bigger than something a few plan adjustments can solve. Sometimes, you must collect your courage and approach your project sponsor with a tough discussion about cutting scope, increasing the project's time or budget, or adding resources. It's where the priorities of your *project triangle* of scope, time, and cost come into stark focus.

When you've refined all the elements of your plan and you believe it's as perfect as it can be, you set the project baseline. When you save baseline information, you have a point of comparison after the project starts and you start tracking its progress. Your original baseline information can help you make adjustments and improve the plan as you go along.

Check the Project Finish Date

A major indicator of project success is whether it finishes on time. In this section, you learn how to view the finish date and to view whether it meets your target. If it doesn't, you can try several techniques to bring in the finish date.

Review the Project Finish Date

The easiest way to keep an eye on your project finish date is to add the project summary task. The *project summary task* shows all summarized or *rolled-up values* for the project as a whole, including the project finish date.

All levels of summary tasks show the rolled-up information of their subtasks. If you show the project summary task in a task sheet that shows the Finish field, you can view the rolled-up finish for the entire project, which is the finish date of the last project task to be completed.

To see the project finish date by adding the project summary task:

1. Switch to the Task Sheet or Gantt Chart.

2. On the Format tab, in the Show/Hide group, select the **Project Summary Task** check box.

   The project summary task appears as row 0 in the task sheet and uses your project file-name as the project summary task name. It appears in most other task sheets as well, like the Leveling Gantt and the Task Sheet.

3. If you want, click in the project summary task name to change it.

4. Review the Finish field in the project summary task.

   This is the finish date for the entire project, based on the schedule of the individual tasks throughout the project.

You can also find your finish date in the Project Information dialog box. On the Project tab, in the Properties group, click **Project Information**. The Finish Date field is dimmed, indicating that it's a calculated field, which is not editable. Again, the finish date is calculated from the schedule of individual tasks throughout the project.

Edit Task and Resource Names with the Project Entry Bar

When you need to change a task or resource name in a view, double-click it. Doing so opens the Task Information or Resource Information dialog box, where you can edit the Name field. You can also click the task or resource name and then click it again to switch to the edit mode within the field. Be sure to click it twice slowly so that Project doesn't interpret your action as a double-click.

One way to quickly edit task and resource names is by adding the project entry bar. This adds an editing bar between the ribbon and the view, similar to the formula bar in Microsoft Excel.

To add the project entry bar to your project:

1. On the File tab, click **Options**.

2. In the left pane, click **Display**.

3. Under Show These Elements, select the **Entry Bar** check box.

4. Click OK.

The entry bar appears in your Project window for this and any other projects (see the following graphic).

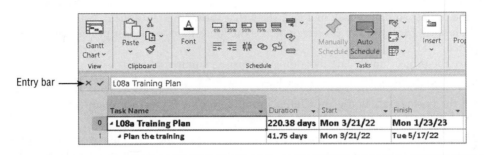

View How the Critical Path Affects the Project Finish Date

The project finish date is the finish date of the project's last scheduled task. The last task is typically the end of a string of linked tasks.

In a waterfall project, you link tasks that depend on each other. This means that a later, or *successor*, task cannot start or finish until the earlier, or *predecessor*, task finishes or starts. A series of linked tasks creates a path of tasks through the project. Most projects have more than one path of tasks. For example, a training project might have five different paths for the development of five separate training modules.

The longest path of tasks through the project is called the *critical path*. This path represents the minimum amount of time needed to accomplish all the tasks in the project. It's considered "critical" because it dictates the overall project finish date. The critical path warrants your attention because when you must bring in the finish date, you can do so by adjusting the tasks on the critical path so that they finish earlier. In other words, when you shorten the critical path, you bring in the finish date.

Be aware that when you shorten the critical path, it's possible that another task path can become the critical path. You can shorten the new critical path as well, continuing in this manner until your schedule reflects your targeted finish date.

This scheme of task paths and the one critical path is a key feature of traditional waterfall projects. In fact, the waterfall methodology is also known as *critical path method*, or *CPM*.

The individual tasks along the critical path are considered *critical tasks*.

Show the Critical Path

To view the critical path on the Tracking Gantt:

1. Right-click the view bar on the left edge of the Project window, then click **Tracking Gantt**.

The table side of the Tracking Gantt shows the same fields as the regular Gantt Chart. However, the timescale side shows two major differences. One is that the Gantt bar labels show percent complete instead of resource names (see Figure 8.1). The other big difference is that the critical path is highlighted in red.

FIGURE 8.1 Critical path on the Tracking Gantt

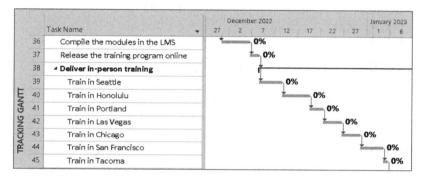

2. Scroll through the timescale side of the Tracking Gantt until you see the start and finish of the critical path for your project. Notice that this is the path of tasks that ends later than any of the other series of linked tasks.

You might prefer to stay in the regular Gantt Chart for much of your work, rather than switching to the Tracking Gantt (or Detail Gantt) whenever you want to examine the critical path. You can easily highlight the critical path on the Gantt Chart.

To view the critical path by changing the format:

1. Switch to the Gantt Chart.

2. On the Format tab, in the Bar Styles group, select the **Critical Tasks** check box.

The Gantt bars representing the critical path through your project turn red. If you don't see the critical path right away, scroll through the timescale side of the view until you see the start and finish of the critical path for your project.

Flag Critical Tasks

If you're reviewing tasks in a view other than a Gantt Chart, or if you're sorting or filtering or grouping tasks in various ways, you might find it helpful to know which tasks are critical. Knowing the critical tasks is important if you're increasing or decreasing the schedule of a critical task, because this affects the overall project schedule. You can add a field to a task table, which indicates a Yes flag for critical tasks.

To add the Critical field to a task sheet view:

1. In any task sheet view like the Task Usage view or Task Sheet, right-click the column heading next to where you want to add the Critical field, and then click **Insert Column**. Project adds a new column to the left of the one you selected and lists all available fields.

2. Type **critical** and then press Enter.

    The Critical column appears. "Yes" appears in the field for any critical tasks; "No" appears in the others.

Bring In the Project Finish Date

If the project finish date shows a date later than your target finish date, determine whether that's acceptable, keeping in mind the priorities of your project triangle.

Remember that having a later finish date can affect your costs; they can go down if you don't have to pay rush fees or overtime, but they can go up if you need to keep resources on the project longer than expected. Having a later finish date can also help you balance your resources, but they might also be committed to move on to other projects after a certain date.

If you need to bring in your finish date, you can shorten the critical path or adjust how your tasks are linked.

If neither of these techniques brings in the finish date enough, you can go to your project sponsor or customer and ask to either accept the later finish date or cut the project scope. If it will bring in the finish date, you might also ask for more money in the budget or more resources.

You might find yourself in the enviable position of showing a finish date earlier than expected. Maintaining this extra time as a schedule buffer is a wise way to use that extra time. A *schedule buffer* is extra time built in to a project plan that you can use like an "emergency time savings account" as project conditions change over time. You can also use the extra time to add scope to the project, add quality checks, reduce costs, or balance resources.

Shorten Durations of Critical Tasks

An easy way to bring in the finish date is to shorten the duration of critical tasks. Make sure the durations are still realistic, though; otherwise, you'll have to make adjustments later when you're tracking actual progress on the tasks.

To shorten durations of a critical task:

1. In the Gantt Chart or other Gantt view, click in the Duration field for the critical task.

2. Change the duration amount, remembering to include the number and time unit—for example, **3d** for three days or **2w** for two weeks.

3. Press Enter.

    The duration changes for the task, and the Gantt bar changes accordingly.

4. Repeat these steps for any other critical tasks whose duration you want to shorten.

5. When finished, review the finish date of the critical path to see if you're achieving your project finish date goal.

Review Links of Critical Tasks

You might have Finish-to-Start task links where they're not really needed. Scrutinize your links and see where you can save time. Focus on links in the critical path and other paths that are nearly as long as the critical path. Look for the following:

- Can the successor task start without the predecessor task being finished? Maybe the successor can start sooner, either by linking to another task scheduled earlier or by removing the link altogether so that the task starts on the project start date.

- Did you link tasks because you assumed they're being done by one person? Maybe if you add one or more resources, different tasks or sets of tasks can be done at the same time. You can either remove the link or link the task to a more realistic predecessor task that's scheduled earlier.

- Although Finish-to-Start is the most common link type, you might find that another link type like Start-to-Start or Finish-to-Finish is a more accurate relationship between two tasks, which can actually help bring in the finish date. You can change the Finish-to-Start link to a different link type.

Review the task links in your project graphically by reviewing the Gantt bars, task paths, and links in a Gantt view. See if any links can be removed or changed to a different link type that can save you time.

To remove a task link:

1. In the Gantt Chart or other Gantt view, select the pair of tasks that contain the link you want to remove.

   If the tasks are next to each other in the table, click anywhere in the task sheet row for the first task, hold down the Shift key, and then click the second task.

   If the tasks are separated in the table (nonadjacent), click in the row for one task, hold down the Ctrl key, and then click the other task.

   If you want to remove the link for more than a series of two tasks, use the Shift or Ctrl key to select as many tasks as is appropriate.

2. On the Task tab, in the Schedule group, click **Unlink Tasks**.

   The link between the selected tasks is removed, and the task schedule and Gantt bar change accordingly.

   If the selected tasks are linked to other tasks that were not selected, those links remain intact.

   If you select just one task, all links to and from that task are removed.

To change a task link to a different link type:

1. In a Gantt view, double-click the successor to the pair of tasks whose link type you want to change.

2. In the Task Information dialog box, click the **Predecessors** tab.

   The table shows the name of the selected task's predecessor along with the current link type between the predecessor and successor.

3. Click the arrow in the **Type** field, then click the link type you want between the selected task and its predecessor, as shown in Figure 8.2.

FIGURE 8.2   Link type choices in the Task Information dialog box

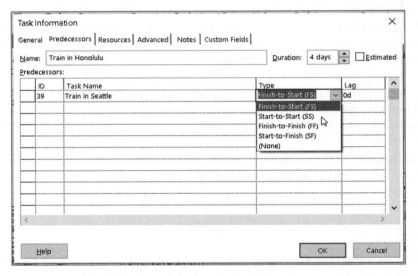

4. Click **OK**.

Look at your task finish date, summary task finish date, and project summary task finish date, and see if your changed links made the difference you need.

Cut Scope

If you've tried reducing durations and refining links and the forecasted project finish date is still beyond your target, you might need to propose either accepting the later date or cutting project scope—two sides of your project triangle. At the outset, you probably had carefully established the scope and finish date with the project sponsor or customer in the project initiating process. Because of this, you'll probably need to get approval for such a significant change.

If your project sponsor chooses to cut scope rather than accept a later finish date, you have three major ways to cut scope to bring in the finish date:

- Cut phases of the project, like the development of optional features of a product or service.

- Cut tasks, like review cycles or quality checks.

- Cut the duration of tasks, like review cycles or quality checks, so that you're still doing them but not spending as much time on them.

Cutting scope along the critical path will have the most impact on the finish date. If you're removing entire project phases, adjust the project linking as necessary and see if the critical path has changed to a different path.

Check Costs

Just like completing a project by the scheduled finish date, a second major indicator of project success is whether it finishes within budget. Along with scope and time, remember that cost is the third side of your project triangle. You need to continually keep these three factors in balance, and you need to know which of these have the highest priority when you have to make adjustments.

In this section, you learn how to view the overall project cost and see whether it meets your project budget. If necessary, you can try several techniques to reduce costs.

Review the Total Project Cost

To review the total project cost, first add the Cost column to a task sheet view, and then show the project summary task. The project summary task will show the total project cost in the Cost field.

Add the Cost Column

None of the task views include Cost as a default field. To keep your eye on project costs, you must add the Cost column to a task sheet view. For each task, this column totals the costs of all assigned resources.

To see task costs based on resource assignments:

1. Switch to the Task Sheet or Gantt Chart.

2. Right-click the column heading next to where you want to add the Cost field, and then click **Insert Column**.

   Project adds a new column to the left of the one you selected, and lists all available fields.

3. Type **cost** and then press Enter.

The Cost column appears. Based on the cost of assigned resources, task costs appear in the field, as shown in Figure 8.3.

FIGURE 8.3   Cost column added to the Task Sheet

		Duration	Start	Finish	Resource Names	Cost	Add New Column
	0	140.38 days	Mon 3/21/22	Mon 10/3/22		$41,720.00	
	1	41.75 days	Mon 3/21/22	Tue 5/17/22		$7,504.00	
	2	1 wk	Mon 3/21/22	Fri 3/25/22	Eduardo	$1,040.00	
	3	2 wks	Mon 3/28/22	Fri 4/8/22	Nicole	$1,920.00	
TASK SHEET	4	7 days	Mon 4/11/22	Tue 4/19/22		$1,456.00	
	5	4 days	Mon 4/11/22	Thu 4/14/22	Eduardo	$832.00	
	6	3 days	Fri 4/15/22	Tue 4/19/22	Eduardo	$624.00	
	7	2 wks	Wed 4/20/22	Wed 5/11/22	Neveah	$2,240.00	

See Total Cost in the Project Summary Task

Now with the Cost field added to your task sheet, use the project summary task to see the total project cost. If it's not already showing, switch to any task sheet like the Gantt Chart or Task Usage view. On the Format tab, in the Show/Hide group, select the **Project Summary Task** check box.

Now look at the Cost field in the project summary task. This is your total project cost, rolled up from the costs of resources assigned to tasks throughout your project.

Reduce Costs

Rarely does a project have an unlimited budget. If the total project cost field shows an amount greater than your allotted or targeted budget, you probably must find ways to bring the costs down.

Standard methods for bringing down project costs are cutting back on resources or adjusting the finish date.

If neither of these techniques cuts the total cost enough, you have to ask your project sponsor to either give you a larger budget or allow you to cut scope.

Work with a Surplus Budget

If your total project shows a figure significantly less than your project budget, first of all, congratulations! With extra funds, you have more flexibility. This gives you a *cost buffer*, which is extra funding or contingency built into a project plan to stay within budget if and when future cost overruns happen.

You might also use the extra funding to add scope to the project, adjust the schedule to be more comfortable, or balance resources.

Review Resource Costs

Resources are invariably the largest costs for a project. Usually this means human resources—the team members carrying out the tasks. Resources can also be the equipment that is fulfilling tasks. Project considers people and equipment your *work resources*. The cost of consumable *material resources* like lumber or paint can drive up your project costs, as can your *cost resources*—those items like travel expenses and space rentals. If you can cut expenses for some or all of these resources, you can cut your overall project costs.

Start looking for cost savings by reviewing the Cost column in a task view. You can scan costs throughout the project in logical order. You might also find it efficient to sort the costs from highest to lowest so that you can focus on the tasks with the largest costs and scrutinize those for ways to trim expenses that would have the biggest impact.

To sort cost from highest to lowest:

1. Show the task sheet view that contains the Cost column you added.

2. On the View tab, in the Data group, click **Sort**, and then click **by Cost**.

    Project sorts the view to show tasks (including summary tasks) by highest to lowest cost, as shown in Figure 8.4.

    Subtasks are kept together under their summary task—that is, the outline structure is retained through the sorting operation.

FIGURE 8.4   Tasks sorted by highest to lowest costs

	Task Name	Duration	Cost
12	◢ Develop Module 1	56.75 days	$10,640.00
13	Research Module 1 topics	3 wks	$3,000.00
17	Test Module 1 topics	3 wks	$2,640.00
14	Write Module 1 topics	2 wks	$2,000.00
16	Revise Module 1 topics	2 wks	$2,000.00
15	Have Module 1 topics reviewed	1 wk	$1,000.00
18	◢ Develop Module 2	40 days	$8,240.00
19	Research Module 2 topics	3 wks	$3,120.00
20	Write Module 2 topics	2 wks	$2,080.00
21	Have Module 2 topics reviewed	1 wk	$1,040.00
22	Revise Module 2 topics	1 wk	$1,040.00
23	Test Module 2 topics	1 wk	$960.00
30	◢ Develop Module 4	35 days	$7,200.00

3. Take note of the tasks with the highest costs, and also note the resources assigned to those tasks. Focus on these tasks and resources to cut costs.

To restore the order of tasks, on the View tab, in the Data group, click **Sort**, and then click **by ID**. If you prefer, you can leave the task sort by Cost while you work on your cost-cutting strategies, and then sort by ID when you're done.

Review Cost Reports to Prioritize Cuts

Another way to find cost-cutting candidates is to run a cost report.

To run an assigned resource cost report:

1. On the Report tab, in the View Reports group, click **Costs**, and then click **Resource Cost Overview**.

    The Resource Cost Overview report appears and looks similar to the following figure.

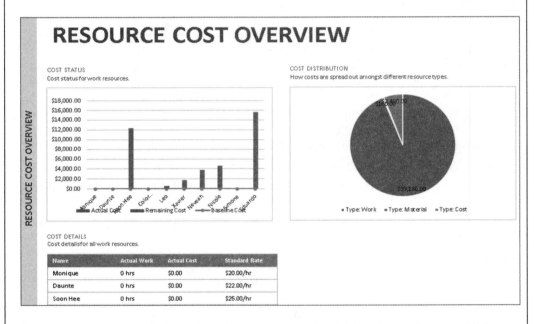

2. Review the Cost Status and Cost Details areas to see which resources have the highest costs based on the tasks to which they're assigned.

Note that these are not necessarily the resources with the highest hourly rates. Your least expensive work resource could show as the most expensive if they're assigned to more tasks or longer tasks than the others.

You can also run the Task Cost Overview report to see which top-level summary tasks have the highest costs.

Cut Resource Costs

Now that you've reviewed which tasks have the highest costs, you can focus your efforts on cutting costs where those reductions will have the greatest effect on your meeting the budget goal.

Reduce Costs in a Task Sheet

Review the task sheet containing the Cost column. For the higher-cost tasks you've noted, you can:

- Reduce the duration for tasks with work resources assigned.
- Reduce the quantity of material resources assigned to tasks.
- Reduce expenses for cost resources assigned to tasks.

To reduce the duration for a task with work resources assigned:

1. Go to a higher-cost task you've noted that has work resources assigned.
2. Determine whether you can realistically reduce the duration and still allow the assigned resources sufficient time.
3. If you can, edit the value in the Duration field to a shorter time.

   An alert appears next to the Duration field asking whether you want to decrease work or decrease units.
4. Keep the default option labeled **Decrease work but keep the hours resources work per day (units) the same**.

   You don't need to click anything to keep the default. The option will be set as soon as you move on to your next action. Reducing work is what reduces cost on a task with people or equipment assigned to it.

To reduce the quantity of a material resource assigned to a task:

1. Go to a higher-cost task you've noted that has a material resource assigned.
2. Determine whether you can trim the quantity of material and still fulfill the task as specified.
3. If you can, double-click the task to open the Task Information dialog box.
4. On the Resources tab, click in the Units field for the material resource, and edit the quantity to the lower amount.

5. Click **OK**.

The quantity changes in the Resources field, and the Cost field is recalculated to a lower amount.

To reduce the expense of a cost resource assigned to a task:

1. Go to a higher-cost task you've noted that has a cost resource assigned.
2. Review the amount specified for the task like travel costs or venue rental. Determine whether you can confirm better rates or develop alternatives to travel, rentals, or other such expenses.
3. If you can, double-click the task to open the Task Information dialog box.
4. On the Resources tab, click in the Cost field for the cost resource, and edit the expense to the lower amount.
5. Click **OK**.

The cost changes in the Resources field and the Cost field is recalculated.

Reduce Costs in the Resource Sheet

You can also reduce costs with adjustments in the Resource Sheet. For the resources assigned to higher-cost tasks, you can:

- Review base costs of the work and material resources.
- Review the material labels, or units, of material resources.
- Determine whether less expensive resources can replace or assist more expensive resources.

As in a task sheet, you can add the Cost field to the Resource Sheet. This field shows the costs accrued for each resource based on assigned tasks. As you adjust resource information, that cost per resource is recalculated.

To add the Cost field to the Resource Sheet:

1. Switch to the Resource Sheet.
2. Click the arrow in the **Add New Column** heading at the far right edge of the sheet, type **cost**, and then press Enter.

The Cost column appears. The total accrued cost of each resource appears in the field, based on all the tasks to which the resource is assigned.

3. If you want to move the Cost column to a different place in the sheet, drag the Cost column heading to that location (see Figure 8.5).

If your Resource Sheet lists generic resources—that is, titles rather than specific team member names—research the range of rates for specialists with those skills. You might be able to find people at rates more compatible with your budget.

FIGURE 8.5   Cost column added to the Resource Sheet

	Resource Name	Type	Material Label	Cost	Max. Units	Std. Rate
1	Monique	Work		$160.00	100%	$20.00/hr
2	Daunte	Work		$0.00	50%	$22.00/hr
3	**Soon Hee**	**Work**		**$14,400.00**	**100%**	**$25.00/hr**
4	Color Printer	Work		$0.00	100%	$10.00/hr
5	Binders	Material	each	$160.00		$4.00
6	Scratchpads	Material	each	$0.00		$1.00
7	Pens	Material	package	$0.00		$12.00
8	Airfare	Cost		$2,400.00		
9	Hotel	Cost		$0.00		
10	Conference Room	Cost		$0.00		
11	Leo	Work		$600.00	100%	$25.00/hr
12	Xavier	Work		$3,520.00	100%	$22.00/hr
13	Neveah	Work		$3,808.00	100%	$28.00/hr
14	Nicole	Work		$4,608.00	100%	$24.00/hr
15	Simone	Work		$224.00	100%	$28.00/hr

To reduce base rates of a work resource:

1. In the Resource Sheet, go to a work resource with a higher accrued cost.

2. For that resource, review the values in the Std Rate, Ovt Rate, and Cost/Use fields.

3. Determine whether you can reduce any of these values.

4. If so, edit the field(s).

   The Cost field for the resource is recalculated to a lower amount.

To reduce the unit and base rate of a material resource unit:

1. In the Resource Sheet, go to a material resource with a higher accrued cost.

2. For that material resource, review the unit in the Material Label field—for example, boxes, gallons, or yards.

3. Determine whether that unit label is really the best size for the tasks in your project and change it if appropriate.

   If the unit is too large, you might be spending too much and wasting excess material. For example, maybe you've specified a carton of 60 items when you really just need a box of 12.

4. Review the value in the Std Rate field, and determine whether it can be reduced.

   If you changed the Material Label field, you most certainly need to change the cost for that unit.

   Even if you didn't change the material label, maybe you can get a better cost per unit.

5. If you can change the cost, edit the field.

   For the material resource, Project recalculates the Cost field to a lower amount.

In your Resource Sheet, if you've identified multiple resources with the same or similar skill set, consider whether you can replace a more expensive resource with a less expensive one and still achieve your task goal and quality requirement.

To replace a more expensive resource with a less expensive one:

1. Switch back to any task view.

2. On the Resource tab, in the Assignments group, click **Assign Resources**.

3. In the task view, click the task with the resource assignment you want to replace.

4. In the Assign Resources dialog box, click the name of the resource you want to replace.

   The resources assigned to the selected task appear at the top of the Resources table with a checkmark next to their names.

5. Click **Replace**.

6. In the Replace Resource dialog box that appears, click the name of the resource you want to assign to this task instead.

7. Click **OK**.

   The old resource is removed, and the new resource is added as a resource assigned to this task.

8. If you've replaced a material resource, enter the quantity in the Units field.

   If you've replaced a cost resource, enter the amount in the Cost field.

9. In the dialog box, click **Close**.

Only Make Realistic Resource Cuts

Be judicious when trimming your resource costs and make sure these are changes your project can live with in the long run. If you artificially reduce duration, base costs, or material quantities to achieve your budget target now, you'll probably experience cost over-runs later when the project starts and reality sets in.

In fact, cutting costs inappropriately now can lead to costs that are even higher than they would have been. If you cut duration, for example, you might have to pay overtime or add more resources because the assigned resources didn't have enough time scheduled to properly complete their tasks. If the appropriate quantity of material is not ordered, you might have to pay rush delivery costs or excess quantities later to make up the difference.

Also, consider that less expensive team members might not have the skills or experience necessary to carry out a set of tasks, and they might be slower, which can cost you more over a longer time period. More expensive resources can actually be a bargain if they have the right skills and can work faster and more efficiently.

The key is "right-sizing" your plan for realistic costs. Trim any buffer and make sure your cost items are not too high to exceed the project budget but not so low as to be deceptively deflated. You don't want today's low-cost projection to transform into tomorrow's high-cost recovery.

Change the Finish Date

In some projects, you can cut costs by bringing in the finish date. In other projects, you can cut costs by extending the finish date. However, it depends on how your project is structured, as well as the nature of your resources and their base costs.

If you think that changing the finish date in one direction or the other might improve your budget situation, play with some scenarios and see what works. Having flexibility with your finish date can help you achieve a more inflexible budget.

For techniques, revisit the section "Check the Project Finish Date" at the beginning of this lesson.

Cut Scope

Suppose you've cut resource costs to the bone and also adjusted the finish date to save money, but your costs are still forecasting over your budget. In this case, it's time for a conversation with your project sponsor. Lay out the two choices: increasing the budget or cutting scope—two sides of your project triangle. Either of these definitely requires explicit approval from your sponsor.

If the sponsor chooses to cut scope rather than allow more funding, there are three ways to cut scope that are most likely to reduce costs:

- Cut phases of the project, like the development of optional features of a product or service.
- Cut tasks, like review cycles or quality checks.
- Cut the duration of tasks like review cycles or quality checks so that you're still doing them but the assigned resources are not spending as much time on them.

Check Resource Assignments

Resources assigned to tasks probably make up 90 to 100 percent of your project costs. But cost isn't the only crucial aspect of assignments in your project. You also want your project to use its resources wisely and efficiently. To this end, it's beneficial to check whether:

- Anyone is *overallocated*, meaning they've been assigned more task work than they have availability for
- Anyone is *underallocated*, meaning they have sizable time gaps where they have nothing to do

- Any tasks have no resources assigned
- Any resources have no tasks assigned

You can review assignments for these issues and adjust them to make sure the resources are well balanced and properly used throughout the project.

It's probably easiest to review and resolve assignment problems in either the Gantt Chart or Team Planner.

Resolve Overallocations in a Task Sheet

The Gantt Chart or any task sheet is a good place to find and resolve overallocations.

To find and reschedule an overallocated resource:

1. In the Gantt Chart or other task sheet, look for any tasks with a red overallocation icon in the Indicators column, as shown in Figure 8.6.

FIGURE 8.6 Task with overallocated resource

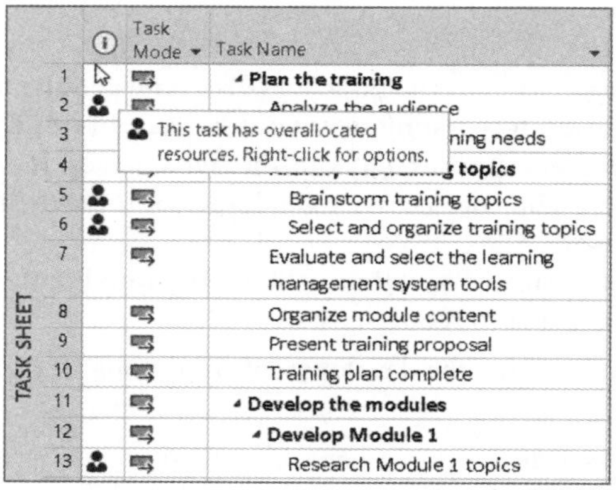

When you see this indicator, it means a work resource assigned to this task has more work assigned during this time period than the resource has availability for.

Remember that work resource *availability* is based on the resource's working times calendar and the Max Units value (full time, part time, or multiples).

2. To quickly resolve the overallocation, right-click the indicator.

3. In the menu that appears, click **Reschedule to Available Date**.

Project moves the task to the resource's next available block of time.

4. Check how the rescheduled task works with the surrounding tasks, dependencies, and other assigned resources.

Note the highlighting that shows the other fields that have changed as a result of this action. If you don't like the change or want to handle the overallocation another way, on the Quick Access Toolbar, click **Undo**. Or just press Ctrl+Z.

The Project Resource Leveling Controls

When you reschedule or reassign tasks to more evenly balance the workload, you're *leveling* resources. In other words, you're rescheduling the assignments of any overallocated resources to use them at 100 percent of their availability rather than 200 or 300 percent.

Project has leveling controls that will balance the workload for you, typically by rescheduling tasks for when the assigned resource has availability. On the Resource tab, in the Level group, click **Leveling Options**. Create a copy of your real project and use the copy as a "sandbox" to explore the different types of leveling, including automatic, manual, and within slack, among others.

Although the Project leveling controls are considered an advanced feature, as you become more comfortable with Project, you might find that using leveling controls can save you a lot of time. Be sure you understand the implications well before leveling resources in a complex project with many tasks and assignments. Learn more in Project Help by searching on "level" and exploring from there.

Resolve Assignment Problems in Team Planner

Team Planner offers a different way to find and resolve overallocations, one that gives you more control. In Team Planner, you can also easily spot work resources that are underused and tasks that have no resources assigned.

To use Team Planner to reschedule an overallocated resource:

1. Right-click the left edge of the Project window, and then on the menu that appears, click **Team Planner**.

    This view shows work resource names along the left edge of the view, and the tasks they're assigned to in the main part of the view along a timescale. Any unassigned tasks are shown near the bottom of the view.

2. To see more of the resource names, drag the divider bar to the right.

3. To adjust the timescale, on the View tab, in the Zoom group, click the arrow in the **Timescale** box, then click the time unit you want for the Team Planner timescale.

4. Review the tasks and look for any overallocations.

    Any tasks with overallocated resources assigned are shown with a red border (see Figure 8.7). The red border indicates multiple tasks are located in the same time period.

FIGURE 8.7   A resource's overallocation shown in Team Planner

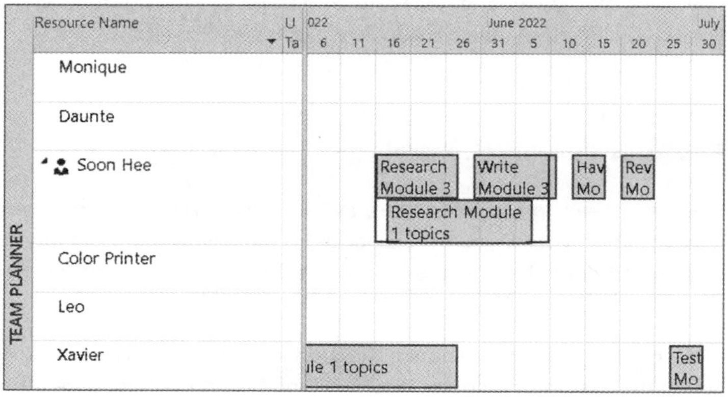

5.   Resolve the overallocation by dragging the task horizontally or vertically to reschedule it.

Reschedule the task to another time period when the resource has availability by dragging the task horizontally along the timescale for the resource.

Reassign the task to another resource by dragging the task vertically to a different resource.

For resources that are underallocated, use the same dragging technique. Again, drag horizontally to reschedule a task for the resource. Or drag other tasks vertically from another resource to the underallocated resource to help more evenly balance the workload.

Drag any task from the Unassigned Tasks area to an appropriate resource with available time for it. Doing so helps balance the workload while ensuring that all tasks have at least one work resource assigned.

When you drag tasks in Team Planner to reschedule or reassign tasks, double-check the results in a task view like the Gantt Chart or Task Sheet. The dragging can modify task links, introduce new date constraints, or affect other resource assignments in ways that you might not want.

Team Planner helps you view at a glance whether you have the right number of the right resource types throughout the timespan of your project.

More Solutions to Assignment Problems

If you have difficulty balancing your resources, determine what you need to solve that problem:

- Your project might need more time for the resources to accomplish all the tasks and requirements.

- The project might need more team members to share the workload. It might need different resources with a different set of skills. Needing more and different resources usually equates to needing more budget.

- If you can't get more time, more resources, or more budget, you'll likely need to cut the project scope.

Set the Project Baseline

At this point, you have refined your project schedule to reflect the best possible plan, with the schedule achieving the targeted finish date and costs within your established budget.

You're just about ready to say "go" to let your team start working on their assigned tasks. Before you do, though, there's one more thing to do—set the project baseline. This is important because as soon as your team takes off and starts executing the project, the plan will start to change. New realities will arise. requiring you to update the plan. Various fields will also change as you enter when tasks are completed.

A project *baseline* is a kind of snapshot of your project schedule and cost information. When you set a baseline, Project saves your original schedule and cost information as they stand at that point. This information changes and adjusts when your project execution process starts and you begin tracking actual information. Your baseline gives you a standard against which you can compare your project status at any moment with your original plan.

When you set a baseline, Project saves the original duration, start date, finish date, work amounts, cost amounts, and other schedule and cost information for each task as they stand at that moment. These values are saved in fields like Baseline Duration, Baseline Finish, and Baseline Cost. Later, you can compare the Baseline Duration field with the scheduled Duration field, for example. The Baseline Duration always stays as it was at the moment you saved it, while the Duration field changes as you update it to reflect changing conditions or enter progress on the task. This comparison offers insights on the project's progress. The baseline fields are also used in several reports to compare with *scheduled values* and *actual values*.

Without a baseline, you lose the data on how you originally scheduled the project or planned the costs. When you save a baseline, you are recording all the information at the moment when everything was "perfect," when your project was still a vision that reality and progress had not yet altered.

To set a project baseline:

1. On the Project tab, in the Schedule group, click **Set Baseline**, and then click **Set Baseline**.

The Set Baseline dialog box appears, as shown in Figure 8.8. In most cases, the default settings of this dialog box will suit your needs. These default settings will save a baseline for the entire project (rather than for selected tasks).

FIGURE 8.8   Set Baseline dialog box

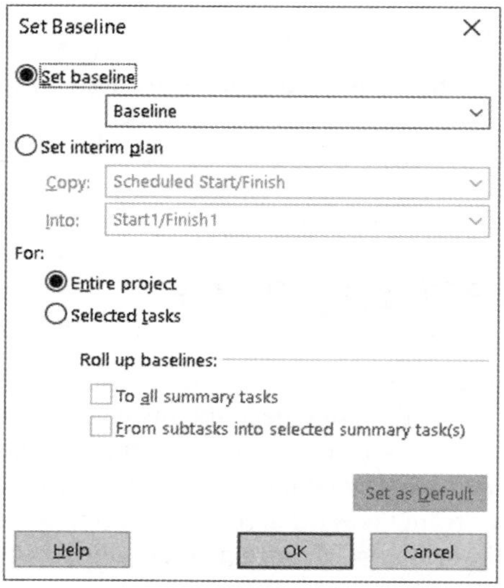

2.   Click **OK**.

After you set the baselines, nothing seems to change on the surface. However, before you set the baseline, the contents of each baseline field was "NA." After you set the baseline, Project copied values from the "scheduled" fields like Duration, Work, and Cost to the corresponding "baseline" fields.

To add a baseline field to a task sheet:

1.   Switch to a task sheet like the Gantt Chart or Task Sheet.

2.   Click the arrow in the Add New Column heading at the far right edge of the sheet, and then type **baseline**. Available baseline fields appear in the menu, as shown in Figure 8.9.

FIGURE 8.9   Menu of available baseline fields

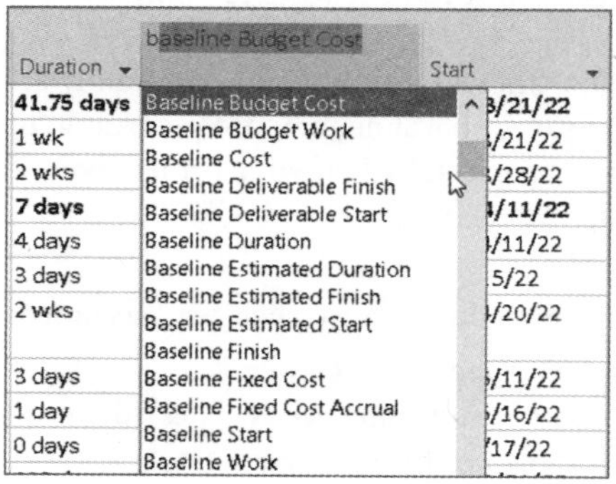

3. Click one of the baseline fields—for example, Baseline Finish.

Project adds the Baseline Finish column to the task sheet, and the dates are exactly the same as those in the Finish field. If you were to change schedule information so that finish dates change, the Finish field would be updated, but the Baseline Finish field would retain the original date.

You can clear a baseline, which effectively empties all your saved baseline fields. On the Project tab, in the Schedule group, click **Set Baseline**, and then click **Clear Baseline**. In the dialog box, keep the default settings, and then click **OK**.

You can also overwrite your existing baseline if necessary. This copies your existing schedule and cost information to the baseline fields, overwriting the previous values. On the Project tab, in the Schedule group, click **Set Baseline**, and then click **Set Baseline**. In the dialog box, click **OK**.

For your baseline to be meaningful, though, it's best to set it and keep it when it's really time to save it. You can save additional baselines, which can be useful if you want to compare different setpoints throughout the project.

To set an additional baseline while retaining the first one:

1. On the Project tab, in the Schedule group, click **Set Baseline**, and then click **Set Baseline**.

2. Click the arrow in the box under Set Baseline, and then click **Baseline1**.

3. Click **OK**.

Project saves all existing schedule and cost information into the Baseline1 fields, while retaining any previous baseline you set in the Baseline field.

Through your work in this lesson, you've seen that optimizing your project plan is a delicate balancing act. This is true as you're making the final touches to perfect your project plan before work begins. It continues to be the case after work begins on project tasks, and you enter actuals and other progress information in the plan, which is the topic of Lesson 9, "Track Project Information." In that lesson, you'll work with changing conditions and continue to maintain that careful balance in your project triangle of scope, time, and cost, while also ensuring your resources are properly and efficiently used throughout.

Key Terms

actual values

availability

baseline

cost buffer

cost resources

critical path

critical path method (CPM)

critical tasks
leveling
material resources
overallocated
predecessor
project summary task
project triangle
rolled-up values
schedule buffer
scheduled values
successor
underallocated
work resources

Review Questions

1. What are the steps for viewing at a glance the project finish date and total project cost in a task sheet?

    A. Open the Task Information dialog box, and then click the Advanced tab.

    B. Add the Cost column to a task sheet, and then move the Cost column next to the Finish column.

    C. Use the Format tab to add the project summary task to the task sheet.

    D. Add the Cost column to a task sheet, and then use the Format tab to add the project summary task.

2. Explain what the critical path is in a waterfall project and describe how the critical path affects the project finish date.

    A. The critical path is the set of project milestones and deliverables. It's considered critical because project funding is often tied to these milestones and deliverables.

    B. The critical path is the series of linked tasks that starts the project. It's considered the critical path because it's important to start the project on a strong foundation.

    C. The critical path is the series of linked tasks that is the longest series compared to the other sets of linked tasks. The finish date of this path is the finish date of the entire project.

    D. The critical path is the shortest series of linked tasks through the project. Bringing in the finish date of the critical path brings in the finish date of the overall project.

3. How do you highlight the critical path on the timescale side of the Gantt view?

    A. On the Format tab, in the Bar Styles group, select the **Critical Tasks** check box.

    B. Click any task, and then on the Task tab, in the Editing group, click **Scroll to Task**.

    C. Click **Insert Column**, type **critical**, and then press Enter to add the Critical Column to the view.

    D. On the Format tab, in the Bar Styles group, click **Task Path**.

4. Which of the following describe three effective methods for bringing in the overall project finish date?

    A. Sort a task sheet by duration, see where you can shorten the longer durations, and unlink tasks so that more tasks are being done concurrently.

    B. Unlink tasks so that more tasks are being done concurrently rather than one after the other, remove resource assignments, or cut scope.

    C. For tasks on the critical path, set date constraints on longer tasks, cut scope, or trim costs.

    D. For tasks on the critical path, shorten the duration of tasks, adjust how the tasks are linked, or cut scope.

5. Which of the following describe three effective methods for cutting project scope?

   A. Cut critical path tasks, reduce the longest durations, and reassign resources.

   B. Cut project phases, cut individual tasks, and cut task durations.

   C. Cut quality checks, remove resources, and switch to estimated durations.

   D. Cut individual tasks, unlink tasks, and cut project costs.

6. Working in the Resource Sheet, what are two good techniques for reducing costs of resources assigned to higher-cost tasks so that overall project costs can be trimmed?

   A. Always replace the more expensive resources with less expensive resources and also remove material resources from the project.

   B. Remove cost resources from the project and also reduce the quantity of material resources assigned to tasks.

   C. Reduce hourly, overtime, and per-use costs of resources and also determine whether less expensive resources can replace or assist more expensive resources on tasks.

   D. Add the Cost column to the Resource Sheet and extend the project finish date so you spend less on team member overtime, and therefore, reduce overall project costs.

7. What are you checking for when reviewing resource assignments to optimize your project plan?

   A. Whether you have to use the leveling feature and whether task durations affecting work values are at the right level

   B. Tasks with no resources assigned, resources with availability less than 100 percent, and resources that include overtime

   C. Overallocations, underallocations, tasks with no resources assigned, and resources not assigned to any tasks

   D. Tasks with only material or cost resources assigned, and work resources with working times calendars showing exceptions

8. How do you set your project baseline?

   A. On the Project tab, in the Schedule group, click **Set Baseline**, and then click **Set Baseline**. Under the For section, click **Selected Tasks**, and then click **OK**.

   B. On the Project tab, in the Schedule group, click **Set Baseline**, and then click **Set Baseline**. Keep the default settings, and then click **OK**.

   C. On the File tab, click **Save As**, and then save the project with "Baseline" in the filename.

   D. In a task sheet, add the Baseline column, and then enter the baseline values you want to save.

Monitor and Control Your Project

Lesson 9

Track Project Information

LESSON OBJECTIVES

✓ Describe the differences between the planning, executing, monitoring, and controlling processes.

✓ List three methods for communicating progress information with your team.

✓ Name three of five progress measures often used with waterfall projects and demonstrate how to enter these measures.

✓ Identify three of four progress measures often used with agile projects and demonstrate how to enter these measures.

✓ Specify how a task is proceeding exactly according to schedule.

✓ Define baseline, scheduled, and actual data in a project and the effect they each have on the project.

✓ Explain the four project elements that should be monitored after entering progress information.

Everything you've done with your project to this point has been planning—looking at the tasks, scheduling, resources, and costs for the project you knew would take place sometime in the near future.

You've optimized the plan to achieve the established finish date and budget, and you've checked and balanced the efficient use of resources throughout the project. With all conditions seemingly perfect, you've set the project baseline, which captures the details of your ideal plan. You're now revving at that special moment in the project when you can actually shift into gear and *go*!

Some project managers feel that, at this point, the heavy lifting is finished. They've built a lovely Gantt Chart or Task Board and all signs point to a successful project that achieves its goals while coming in on schedule and within budget.

The fact is that project implementation ushers in a whole new set of responsibilities. The plan you developed in the *planning process* created the vision of the ideal project. Now, in the *executing process*, when your team members start working on their tasks, the project "gets real." The project moves from the "future" to "now," and as the project manager, you oversee team activities and face day-to-day challenges requiring constant adjustment and rebalancing.

In this lesson, you explore the *monitoring process*, which has you collecting information from your team members about the current status of tasks being carried out. You record that status in your project plan, whether it's specifying a task's percentage complete or moving an agile task card from the In Progress column to the Done column. This monitoring is essential for good communication and reporting within the team, as well as with the project sponsor and other stakeholders beyond the project team.

Your monitoring will no doubt reveal that some aspect of the project isn't going exactly as planned. This is a normal and expected part of the project life cycle. When this happens, the *controlling process* has you responding to changes and making the necessary adjustments to bring the project back in line with its goals. This can mean recovering the schedule when a set of tasks has come in late or cutting future costs to compensate for recent cost overruns. You might also need to adjust resource assignments. Sometimes controlling also means identifying scope creep and either halting it or absorbing it into the plan.

To revisit the overview of the executing, monitoring, and controlling processes, see "Project Processes" in Lesson 1, "Project Management Basics."

Collect Progress Information

With your tasks carefully scheduled and resources thoughtfully assigned, as soon as the project start date arrives, your team members aptly launch into their assigned tasks as scheduled. At that moment, your waterfall project officially enters the executing process and you're all off and running. While your team members carry out their tasks, as the project manager you're regularly monitoring status.

To effectively collect progress information from your team, you must establish your method and frequency of communicating progress, and also identify the types of information you're collecting.

- Decide on the communication method that works best for you and your team:
  - Emails, whether daily, weekly, or on task due dates
  - Online tracking, for example, directly in Project itself or in Microsoft Teams
  - Regular online or in-person meetings, like in *daily scrums* or *standups* (brief agile status meetings) or with weekly check-ins
  - Written status reports
- Choose daily, weekly, or monthly reporting depending on the *scope* and pace of your project and how quickly you anticipate that adjustments and issues must be addressed.
- Determine how you want progress to be reported. This is the data you'll enter into Project to record progress on assigned tasks. Choose from one or more of the following progress measures for each task:
  - Percentage complete
  - Time already spent on the task (actual duration or actual work)
  - Time left to spend on the task (remaining duration or remaining work)
  - Date the task was started (actual start)
  - Date the task was finished (actual finish)
- Set the format for the information you want on tasks assigned during the time period you've chosen:
  - Completed tasks; what was accomplished in the last time period
  - Upcoming tasks and tasks in progress; what will be accomplished in the next time period
  - Any obstacles or issues preventing completion of tasks

Enter Actuals in a Waterfall Project

When you use Project to enter progress in a waterfall project, durations and dates are adjusted automatically for downstream tasks—the linked *successor* tasks. Those successors are affected by how early or late their linked *predecessor* tasks started or finished. Associated resource costs are also automatically adjusted, because if a task doesn't take as long as expected, the cost for the task is reduced.

You can enter progress by saying a task is proceeding exactly on schedule. You can also enter more detailed progress information like actual duration, remaining duration, actual start date, or actual finish date.

As soon as you start to enter progress, you have information for three different versions of your plan: the baseline (or original values), the scheduled (or current values), and the actual values.

Enter Progress as Expected

If a task is proceeding or has completed according to plan with the expected duration, start date, and finish date, you can quickly enter progress by using either the Mark on Track or Percent Complete function.

To specify that a task is progressing according to its planned schedule:

1. In a Gantt view or other task view, select the task.

2. On the Task tab, in the Schedule group, click **Mark on Track**.

   The task is marked as completed as far as it should be according to its planned schedule. That is, if it was supposed to start on October 26, and you click **Mark on Track**, Project will record that the task indeed started on October 26. Likewise, if the task was scheduled to finish on November 14, and you click **Mark on Track**, Project will record that the task finished on November 14. The current date is not taken into account.

To specify a task's percent complete by using the ribbon:

1. In a Gantt view or other task view, select the task.

2. On the Task tab, in the Schedule group, click **25%, 50%, 75%,** or **100%**.

   If you're working in a Gantt view, a dark progress line in the center of the Gantt bar reflects the percent complete (see Figure 9.1).

FIGURE 9.1   Gantt bar for a task that's 50 percent complete

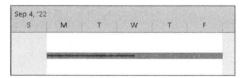

Regardless of the current date when you mark a task complete, Project indicates that the actual finish date is the same as the scheduled finish date shown in the Finish field.

To specify a task's percent complete by using the Task Information dialog box:

1. In any task view, double-click the task.

2. In the Task Information dialog box that appears, click the **General** tab.

3. In the Percent Complete box, enter the task's percent complete, such as 50%, as shown in Figure 9.2.

FIGURE 9.2   Percent complete in the Task Information dialog box

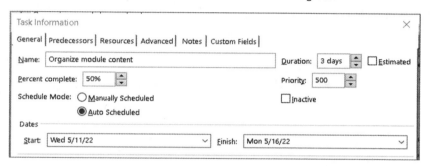

Enter Different Types of Progress Information

It's quick and easy to use Mark on Track or Percent Complete to enter progress, but if a task proceeded differently from the plan, you probably want to record that difference in Project. Specifying how long a task really took to complete, or the real start and finish dates, gives you accurate data about your project. This is important for a true picture of the ripple effects that delayed tasks are having on the rest of the schedule, how much your resources are being used, and project costs.

Use the Update Tasks dialog box to enter one or more different progress measures: *percent complete*, *actual duration*, *remaining duration*, *actual start date*, or *actual finish date*. Experiment with entering different types of progress to determine what works best for you, your team, and the project. You can mix and match how you enter projects on different tasks. With one or more pieces of progress information, Project calculates the rest.

Percent Complete   Is easy and quick to enter. Project assumes that the actual duration, start, and finish were exactly as planned, which may or may not be accurate.

Actual or Remaining Duration   Records more accurately how long a task took or will take. If you enter only actual duration, Project calculates the remaining duration. If you enter actual and remaining duration, Project calculates the scheduled duration.

Actual Start and Actual Finish   Records more accurately when the task was worked on and calculates the actual duration from the period between the actual start and finish dates. If you enter the actual start date, Project calculates the scheduled finish date. If you enter the actual start and actual finish, Project calculates the actual duration.

To record progress in the Update Tasks dialog box:

1. Open any task view, like the Gantt Chart or Task Board.

2. On the Task tab, in the Schedule group, click the arrow next to Mark on Track, and then click **Update Tasks** (Figure 9.3).

FIGURE 9.3   Update Tasks dialog box

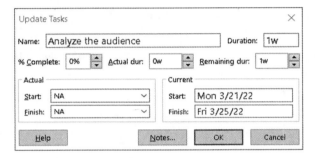

3. In the Update Tasks dialog box, enter the progress information for the selected task. You can enter information in one or more of the percent complete, actual duration, remaining duration, actual start date, or actual finish date fields.

4. Click **OK**.

If you're working in a task sheet, and if your progress information changed any scheduled information for the current or successor tasks, blue shading appears in those changed fields. Also, if you reopen the Update Tasks dialog box, you can see any calculations Project has made based on your progress information.

Distinguish Baseline, Scheduled, and Actual Values

Now that you're tracking progress, you're telling Project when tasks actually started and finished as well as how much time they took. With these status updates, you're creating a new set of useful information. The information reflecting what really happened with the task is called the actual data, the *actual plan*, or *actuals* for short. You can see your actuals by adding "Actual" fields to a column in a task sheet, such as Actual Duration, Actual Start, and Actual Finish.

Your actuals are always distinct from the current or scheduled values for your plan, which you see in the Duration, Start, and Finish fields. These values are considered the *scheduled plan.* You set these values in Project as soon as you started adding durations, task links, and other schedule controls to your project, as described in Lesson 5, "Build the Schedule." The scheduled plan can change as you enter actuals, because a task finishing earlier or later than originally scheduled can change the start and finish dates of successor tasks that are linked to it. The scheduled plan shown in the Duration, Start, and Finish fields reflects the project as it stands today based on actuals entered so far. So, these fields do not necessarily retain their original values from when you started the project; they are fluid and are likely to change as you enter actuals.

Your original duration and dates are saved when you set the project baseline, as described in "Set the Project Baseline" in Lesson 8, "Check and Adjust the Project." The values in your scheduled Duration, Start, and Finish dates were saved at that moment, like a snapshot. They're copied into the *baseline plan* and can be viewed in "Baseline" fields like Baseline Duration, Baseline Start, and Baseline Finish. These fields do not change as you enter actuals but always retain their original values from the point when you saved the baseline.

Think of the baseline as your original plan, the scheduled plan as the fluid and ever-changing plan that you work with day to day, and the actuals as the record of what really happened. See Figure 9.4 for an example of how you might show and compare this information in the Task Sheet.

FIGURE 9.4   The Task Sheet customized to show the baseline, scheduled, and actual finish dates

The Actual Finish field contains the date you recorded in Project that the task was completed in real life.

The Finish field contains the current, or scheduled, finish date and can change throughout the project as actual schedule information is added.

The Baseline Finish field shows the original scheduled finish date as it was when you set the project baseline.

Task Name	Baseline Finish	Finish	Actual Finish
◢ **Plan the training**	**Tue 5/17/22**	**Tue 5/17/22**	**NA**
Analyze the audience	Fri 3/25/22	Thu 3/24/22	Thu 3/24/22
Assess audience training needs	Fri 4/8/22	Tue 4/5/22	Tue 4/5/22
◢ **Identify the training topics**	**Tue 4/19/22**	**Sun 4/17/22**	**Sun 4/17/22**
Brainstorm training topics	Thu 4/14/22	Thu 4/14/22	Thu 4/14/22
Select and organize training topics	Tue 4/19/22	Sun 4/17/22	Sun 4/17/22
Evaluate and select the learning management system tools	Wed 5/11/22	Wed 5/11/22	NA
Organize module content	Mon 5/16/22	Mon 5/16/22	NA
Present training proposal	Tue 5/17/22	Tue 5/17/22	NA

The distinction between the baseline, scheduled, and actual data is important as you analyze progress, report the status, and compare where the project stands with your original schedule. Several reports include baseline, scheduled, and actual data to help with these comparisons and analysis.

Cost and work information also work on the same principles. You can access Project data for baseline costs, scheduled costs, and actual costs. For tasks assigned to work resources, you have baseline work, scheduled work, and actual work.

Don't Enter Actuals in the Start and Finish Fields

It might be tempting to just enter your actual start and finish dates in the Start and Finish fields that appear in the Gantt Chart and many other task sheets. However, remember that entering a date in the Start field creates a Start No Earlier Than constraint and entering a date in the Finish field creates a Finish No Earlier Than constraint. These constraints can interfere with linked successor tasks and bring up confusing alerts.

Instead, enter actual start and finish dates in the Update Tasks dialog box.

You can also add the Actual Start and Actual Finish columns to a task sheet. Click in the **Add New Column** heading in any task sheet, and then click **Actual Start** or **Actual Finish**.

Update Status in an Agile Project

Recording updates to agile project tasks can be as simple as dragging a task card from one column to another on the Task Board or Current Sprint Board. You can quickly update progress during or after your daily scrum huddles or standups. Your updates can be as detailed or as broad as suits your tracking style and the needs of your team and project.

Enter Progress on the Task Board

The Task Board is made up of columns that indicate current task status. The default progress columns are Not Started, Next Up, In Progress, and Done. All tasks originate in the Not Started column. To update progress, simply drag a task card from one column to another.

To update progress on the Task Board:

1. On the View tab, in the Task Views group, click **Task Board**. Or right-click the left edge of the Project window where the name of the current view shows, and then click **Task Board** on the menu that appears.

2. Drag a task card to the column that indicates its current progress, for example, from the Next Up to the In Progress column or from the Not Started to the Done column.

   This gives you the visual representation of agile task progress, as shown in Figure 9.5.

FIGURE 9.5   Drag task cards on the Task Board to the appropriate column to indicate current status.

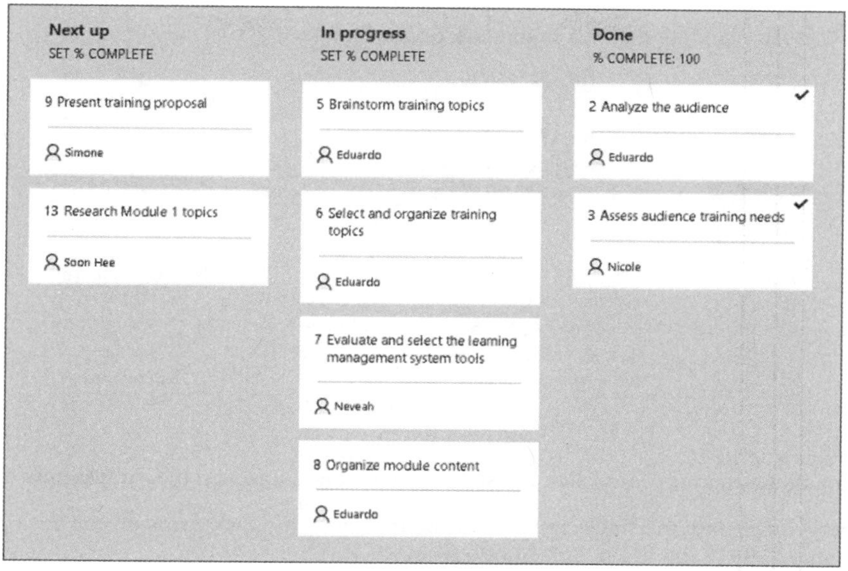

Note that by default, moving task cards to a progress column on the Task Board does not automatically change the task status fields in the Project scheduling engine. For example, moving a task card to the Next Up or In Progress column does not change the task's Actual Start date or the % Complete fields.

The exception to this is when you move a task card to the Done column. This updates the task to 100 percent complete and the actual start and finish fields are entered as scheduled.

Also, if you update a task elsewhere in Project, like on the Gantt Chart, to indicate that it's in progress or completed, the task card does not move automatically on the Task Board. You always need to drag the task card yourself.

You can add custom columns to the Task Board if you want to add more incremental columns to show progress. You can also move and rename Task Board columns. See "Customize a Board View" in Lesson 11, "Customize Project Information."

Enter Progress in the Task Board Sheet

Another way to update progress on an agile project is by using the Task Board Sheet. Instead of dragging task cards from one column to another, you update the Board Status field for each task.

To enter progress in the Task Board Sheet:

1. On the View tab, in the Task Views group, click **Task Board,** click **More Views,** and then double-click **Task Board Sheet.**

2. In the Task Board Sheet, click in the Board Status field for the task you want to update, and then click the arrow in the field, as shown in Figure 9.6.

FIGURE 9.6   Updating status in the Task Board Sheet

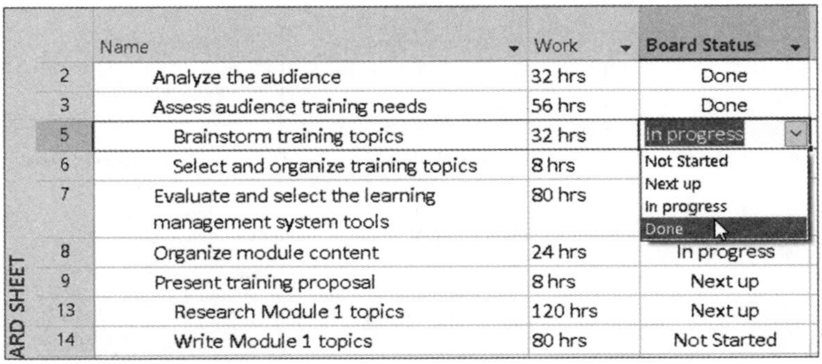

3. In the menu that appears, click the status for the task, for example, **In Progress** or **Done**.

When you update the status in the Task Board Sheet, the task cards on the Task Board automatically move to the indicated status column.

Specify Percent Complete on the Task Board

You can take the visual representation on the Task Board a step further by specifying the percent complete that a column represents. If you do this, when you drag a task card to the column, Project updates the task to the specified percent complete. If the percent complete for a column is not specified, the task's percent complete is unchanged.

To specify the percent complete represented by a Task Board column:

1. Open the Task Board.

2. Under the column heading, click in the **Set % Complete** label.

3. In the white box that appears with a blinking cursor, enter the percent complete you want this column to represent.

For example, suppose you want tasks in the Next Up column to always show as 10 percent complete. Enter **10** in the **Set % Complete** box. Now, when you drag a task card to this column, Project automatically updates the task's percent complete to 10 percent.

You cannot set a percent complete range, like 5 to 95 percent, for one column. If you set a percent complete, any tasks in that column adopt that percent complete.

The Done column is already set to 100 percent complete. When you drag a column to the Done column, Project automatically updates the task percent complete to 100 percent, and checks it as a completed task.

You might find it helpful to show percent complete on all task cards.

To show percent complete on all task cards:

1. With the Task Board open, on the Task Board Format tab, in the Customize group, click **Customize Cards**.

   The Customize Task Board Cards dialog box appears.

2. Under Additional Fields, click the arrow in the next available **Select Field** box.

3. Click **% Complete**, and then click **OK**.

   The % Complete field appears under the task name on every task card, as shown in Figure 9.7.

FIGURE 9.7 The % Complete field added to every task card

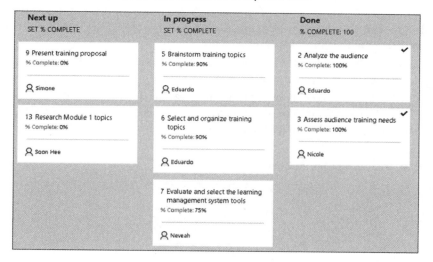

To enter percent complete on an individual task:

1. Double-click the task card whose percent complete you want to update.

   The Task Information dialog box appears. Make sure the General tab is showing.

2. In the Percent Complete box, enter the percent complete for this task.

3. Click **OK**.

Update Task Progress Details from the Task Board

You can update task progress details like percent complete, actual and remaining duration, and actual start and finish dates from the Task Board, just as you can from any task sheet in Project. To do this, click the task card whose progress information you want to update. On the Task tab, in the Schedule group, click the arrow in **Mark on Track**, and then click **Update Tasks**.

For more information on updating the task progress, see "Enter Different Types of Progress Information," earlier in this lesson.

Enter Progress on the Current Sprint

If you have created *sprints*, for example, two-week or four-week sprints, and identified the tasks within each sprint, you can enter progress on the current sprint by updating tasks on the Current Sprint Board.

For a refresher on adding sprints to your project and adding tasks to the sprints, see "Schedule Sprints for an Agile Project" in Lesson 5.

To update tasks in the current sprint:

1. On the View tab, in the Task Views group, click **Task Board**, click **More Views**, and then double-click **Current Sprint Board**.

    The Current Sprint Board shows all tasks in the sprint scheduled for the current time period. The Current Sprint Board shows the same progress columns and task card customizations as on the Task Board and other board views (see Figure 9.8).

FIGURE 9.8   Current Sprint Board

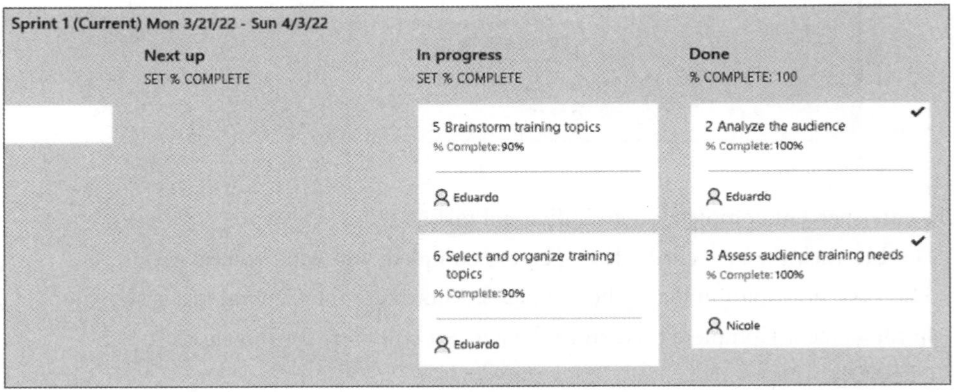

2. Drag a task card to the column that indicates its current progress, for example, from the Not Started to the Next Up column or from the In Progress to the Done column.

Update Sprint Progress in the Current Sprint Sheet

You can also use the Current Sprint Sheet to update progress for the current sprint. On the View tab, in the Task Views group, click **Task Board**, click **More Views**, and then double-click **Current Sprint Sheet**. In the sheet, click in the Board Status field for the task you want to update, and then click the arrow in the field. In the menu that appears, click the status for the task, for example, **Next Up** or **Done**.

Move Tasks from One Sprint to Another

If necessary, you can move tasks from one sprint to the next by using the Sprint Planning Board.

To move a task to another sprint:

1. On the View tab, in the Task Views group, click **Task Board**, click **More Views,** and then double-click **Sprint Planning Board**.

   The Sprint Planning Board shows all tasks arranged by sprint (see Figure 9.9).

FIGURE 9.9   Sprint Planning Board

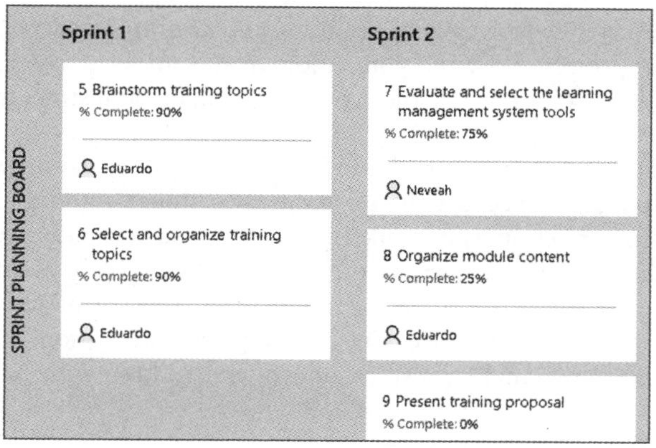

2. Drag a task card to a different sprint to schedule it for that sprint period.

Move Tasks to Another Sprint by using a Sprint Sheet

You can also use the Sprint Planning Sheet or Current Sprint Sheet to move a task to a different sprint. On the View tab, in the Task Views group, click **Task Board**, click **More Views**, and then double-click **Sprint Planning Sheet** or **Current Sprint Sheet**.

In the sheet, click in the Sprint field for the task you want to move to another sprint, and then click the arrow in the field. In the menu that appears, click the name of the sprint where you want to move the task, for example, **Sprint 2** or **Sprint 3**.

Respond to Changes

As you enter progress information into your project to reflect what's really happening, task start and finish dates can change along with costs. If a task takes longer than expected, for example, the schedule for successor tasks moves out and can get in the way of other tasks that might have specific date constraints. This can result in other tasks coming in late or resources being scheduled for two major activities at the same time. Either of these can result in the project finish date moving beyond the authorized deadline, increases in the project cost beyond the allocated budget, or resources out of balance.

Because of this, every time you update progress, you need to check your project finish date, your forecasted project costs, and your resource allocations to see whether you're still within your project boundaries or whether you need to make adjustments to compensate for these changes.

If checking and adjusting for the project finish date, project cost, and well-balanced resources sounds familiar, it's because these are the same things you did in Lesson 8 to get the project as close to perfection as possible right before you started executing the project. After you execute the project and start monitoring progress, you check and adjust the project again, and continuously, to control the priorities of scope, time, cost, and resources.

The difference is that now you're working with a project in motion. It's like riding a bicycle—while you steer, you make constant adjustments to keep your balance.

Check the Project Finish Date

The easiest way to monitor the project finish date as you update progress in your schedule is to add the *project summary task*.

To do this, with any task sheet open, on the Format tab, in the Show/Hide group, select the **Project Summary Task** check box. Once you add it, it appears on most other task sheets as well. The Finish field in the project summary task indicates the overall project finish date.

If necessary, see "Bring in the Project Finish Date" in Lesson 8. There you have specifics on:

- Shortening durations of *critical tasks*
- Reviewing and adjusting links between critical tasks
- Cutting scope

Check the Project Cost

To monitor the overall project cost as you update progress in your schedule, add the Cost column to the task sheets you use most frequently, for example, the Gantt Chart or Task Sheet.

To do this, open the task sheet, scroll to the far right edge of the sheet, and then click the **Add New Column** heading. Type **cost** and then press Enter. The Cost field is added to the sheet. The cost showing in the project summary task indicates the overall project cost.

If necessary, see "Reduce Costs" in Lesson 8. There you can follow procedures on:

- Cutting resource costs based on task information
- Cutting resource costs based on resource information
- Changing the finish date
- Cutting scope

Check Resource Allocations

When resources are overallocated, that is, scheduled for more work than they have available time to work on, their resource information or assigned task is flagged with the red overallocation icon in the Indicators column.

To resolve *overallocations*, see "Check Resource Assignments" in Lesson 8. There you'll see techniques on resolving overallocations in a task sheet or in Team Planner. You'll also see how to use Team Planner to better balance the resource load between overallocated and *underallocated* resources.

By keeping an eye on the overall resource load, along with monitoring the project cost and finish date while updating progress on a regular basis, you can be sure that you detect resolvable issues before they become big problems. You can take the necessary steps to adjust the project to set it up for success in meeting its goals, preventing team burnout, coming in under budget, and finishing on time.

Key Terms

actual duration
actual finish date
actual plan
actual start date
actuals
baseline plan
controlling process
critical task
daily scrum
executing process
monitoring process
overallocation
percent complete
planning process
predecessor
project summary task
remaining duration
scheduled plan
scope
sprint
standup
successor
underallocated

Review Questions

1. What's the difference between the planning and executing processes?

   A. Planning is the process for transforming the goals and constraints agreed upon by the project sponsors or customers. Executing is the process for gathering information from the team about task progress.

   B. Planning is the process when the project sponsors or customers agree to the project objectives and requirements, and when the project manager is first assigned. Executing is the process for starting and updating the project according to actual results.

   C. Planning is the process for transforming the goals and constraints identified in the initiating process into a roadmap for achieving those goals, task by task. Executing is the process for when the project actually starts being implemented and tasks are being accomplished.

   D. Planning is the process for outlining the project requirements and negotiating the project finish date and budget with the project sponsor. Executing is the process for actually implementing the project and carrying out the tasks.

2. What's the difference between the monitoring and controlling processes?

   A. Monitoring is about working with the appropriate Microsoft Project views. Controlling is about entering the right information in the right views.

   B. Monitoring is about collecting information about project progress and comparing it against the plan. Controlling is about printing views and reports based on that comparison.

   C. Monitoring is about designing and generating reports for the team and stakeholders. Controlling is about watching the project schedule and budget.

   D. Monitoring is about collecting status information from team members. Controlling is ensuring the project stays within bounds of finish date, cost, scope, and resource balancing.

3. List two of four methods for regularly communicating progress information with your team.

   A. Any two of the following: email, percent complete, actual duration, remaining cost

   B. Any two of the following: daily scrum huddles, remaining duration, actual work, completed tasks

   C. Any two of the following: email, online tracking, meetings, status reports

   D. Any two of the following: Microsoft Teams, Project on the web, remaining work, obstacles or issues

4. List three of five progress measures often used with waterfall projects.

   A. Any three of the following: Percent Complete, Actual Duration, Remaining Duration, Actual Start, Actual Finish

   B. Any three of the following: Not Started, Next Up, Percent Complete, In Progress, Done

   C. Any three of the following: Not Started, Actual Duration, Actual Finish, In Scrum, Done

   D. Any three of the following: Actual Start, Actual Finish, In Baseline, In Progress, Critical Task

5. What's one of the best ways to enter one or more of the five progress measures for water-fall projects?

A. Open the Update Tasks dialog box.

B. Open the Task Information dialog box.

C. Enter the percent complete on the Task tab.

D. Insert the Baseline Duration column in the Gantt Chart.

6. List three of four progress measures often used with agile projects.

A. Any three of the following: Next Up, In Progress, 25% Complete, Actual Work

B. Any three of the following: Not Started, Next Up, In Progress, Done

C. Any three of the following: Not Started, In Scrum, 50% Complete, Done

D. Any three of the following: In Baseline, In Progress, Critical Task, Done

7. What's one of the best ways to update progress for an agile project in Microsoft Project?

A. Move the baseline start date to the appropriate column on the Task Board.

B. Add the % Complete field to all task cards in the project.

C. Drag task cards to the appropriate sprint number on the Sprint Planning Board.

D. Drag task cards to the appropriate progress column on the Task Board or Current Sprint Board.

8. How does actual data affect current, scheduled data?

A. Entering actual duration, actual start, or actual finish can change the schedules for linked successor tasks.

B. Entering actual duration, actual start, or actual finish can change the baseline for linked predecessor tasks.

C. Entering actual work and actual cost can change the scheduled work and cost date for tasks already completed.

D. Entering actual baseline and scheduled plan can change the linked successor tasks.

9. How do you see the original schedule data for your project?

A. Review the actual data, like Actual Duration or Actual Finish, which show how the task was originally scheduled.

B. Review the baseline data, like Baseline Start or Baseline Cost, that saved a snapshot of the scheduled data when you originally set the baseline.

C. Review the currently scheduled data, like the Start and Finish fields, because these always retain their original values, regardless of actuals entered.

D. Review the baseline data, like Baseline Duration or Baseline Finish, because these indicate how long a task actually took to complete.

10. What are the three of the four project elements that should be monitored after entering progress information?

A. Any three of: project finish date, overall project cost, scheduled start, actual work

B. Any three of: project finish date, overall project cost, scope, resource allocation

C. Any three of: overall project cost, quality, scope, material resources

D. Any three of: scope, material resource units, overall project cost, completed tasks

Lesson 10

View Project Information

LESSON OBJECTIVES

✓ Tailor the display of project information by zooming a view, adjusting a timescale, and showing selected outline levels.

✓ Rearrange project information by sorting and grouping by a selected field.

✓ Filter and highlight tasks and resources to show information that meets your selected criteria.

✓ Add or remove a column in a sheet view.

✓ Format, preview, and print a view on paper and as a PDF file.

✓ Explore the variety of Project views, along with their layout, functions, and formatting options.

As soon as you start executing the project plan, you're constantly monitoring and controlling the project. Like the driver on a journey, you're continually monitoring your vehicle's speed, fuel level, road conditions, and traffic. You make adjustments for changes like construction, route detours, needs of fellow travelers, and traffic jams.

The views in Microsoft Project play a huge part in your ability to monitor the project. Views like the Gantt Chart, Resource Sheet, Task Board, and Sprint Board are like gauges you use to assess your project information from various points of view.

In this lesson, you learn how to home in on the project information you need, whether it's by adjusting a timescale or by grouping information by specific data. You learn how to work with tables and sheets, including adding and removing columns. You see how to effectively print a view, and you step through a guided tour of some of the many other views available in Project.

See the Data You Need

The larger and more complex your project, the more you'll find it necessary to focus on specific aspects of project information for various needs. You can zoom a *view* in or out, adjust the view's timescale from days to weeks, or see just the first and second outline levels in your task hierarchy. You can also rearrange your task or resource information into groups, and filter or highlight by a specific field.

Zoom a View In or Out

You can *zoom* any timescale or graphically oriented view in or out by using the *Zoom slider* available in the lower-right corner of the Project window. This means you can zoom the following views and types of views:

- The *timescale* (right) side of any Gantt view or usage view
- Team Planner
- The Timeline
- The Calendar view
- Network Diagram
- The Resource Graph

Click the minus sign to zoom out or the plus sign to zoom in. Or drag the Zoom slider to the level of zoom you want.

The Zoom slider does not work on the following views or types of views:

- Board views, for example, the Task Board or Sprint Planning Board
- Sheet views, for example, the Resource Sheet or Task Sheet
- Form views, for example, the Task Form or Resource Form

You can also use the Zoom controls on the ribbon.

To Zoom in or out using ribbon commands:

1. Display the view you want to zoom in or out.
2. On the View tab, in the Zoom group, click **Zoom**.
3. On the menu that appears, click **Zoom Out** to see a broader view of the project information. Click **Zoom In** to see more detail.

   Using these controls is similar to using the Zoom slider. Note that if the Zoom controls are dimmed on the View tab, zooming is not available for the current view.

To zoom to see the entire project on one screen:

1. Display the view with which you want to zoom to see the entire project.
2. On the View tab, in the Zoom group, click **Entire Project**.

   The view adjusts to show the entire project on one screen.

Adjust the Timescale

In the timescale-oriented views, like any Gantt view or usage view, zooming has the effect of adjusting the timescale. For example, when you zoom in, you might change the timescale from weeks to days. When you zoom out, you might change the timescale from weeks to months.

You can adjust the timescale by clicking the minus or plus sign on the Zoom slider. You can also use the Timescale controls on the ribbon.

To adjust the timescale by using the ribbon:

1. Display the view whose timescale you want to adjust.
2. On the View tab, in the Zoom group, click the arrow in the **Timescale** box.

   The Timescale drop-down menu appears, as shown in Figure 10.1. Note that if the Timescale control is dimmed on the View tab, timescale adjustments are not available for the current view.
3. Click the period of time you want to see in the current view.

FIGURE 10.1   Timescale drop-down menu

Show a Specific Outline Level

When you organize your task list with levels of *summary tasks* and *subtasks*, you can have two, three, or more outline levels. You might want to see just the first or second *outline level* to see a broader overview of the project.

This can be useful if you want to print a task sheet for a management report, for example. In other cases, you might want to see all outline levels of just one or two sets of tasks. This is helpful when you need to focus on the details of a specific phase of the project. Either way, you can specify the outline levels to show as many or as few outline levels as you need.

To show a specific outline level of the task hierarchy:

1. Display the task sheet, such as the Gantt Chart or Task Sheet, that shows the outline hierarchy (see Figure 10.2).

2. On the View tab, in the Data group, click **Outline**.

3. On the drop-down menu that appears, click the outline level you want to show, for example, **Level 2** or **Level 3**.

    The task list changes to show only those tasks at the outline level you selected (see Figure 10.3).

In this way, you can hide many subtasks to just show the higher-level tasks. You can still show the detail for one summary task.

FIGURE 10.2   Full task hierarchy

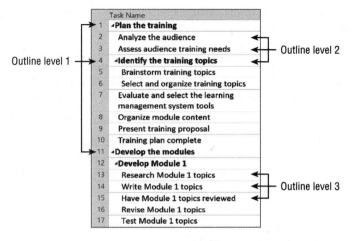

FIGURE 10.3   Task list showing only Level 1 of the outline

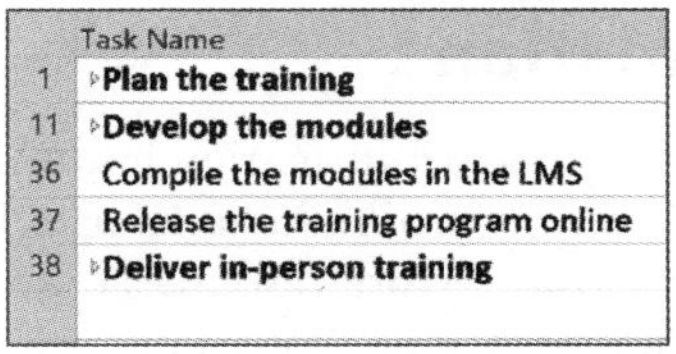

To expand the subtasks under just one summary task:

1.   In a task sheet with subtasks hidden, click the summary task whose subtasks you want to show.

2.   On the View tab, in the Data group, click **Outline**, and then click **Show Subtasks**.

The subtasks under the selected summary task are displayed.

To return your task list to its original state of showing all subtasks under all summary tasks, on the View tab, in the Data group, click **Outline**, and then click **All Subtasks**.

Sort Project Information

Having your tasks in the hierarchical order in which you've arranged them is typically the most logical order for your day-to-day project management work. Sometimes, however, it's useful to arrange the tasks in a different order.

For example, you might want to *sort* tasks from highest to lowest cost, especially if you're looking for the best opportunities to cut costs. Or you might want to sort resources alphabetically by name. You can always return the tasks or fields to their original order—that is, their order by Task ID or Resource ID.

To sort project information by a specific *field*:

1. Display the sheet view containing the information you want to sort, for example, the Task Sheet or Resource Sheet.

2. On the View tab, in the Data group, click **Sort**.

   The drop-down menu lists some of the more frequently used fields for sorting the current sheet. For example, for any task sheet, the sort fields shown are Start Date, Finish Date, Priority, and Cost. For any resource sheet, the default sort fields are Cost and Name.

3. Click the field by which you want to sort the information in the current sheet view.

   If the field by which you want to sort is not on the drop-down menu, click **Sort By** to open the Sort dialog box. Click in the **Sort by** field, then click the field you want. You can sort a task sheet by any task field available in Project. Likewise, you can sort a resource sheet by any resource field. Click **Sort**.

   The tasks or resources are sorted by the field you select.

To return the information in the sheet view to its original order, on the View tab, in the Data group, click **Sort**, and then click **by ID**.

Group Project Information

You can temporarily rearrange sheet view information into helpful categories. For example, if you want to see critical tasks, you can *group* the tasks by critical tasks. If you want to rearrange the Resource Sheet to show all work resources together and all material resources together, you can group the resources by type. You can group tasks by any task field and resources by any resource field.

To group project information by a specific field:

1. Display the task sheet or resource sheet containing the information you want to group.

2. On the View tab, in the Data group, click the arrow in the **Group By** box, and then click the field by which the information should be categorized.

   Your information is grouped by the field you selected, as shown in Figure 10.4.

To remove a grouping, on the View tab, in the Data group, click the arrow in the Group By box, and then click [**No Group**].

Filter Project Information

You can *filter* information in a task or resource sheet to show only the information you specify. For example, you can filter your Gantt Chart to show only late tasks. Or, you can filter your Resource Sheet to show only overallocated resources. You can filter a task sheet by any task field and filter a resource sheet by any resource field.

FIGURE 10.4   Task sheet grouped by resource

	Task Name	Duration	Start
	Resource Names: Leo	**3d**	
46	Train in Eugene	3 days	Thu 9/22/22
	Resource Names: Monique	**1d**	
45	Train in Tacoma	1 day	Wed 9/21/22
	Resource Names: Neveah	**92.38d**	
7	Evaluate and select the learning management system tools	2 wks	Wed 4/20/22
36	Compile the modules in the LMS	3 days	Mon 8/22/22
	Resource Names: Nicole	**105d**	
3	Assess audience training needs	1.4 wks	Mon 3/28/22
23	Test Module 2 topics	1 wk	Mon 5/9/22
35	Test Module 4 topics	1 wk	Mon 8/15/22
	Resource Names: Nicole,Neveah	**6.75d**	
48	Train in Monterey	6 days	Thu 9/29/22
	Resource Names: Simone	**1d**	
9	Present training proposal	1 day	Mon 5/16/22
	Resource Names: Soon Hee	**138.63d**	
13	Research Module 1 topics	3 wks	Tue 5/17/22
14	Write Module 1 topics	2 wks	Mon 3/21/22

(GANTT CHART)

To filter project information by a specific field:

1. Display the task sheet or resource sheet containing the information you want to filter.
2. On the View tab, in the Data group, click the arrow in the **Filter** box (which displays [No Filter]).
3. On the drop-down menu, click the field by which the information should be filtered.

If you don't see the field you want, click **More Filters** on the drop-down menu to open the More Filters dialog box. Click the field you want, then click **Apply**.

Your information is filtered by the field you selected.

To clear a filter, on the View tab, in the Data group, click the arrow in the **Filter** box (which shows the name of the current filter), and then click **[No Filter]**.

Highlight Project Information

Similar to using a filter, you can *highlight* information in a task or resource sheet. However, instead of the filtered information being the only information showing, all information still shows, but the filtered information is highlighted in yellow.

For example, you can highlight critical tasks in your Task Usage view. Or, you can highlight material resources in your Resource Sheet. You can highlight a task sheet by any task field and highlight a resource sheet by any resource field.

To highlight project information by a specific field:

1. Display the task sheet or resource sheet containing the information you want to highlight.
2. On the View tab, in the Data group, click the arrow in the **Highlight** box (which displays [No Highlight]).

3. On the drop-down menu, click the field that indicates which information in the sheet should be highlighted.

If you don't see the field by which you want to highlight your information, click **More Highlight Filters** on the drop-down menu to open the More Filters dialog box. Click the field you want, then click **Highlight**.

Your information is highlighted according to the field you selected (see Figure 10.5).

FIGURE 10.5   Resource sheet with cost resources highlighted

	ⓘ	Resource Name	Type	Material Label	Max. Units	Std. Rate
1		Monique	Work		100%	$20.00/hr
2		Daunte	Work		50%	$22.00/hr
3	👤	Soon Hee	Work		100%	$25.00/hr
4		Color Printer	Work		100%	$10.00/hr
5		Binders	Material	each		$4.00
6		Scratchpads	Material	each		$1.00
7		Pens	Material	package		$12.00
8		Airfare	Cost			
9		Hotel	Cost			
10		Conference Room	Cost			
11		Leo	Work		100%	$25.00/hr
12		Xavier	Work		100%	$22.00/hr
13		Neveah	Work		100%	$28.00/hr
14		Nicole	Work		100%	$24.00/hr

RESOURCE SHEET

To clear a highlight, on the View tab, in the Data group, click the arrow in the **Highlight** box (which shows the name of the current highlight), then click [**No Highlight**].

Change Columns in a Sheet View

Any Project view that includes a grid of rows and columns is considered a *sheet view*. Examples include the Task Sheet, Resource Sheet, and Current Sprint Sheet.

Any Project view that includes a sheet view on the left side and a timescale view on the right side is considered a *combination view*. Examples include all the Gantt views, the Task Usage view, and the Resource Usage view. In sheet views or in the sheet side of a combination view, you can add or remove columns to see just the fields of information you want.

Add a Column

To add a column to a sheet view:

1. Display the sheet view or combination view to which you'd like to add a column.

2. Scroll to the far right edge of the sheet view until you see the last column, labeled Add New Column.

3. Click the **Add New Column** heading.

A list of all available fields appears alphabetically in a drop-down menu, as shown in Figure 10.6.

FIGURE 10.6 Add New Column drop-down menu

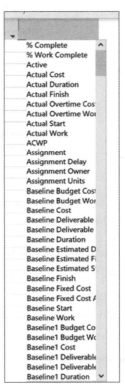

4. In the menu, scroll to the field you want to add as a new column, or type the first couple letters of the field name to quickly find it.

5. Click the field name.

The field appears as a new column in your sheet view (see Figure 10.7).

If your project plan is structured into a series of sprints, consider adding the Sprint, Sprint Start, or Sprint Finish column to any task sheet. This is a useful way to see the sprint number and associated dates amid other related task information. For more information, see "Schedule Sprints for an Agile Project" in Lesson 5, "Build the Schedule."

FIGURE 10.7   Cost column added to the Task Sheet

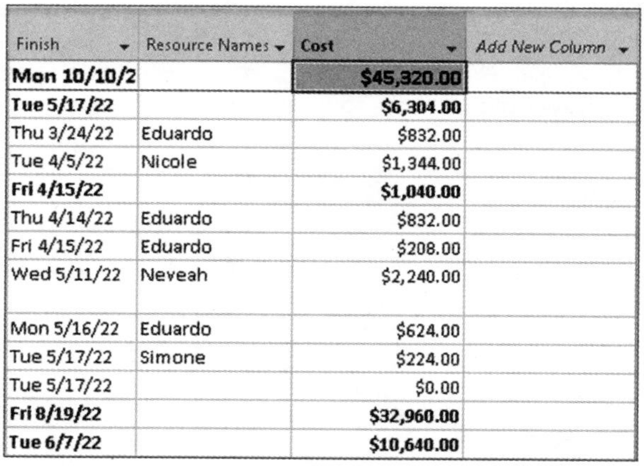

Finish	Resource Names	Cost	Add New Column
Mon 10/10/2		$45,320.00	
Tue 5/17/22		$6,304.00	
Thu 3/24/22	Eduardo	$832.00	
Tue 4/5/22	Nicole	$1,344.00	
Fri 4/15/22		$1,040.00	
Thu 4/14/22	Eduardo	$832.00	
Fri 4/15/22	Eduardo	$208.00	
Wed 5/11/22	Neveah	$2,240.00	
Mon 5/16/22	Eduardo	$624.00	
Tue 5/17/22	Simone	$224.00	
Tue 5/17/22		$0.00	
Fri 8/19/22		$32,960.00	
Tue 6/7/22		$10,640.00	

Move a Column

When you use Add New Column, the new field appears near the far-right edge of the sheet view. You can move it to another position in the sheet.

To move a column:

1. Display the sheet or combination view containing the column you'd like to move.

2. Click in the column heading, then click a second time to activate the move function.

3. Drag the column to the place you want in the sheet.

   A gray vertical bar shows where the column will be placed.

4. Release the mouse button.

   The column appears in your specified location.

Hide a Column

If your sheet view includes a column you never use and it just seems to be in the way, you can hide it to remove it from the sheet. Hiding a column never deletes the field information; you can always show the information again in this or another view.

To hide a column:

1. Display the sheet or combination view containing the column you'd like to hide.

2. Right-click in the column heading.

3. On the drop-down menu, click **Hide Column**.

   To show a column again, follow the steps in the previous section titled "Add a Column."
   Or, click anywhere in the column, then on the Format tab, in the Columns group, click **Column Settings**, then click **Hide Column**.

Print a View

You can print any Project view on paper or as a PDF file to share with others on the team or to have as a ready reference.

To format a view to prepare it for printing:

1. Display the view you want to print.

2. Arrange the view to show the information you want in the printout.

This might mean adjusting the split bar between two sides of a combination view, adding or removing columns, or adjusting the font or text alignment.

3. On the File tab, click **Print**.

The view shows a preview of the view as it will be printed (see Figure 10.8).

FIGURE 10.8   Print window with preview and controls

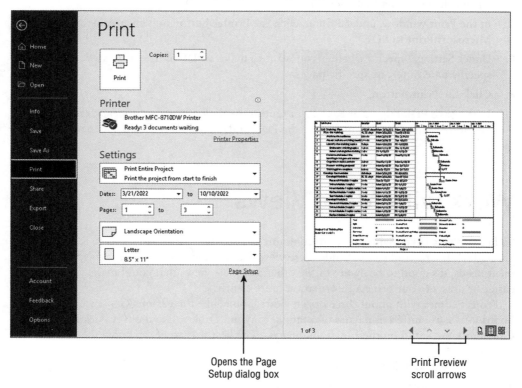

Opens the Page
Setup dialog box

Print Preview
scroll arrows

4. If the preview includes multiple pages, click the right and left arrows to scroll through the pages horizontally. Click the down and up arrows to scroll through the pages vertically.

5. To change the page orientation, in the Print window, under Settings, click whether you want the view to print in Portrait or Landscape orientation.

6. To set the printed page margins or add a header or footer to the printed view, click **Page Setup**.

  In the Page Setup dialog box, use the tabs to set your preferences for page scaling, margins, header, or footer. When finished, click **OK**.

  After the view is laid out the way you want, you're ready to print the view.
  To print the view on paper:

1. In the Print window, under Printer, make sure the proper device is showing. If not, click the **Printer** button and select the printer.

2. Under Settings, specify whether you want to print the entire view, only a specific date range, or specific pages.

3. Click the **Print** button.

  It's often easier to print the view as a PDF file, so you can easily email or share the view in a format that everyone in the team can view, even if they don't have access to Project.
  To print the view as a PDF file:

1. In the Print window, under Printer, click the **Printer** button and click **Adobe PDF** or **Microsoft Print to PDF**.

2. Under Settings, specify whether you want to make a PDF of the entire view, or only a specific date range, or specific pages.

3. Click the **Print** button.

4. In the Save PDF File As or Save Print Output As dialog box that appears, select the drive and folder where you want to save the PDF, and enter a name in the File name field.

5. Click **Save**.

Work with More Views

So far, you've worked with the more common Project views: the Gantt Chart, Resource Sheet, Task Board, and so on. While these views can handle much of your project management needs, it's good to be aware of the other available views that could make your life easier or present your project information more clearly.

  Project comes with about three dozen views. Some, like the various Gantt views and board views, are different flavors of a familiar layout. Others, like the Network Diagram or Calendar view, stand on their own uniqueness. The best way to get to know the views is to click around.

  To browse available Project views:

1. Open a project file that has enough tasks, resources, and assignments to let you see what each view can offer.

2. On the View tab, in the Resource Views group, click **Other Views**, then click **More Views**.

  The More Views dialog box lists all available Project views, whether they are task views, resource views, assignment views, or agile-oriented views. See Figure 10.9.

FIGURE 10.9   The More Views dialog box

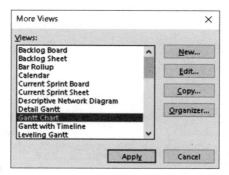

3. Double-click a view name to apply it.

4. Browse the view itself, as well as the controls on the Format tab.

5. Return to the More Views dialog box to select another view to browse.

As before, on the View tab, in the Resource Views group, click **Other Views**, then click **More Views**. You can also right-click the view bar on the left edge of the Project window, then on the drop-down menu, click **More Views**.

The following sections offer a guided tour of some of the available graphical views and combination views.

Browse Graphical Views

The graphically oriented views in Project represent task, resource, or assignment information in a visual layout. Examples include the Timeline, Calendar view, Network Diagram, Resource Graph, and Team Planner.

To tour a variety of graphical views in Project:

1. Open your project file with any task view showing.

2. On the View tab, in the Split View group, select the **Timeline** check box.

The *Timeline view* appears as a narrow horizontal bar above the current view. It's blank until you add tasks to it. The Timeline is useful for highlighting major tasks like phases, sprints, or milestones, giving them more visibility at a glance. To add a task to the timeline, right-click its name in the main view, then click **Add to Timeline**. The task name with its start and finish dates appears as a bar along the timescale in the Timeline view (see Figure 10.10). When you apply the Timeline view, it stays in place as you move to any view throughout Project.

3. To hide the Timeline view, on the View tab, in the Split View group, clear the **Timeline** check box.

FIGURE 10.10   The Timeline view above the Task Board

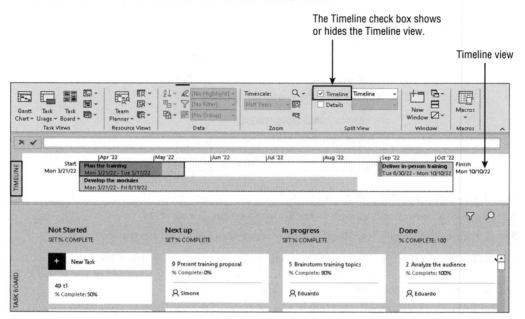

The Timeline check box shows or hides the Timeline view.

Timeline view

4. Right-click the view bar on the left edge of the Project window, then on the drop-down menu, click **Calendar**.

The *Calendar view* appears, showing your tasks arranged across a monthly calendar grid, as shown in Figure 10.11. Use the arrows near the upper-left corner of the view to move across different time periods. Also in the upper-left corner, click **Week** if you prefer to see a week at a time, rather than a month. Within the calendar grid, drag the gray date bars to make a time period narrower or wider to better show the tasks in that time period.

5. Right-click the view bar, then on the drop-down menu, click **Network Diagram**.

The *Network Diagram* appears, showing your tasks arranged in boxes or other shapes, which contain the start and finish dates, duration, assigned resource name, and percentage complete (see Figure 10.12). This view highlights the relationships between tasks—that is, how they're linked from predecessor tasks to successor tasks. Critical tasks are shown in red.

FIGURE 10.11   The Calendar view

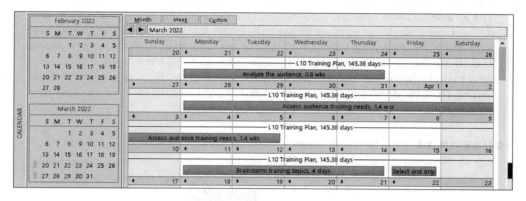

FIGURE 10.12   Network Diagram

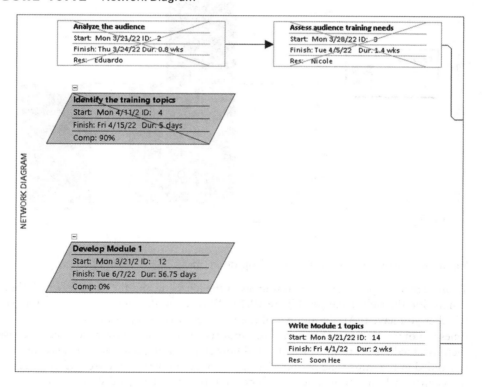

6. Right-click the view bar, then on the drop-down menu, click **Resource Graph**.

The *Resource Graph* appears, showing one resource at a time (see Figure 10.13). Use the horizontal scroll bar to move through the graph side of the view. The graph shows when the current resource is used, not used, or overallocated, and at what percentages of their availability. Click the arrows in the horizontal scroll bar in the left side of the view to cycle through all the resources in your plan and see their individual resource graphs. Drag the divider bar between the left and right sides of the view to show more of the graph.

FIGURE 10.13 The Resource Graph

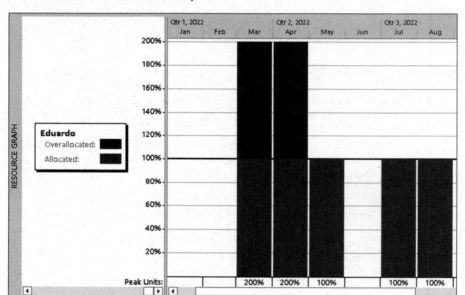

7. Right-click the view bar, then on the drop-down menu, click **Team Planner**.

Team Planner appears, showing resources in the left pane and the tasks to which they're assigned in the right pane (see Figure 10.14). With Team Planner, you can see at a glance whether you have the right number of the right resource types throughout the timespan of your project. You can easily spot resources that are overallocated, because their assigned tasks are shown with a red border, indicating that multiple tasks are scheduled in the same time period. You can also see resources that are underused. Any unassigned tasks are shown near the bottom of the view. Drag a task horizontally to move it to a different time period. Drag a task vertically to assign it to a different resource.

FIGURE 10.14   Team Planner

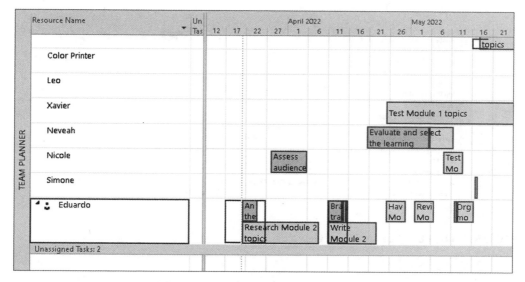

Browse Combination Views

Combination views are those that include two or three views in a single view. These include the Gantt views, Task Entry view, split views, and the two usage views.

To tour a variety of Project combination views:

1. Open your project file.

2. Right-click the view bar, then on the drop-down menu, click **Tracking Gantt**.

   The *Tracking Gantt* view appears. If necessary, drag the divider bar to see as much of the sheet area on the left and the timescale area on the right as you want. Click a task, then on the **Task** tab, in the **Editing** group, click **Scroll to Task** to see the Gantt bar for the selected task. As shown in Figure 10.15, the Gantt bars show visually and textually the percentage complete for each task. Project offers several variations of Gantt views, including the Bar Rollup view, Detail Gantt, Leveling Gantt, Milestone Date Rollup view, Milestone Rollup, and Multiple Baselines Gantt.

3. On the View tab, in the Task Views group, click **Gantt Chart**, click **More Views**, click **Task Entry**, then click **Apply**.

   The *Task Entry view* appears, as shown in Figure 10.16. The Task Entry view is a *split view*. By default, the upper view is the Gantt Chart and the lower view is the Task Form. When you click a task in the Gantt Chart, the details of that task appear in the Task Form. These details include the start date, finish date, and assigned resources. This is a great view for seeing an overview of the project and task details in a single window. To return to the full-screen Gantt Chart, double-click the horizontal divider between the two views. Or, on the View tab, in the Split View group, clear the **Details** check box.

FIGURE 10.15 The Tracking Gantt

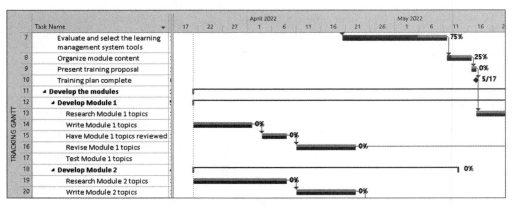

FIGURE 10.16 The Task Entry view

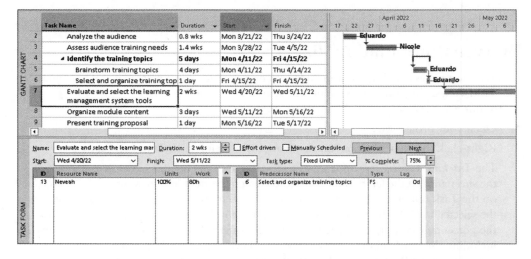

4. Right-click the view bar, then on the drop-down menu, click **Resource Sheet**.

5. On the View tab, in the Split View group, select the **Details** check box.

   A split view similar to the Task Entry view appears, but this one is for resources (see Figure 10.17). When you click a resource in the Resource Sheet, the details of that resource appear in the *Resource Form*. These details include the units, cost, and assigned tasks. Use this view to see an overview of resources and their assignments in a single view. To return to the full-screen Resource Sheet, double-click the horizontal divider between the two views. Or, on the View tab, in the Split View group, clear the **Details** check box.

FIGURE 10.17 Split view of Resource Sheet and Resource Form

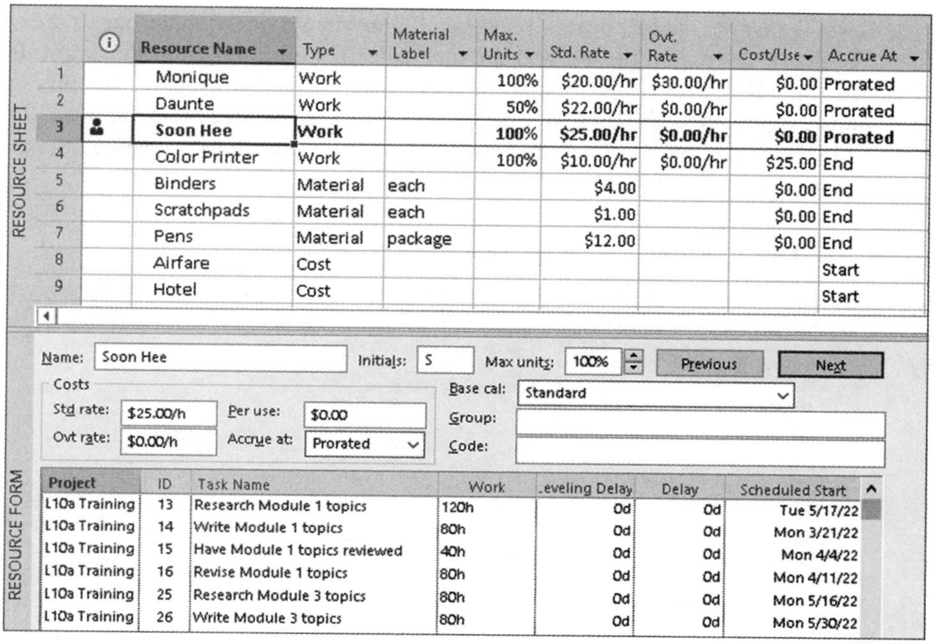

6. Right-click the view bar, then on the drop-down menu, click **Task Usage**.

The *Task Usage view* appears. If necessary, drag the vertical divider bar to see as much of the sheet area on the left and the timescale area on the right as you want. In the sheet area, the Task Usage view shows resource assignments by tasks. The timescale area on the right shows the total amount of work for the tasks and the work for each of the assigned resources (see Figure 10.18). This view is useful for reviewing the details of resource assignments by task.

FIGURE 10.18 The Task Usage view

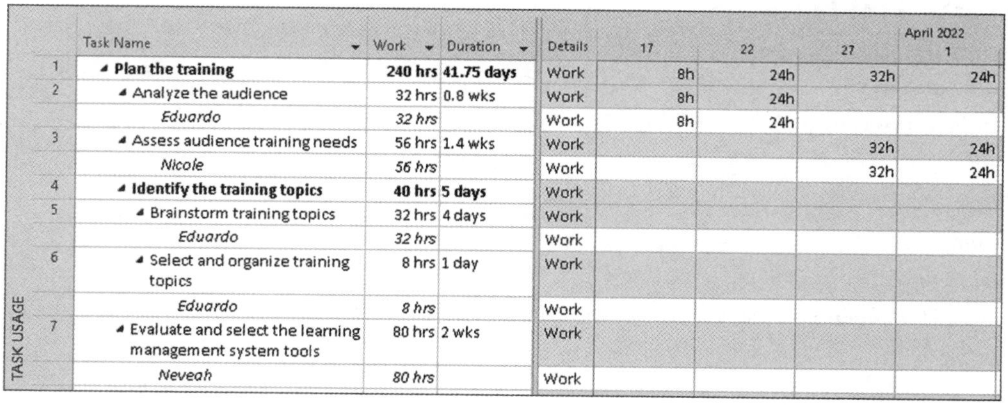

7. Right-click the view bar, then on the drop-down menu, click **Resource Usage.**

   The *Resource Usage view* appears. If necessary, drag the vertical divider bar to see as much of the sheet area on the left and the timescale area on the right as you want. In the sheet area, the Resource Usage view shows task assignments by resource. The timescale area on the right shows the total amount of work for the resources and the work for each of the assigned tasks (see Figure 10.19). This view is useful for reviewing the details of task assignments by resource.

FIGURE 10.19 The Resource Usage view

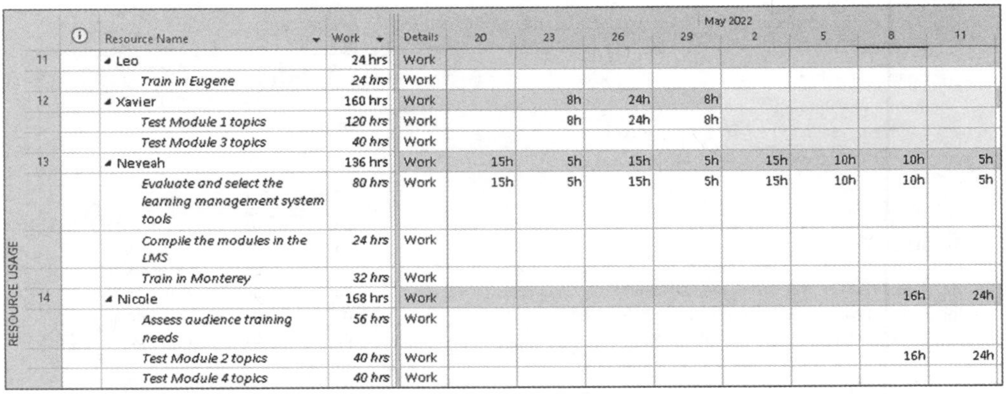

	ⓘ	Resource Name	Work	Details	20	23	26	29	May 2022 2	5	8	11
11		◢ Leo	24 hrs	Work								
		Train in Eugene	*24 hrs*	Work								
12		◢ Xavier	160 hrs	Work		8h	24h	8h				
		Test Module 1 topics	*120 hrs*	Work		8h	24h	8h				
		Test Module 3 topics	*40 hrs*	Work								
13		◢ Neveah	136 hrs	Work	15h	5h	15h	5h	15h	10h	10h	5h
		Evaluate and select the learning management system tools	*80 hrs*	Work	15h	5h	15h	5h	15h	10h	10h	5h
		Compile the modules in the LMS	*24 hrs*	Work								
		Train in Monterey	*32 hrs*	Work								
14		◢ Nicole	168 hrs	Work							16h	24h
		Assess audience training needs	*56 hrs*	Work								
		Test Module 2 topics	*40 hrs*	Work							16h	24h
		Test Module 4 topics	*40 hrs*	Work								

Use these and other Project views to best meet the project monitoring requirements for you, your team, and your project sponsors. By keeping a fixed eye on current road conditions as well as the road ahead, you improve your odds to anticipate and mitigate possible issues and see your way through to successful project completion.

Key Terms

Calendar view

combination view

field

filter

group

highlight

Network Diagram

outline level

Resource Form

Resource Graph
Resource Usage view
sheet view
sort
split view
subtasks
summary tasks
Task Entry view
Task Usage view
Team Planner
Timeline view
timescale
Tracking Gantt
view
zoom
Zoom slider

Review Questions

1. How do you zoom the timescale (right) side of any Gantt view or Usage view?

A. On the View tab, in the Data group, click **Outline**. Then click the outline level you want to show in the timescale.

B. On the View tab, in the Split View group, select the **Timeline** check box.

C. Right-click the view bar, then on the drop-down menu, click **Zoom Out** or **Zoom In**.

D. Click the minus or plus arrow in the Zoom slider located in the lower-right corner of the Project window.

2. What might be a good reason to sort a task sheet?

A. To arrange the tasks by highest to lowest cost so that you can see where you might cut project costs

B. To arrange the tasks into groups by assigned resources

C. To highlight the fields filtered by a field you specify, like completed tasks

D. To see only those fields filtered by a field you specify, like critical tasks

3. What's the difference between filtering a task or resource sheet by a particular field and highlighting it by a particular field?

A. When you filter, the task or resource information is grouped into categories by the field you specify. When you highlight, tasks or resources that meet the field criteria are marked in yellow.

B. Filtering by a specific field results in the sheet displaying only those tasks or resources that meet the criteria of the filter. When you highlight, task or resource information is rearranged, or sorted, by the field you specify.

C. When you filter, all task or resource information is still displayed, while those tasks or resources that meet the criteria are marked in yellow. By contrast, highlighting by a specific field results in the sheet displaying only those tasks or resources that meet the filter criteria.

D. Filtering by a specific field results in the sheet displaying only those tasks or resources that meet the criteria of the filter. By contrast, when you highlight, all task or resource information is still displayed, while those tasks or resources that meet the criteria are marked in yellow.

4. How do you add a new column in a sheet view?

A. Right-click the All Cells cell in the upper-left corner of the sheet, then click the name of the column you want to add.

B. Scroll to the far right edge of the sheet view and click the **Add New Column** heading. Select the name of the field you want to add as a new column.

C. On the Format tab, in the Columns group, select the **New Column** check box.

D. On the View tab, in the Columns group, click **Insert Column**.

5. How do you adjust the margins or add a header or footer to a view you're printing on paper or saving as a PDF file?

   A. On the File tab, click **Print**. Under Settings, click Page Setup. Use the Margins, Header, or Footer tab to specify the layout for the printed view.

   B. On the File tab, click **Print**. Under Settings, click Print Entire Project, then click Print Custom Dates and Pages.

   C. On the File tab, click **Save As**. Click **Browse** and select the drive and folder where you want to save the PDF, then enter a name in the File name field. In the Save as type field, click **PDF Files (.pdf)**, then click **Save**.

   D. On the File tab, click **Export**, then click the **Create PDF/XPS** button. Select the drive and folder, then enter a name in the File name field. Click **OK**.

6. What's the best way to see what a Project view has to offer and whether it might be useful in your project management work?

   A. Working with a project plan containing tasks, resources, assignments, and scheduling information, switch to the new view. On the File tab, click **Export**, then export the view to Excel.

   B. Open Project to a blank project plan, then switch to the new view. Review the layout and fields of information in the view. Click the **Format** tab to see how you can control and customize this view.

   C. Working with a project plan containing tasks, resources, assignments, and scheduling information, switch to the new view. Review the layout and fields of information in the view. Click the **Format** tab to see how you can control and customize this view.

   D. Open Project to a blank project plan, then switch to the new view. On the Report tab, in the Project group, click **Compare Projects**.

Lesson 11

Customize Project Information

LESSON OBJECTIVES

✓ Modify the text format in a sheet view.

✓ Customize Gantt bar colors.

✓ Add a text box and other drawing shapes to the timescale area of a Gantt view.

✓ Rename, add, and move columns on a board view.

✓ Add or remove information on a task card for board views.

✓ Set your preferences for working in Project.

In Lesson 10, "View Project Information," you learned how to manipulate your plan's data in different views to show exactly what you need.

This lesson takes your knowledge of Microsoft Project views a step further. In this lesson, you get an introduction to formatting and customizing sheet views, Gantt views, and board views to better suit your needs. You'll also explore a sampling of basic Project options to fine-tune your project plan to your working preferences.

Customize a Sheet View

Any Project view that includes a grid of rows and columns is considered a *sheet view*. Your most commonly used sheet views in Project include the Task Sheet, Resource Sheet, and Current Sprint Sheet.

As you might expect for any spreadsheet, you can modify the style of text in the cells, rows, and columns. This includes setting the font and size, changing a font or background color, or applying bold or italic. You can also adjust text alignment and text wrapping.

To format individual text in a sheet view:

1. In Project, display the sheet view, then select the text you want to format.

   If the text is in a single cell, just click that cell.

   If the text is across several adjacent cells, drag to select them all.

   If the text is across nonadjacent cells, click the first cell, hold down the Ctrl key, then click or drag across the other cells you want to format.

2. On the Task tab, in the Font group, make the format changes you want.

   For example, click the arrow in the **Font** field, then click the name of the font you want to apply to the selected text. Click **Bold** or **Italic**. Click the arrow in the **Font Color** field, then pick the color you want for the selected text. Click the arrow in the **Background Color** field, then pick the background color you want for the selected cells.

   To format text for an entire sheet view:

1. Display the sheet view whose text you want to modify throughout.

2. On the Format tab, in the Format group, click **Text Styles**.

3. In the Text Styles dialog box, make sure that the **Item to Change** field is set to **All**.

4. Set the format for all text in the current sheet view, using the controls in the dialog box.

   This is a quick way to change the font or font size for all text in the sheet.

5. Click **OK**.

Project formats all text on the current sheet view according to your specifications. The formatting applies to the current sheet view only, and it applies to any new items as they are added to this sheet.

Within a chosen task sheet, you can change the *text styles* for all specified task categories, such as summary tasks, critical tasks, or milestone tasks. Likewise, in the Resource Sheet or Resource Usage view, you can change text styles for all specified resource categories like resources that are assigned to tasks or overallocated resources. This is a timesaver when you want to always highlight specific kinds of tasks or resources with specific formatting, so you don't have to format them yourself one by one.

To modify text styles in a sheet view:

1. Display the sheet view whose text styles you want to modify.

2. On the Format tab, in the Format group, click **Text Styles**.

3. In the Text Styles dialog box, click the arrow in the **Item to Change** field. If a task sheet is displayed, the list appears as shown in Figure 11.1.

FIGURE 11.1   Text Styles dialog box for a task sheet

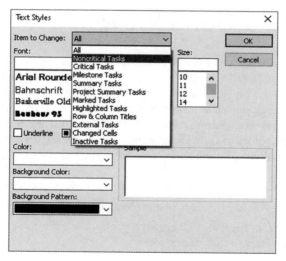

If a resource sheet is displayed, the Item to Change list shows items that apply to resources, such as Allocated Resources and Overallocated Resources.

4. Click the item that you want to have the same formatting throughout the sheet.

5. Set the format for that item, using the controls in the dialog box. Choices include the font, font size, bold, italic, font color, and background color.

6. Click **OK**.

Project formats the tasks or resources that meet your criteria according to your specifications. The formatting of these items applies to the current sheet only, and it applies to any new items as they are added.

Throughout the Project sheet views, columns containing text are left-aligned, whereas columns containing numbers are right-aligned. You can change this alignment.

To change text alignment in a sheet view column:

1. In the sheet view, click anywhere in the column whose alignment you want to change.

2. On the Format tab, in the Columns group, click **Align Left, Center,** or **Align Right.** Project then adjusts the alignment throughout the column.

In the Project sheet views, text typically flows, or wraps, to a second or third line as needed, rather than being cut off from view at the column's right edge.

To change the *text wrapping* in a sheet view column:

1. In the sheet view, click anywhere in the column whose text wrapping you want to change.

2. On the Format tab, in the Columns group, click **Wrap Text.**

Because this button is a toggle control, if the text was wrapped to multiple lines, it is now unwrapped to single lines. Likewise, if the text was unwrapped, it now wraps to multiple lines as needed.

Customize a Gantt View

Project comes with several types of *Gantt views*, including the default Gantt Chart, the Tracking Gantt, and the Detail Gantt. All Gantt views are a combination view, with a sheet view on the left side and a timescale view on the right. The horizontal *Gantt bars* on the right side of the view each represent a task, including the task's start date, duration, and finish date. As you mark progress on tasks, the Gantt bars show the percentage complete.

You can format the colors of Gantt bars, either setting the *bar style* for all Gantt bars of a specific type or for individually selected Gantt bars. You can also add a text box and draw arrows or other shapes on the Gantt area.

To change the color combination of all the Gantt bars in a Gantt view:

1. Display the Gantt view whose Gantt bar colors you want to change.

2. On the Format tab, in the Gantt Chart Style group, click the color combination you want for all Gantt bars in the current view.

The bottom color is the color of the standard Gantt bar, and the top color is the color of the progress line within the Gantt bar.

Project formats the Gantt bars in the current view to the color scheme you select.

You can highlight one specific Gantt bar to bring more attention to it. To change the color of an individual Gantt bar:

1. Display the Gantt view where you want to highlight a specific Gantt bar, then click the task(s) you want to highlight.

2. On the Format tab, in the Bar Styles group, click **Format,** then click **Bar.**

3. In the Format Bar dialog box, click the **Bar Shape** tab.

4. In the section labeled "Middle," click the arrow in the **Color** field, then click the color you want for the selected task's Gantt bar.

5. Check the preview in the Sample box to make sure the Gantt bar looks the way you want.

6. Click **OK**.

The color of the selected task's Gantt bar changes to the color you selected.

Note that if progress is already showing in the Gantt bar, for example, 50 percent complete, the progress bar changes color rather than the Gantt bar. You might find it useful to label specific Gantt bars or add context. You can use the Drawing tools to add text, arrows, and other shapes to a Gantt view.

To add text to the timescale area of a Gantt view:

1. Display the Gantt view where you want to add a text box.

2. On the Format tab, in the Drawings group, click **Drawing**.

3. The Drawing drop-down menu appears, as shown in Figure 11.2.

FIGURE 11.2   Drawing drop-down menu

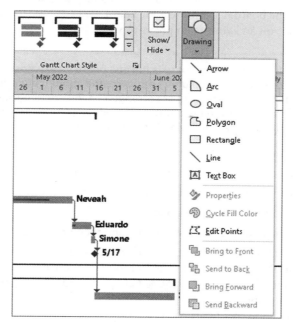

4. Click **Text Box**.

5. With the mouse pointer now shaped like a plus sign, drag in the timescale area on the Gantt view to define where you want to insert the new text box.

6. Type your text in the new text box.

7. If necessary, drag the edges of the text box to better fit the text. You can also drag the text box to a different position.

Customize a Board View

In Project, a *board view* displays tasks as boxes or *task cards* containing key task information. On a board view, these task cards are aligned in columns across the board to show how far along the task is toward completion. Commonly used Project board views are the Task Board, Sprint Board, and Current Sprint Board.

You can customize the columns on most board views. You can also customize the task cards used on the board views.

Modify Board View Columns

On most board views, you can rename a column, add a new column, or move a column to a different position on the board. Customize your board views as needed to reflect the needs of your project and how you and your team prefer to work.

The Sprint Planning Board is the one board view whose columns are not customizable. The column names are the sprint names, like "Sprint 1" and "Sprint 2", and they are arranged on the board by sprint number. For a refresher on adding sprints and modifying sprint names, see "Schedule Sprints for an Agile Project" in Lesson 5, "Build the Schedule."

To rename a column on a board view:

1. Open the board view whose columns you want to rename.

2. Right-click the column heading, such as Next Up or In Progress.

3. On the menu that appears, click **Rename**.

4. In the box, type the new name of the column, and then press Enter.

You can add more columns to a board view if you'd like to see more progress detail. In addition to the default Not Started, Next Up, In Progress, and Done columns, you might want to add columns for 25% Complete, 50% Complete, and 75% Complete to represent incremental stages of completion.

To add a custom column to a board view:

1. Scroll to the right edge of the board view and click the **Add New Column** heading.

2. In the box that appears, type the name of the new column, such as Just Started or Nearly Finished, and then press Enter.

To move any column to a different position on a board view:

1. Right-click the column heading and then click **Move Left** or **Move Right**.

2. Repeat this until the column is in the position you want on the board.

Modify Task Cards

You can add or remove the information included on task cards. In addition to the task name, you can add up to eight fields of task information to each task card. The changes you make to the task card format apply across all board views, whether it's the Task Board or the Sprint Planning Board.

To add information to the task card format:

1. Open any board view, like the Backlog Board or Sprint Board.

2. On the Format tab, in the Customize group, click **Customize Cards**.

    The Customize Task Board Cards dialog box appears as shown in Figure 11.3.

FIGURE 11.3   Customize Task Board Cards dialog box

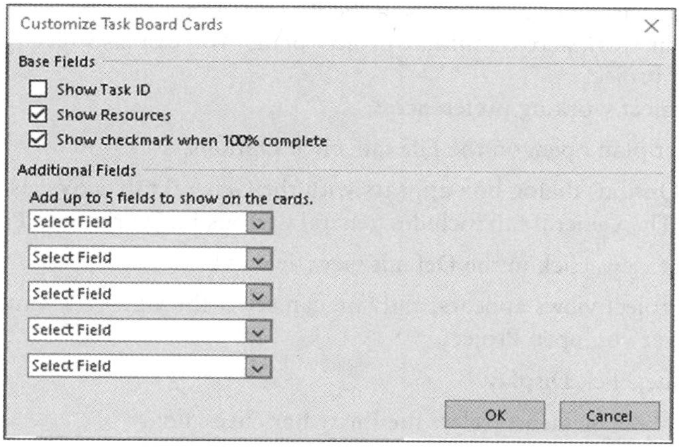

3. Under Base Fields, select any check box for information you want to include on the task cards.

4. Under Additional Fields, click the arrow in the next available **Select Field** box.

    The list of all available task fields appears in a drop-down menu.

5. Scroll to the field you want or type the first couple letters of the field name.

6. Click the field name.

    The selected field name appears in the box.

7. Repeat steps 4–6 for any other fields you want to add.

    Fields particularly useful on task cards include Duration, % Complete, Start, Finish, and Predecessors.

8. When finished adding fields, click **OK**.

   Information for the selected fields appear under the task name on every task card on all board views.

   To remove information from the task card format:

1. With a board view open, on the Format tab, in the Customize group, click **Customize Cards**.

2. Under Base Fields, clear any check box for information you want to remove from the task card format.

3. Under Additional Fields, click the **X** next to the field you want to remove from the task card format.

4. When finished removing information, click **OK**.

Set Options and Preferences

You can set a wide variety of preferences in the Project Options dialog box. You can specify options for all your work across multiple project plans. You can also specify options to apply to the open project.

   To set your Project working preferences:

1. With a project plan open, on the File tab, click **Options**.

   The Project Options dialog box appears with the General tab active, as shown in Figure 11.4. The General tab includes general options for working in Project.

2. Under Project view, click in the **Default view** field.

   A list of all Project views appears, and you can select the view you want to be the first to show whenever you open Project.

3. In the left pane, click **Display**.

4. Under Show these elements, select the **Entry bar** check box.

   This will display the entry bar above every sheet view, which is handy for easily entering and editing text in the sheet.

5. In the left pane, click **Save**.

6. Next to the Default File location field, click **Browse**, navigate to your preferred location for your Project files, then click **OK**.

7. Continue exploring the Project Options dialog box. Whether you make any further changes, it's good to be aware of the available preferences.

8. When you're finished exploring, click **OK**.

   By setting your Project preferences and formatting the views you use frequently to suit your needs, you set up the best project management working environment for yourself.

FIGURE 11.4   The General tab in the Project Options dialog box

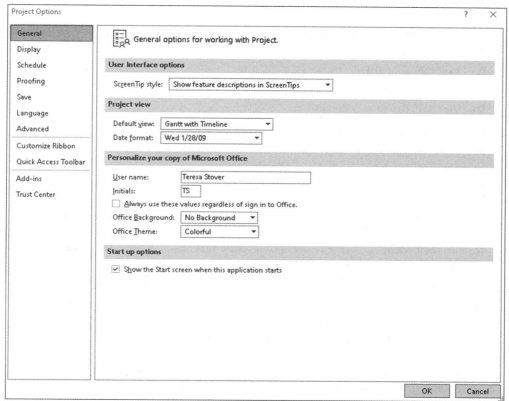

Key Terms

bar styles
board views
Gantt bars
Gantt views
sheet views
task cards
text styles
text wrapping

Review Questions

1. Where do you go to format individual text in a Resource Sheet?

   A. Resource tab, Font group

   B. Task tab, Font group

   C. Format tab, Columns group

   D. View tab, Resource Views group

2. How do you change the font or font size for an entire sheet view?

   A. Click anywhere in the sheet, then on the Task tab in the Font group, change the font or font size.

   B. Right-click anywhere in the sheet, then on the pop-up menu that appears, change the font or font size.

   C. On the View tab, in the Format group, click **Text Styles**, click **All Cells**, then change the font or font size.

   D. On the Format tab, in the Format group, click **Text Styles**, set **Item to Change** field to **All**, then change the font or font size.

3. How do you change the color combination of all the Gantt bars in the current Gantt view?

   A. On the Format tab, in the Drawings group, click **Drawing**, and then click **Cycle Fill Color** until the Gantt bars are the color you want.

   B. On the Format tab, in the Bar Styles group, click **Format**, then click **Bar**. Select the color you want, then click **OK**.

   C. On the View tab, in the Task Views group, click **Gantt Chart Style**, then click the color combination you want for all Gantt bars in the current view.

   D. On the Format tab, in the Gantt Chart Style group, click the color combination you want for all Gantt bars in the current view.

4. How do you add a new column to a board view?

   A. Scroll to the right edge of the board view, click the **Add New Column** heading, type the name of your new column, then press Enter.

   B. On the board view, right-click any existing column heading, click **Insert Column**, then type the name of your new column.

   C. On the Sprints tab, in the Sprints group, click **Manage**. Click **Insert Column**, type the name of the new column, then click **OK**.

   D. On the Format tab, in the Columns group, click **Insert Column**. Click the field name for the new column, then press Enter.

5. How do you add or remove information on the task cards for all board views?

A. On any board view, right-click a task card, then click **Customize Cards**.

B. On any board view, double-click a task card, then in the Task Information dialog box, click **Customize Cards**.

C. With any board view open, on the View tab in the Task Board group, click **Customize Cards**.

D. With any board view open, on the Format tab in the Customize group, click **Customize Cards**.

6. How do you open the dialog box to set general preferences for working in Project, for example, to specify the default view upon opening or to identify where you want Project files to be saved?

A. On the File tab, click **Info**.

B. On the View tab, in the Window group, click **Options**.

C. On the File tab, click **Options**.

D. On the Help tab, click **Info**.

Lesson

12

Report Project Information

LESSON OBJECTIVES

✓ Run a built-in report or dashboard.

✓ Adjust the design of a report or dashboard.

✓ Create a new report or dashboard.

✓ Print a report or dashboard.

✓ Save a report or dashboard as a PDF.

As the project manager, one of your major responsibilities throughout the monitoring and controlling processes is to review a project's ongoing status and regularly communicate it with everyone involved. Using the reporting tools in Microsoft Project, you can review information about the schedule, budget, and resource assignments, and also share meaningful reports with your team, sponsors, and other stakeholders.

In this lesson, you explore the built-in reports and dashboards available in Project. You learn how you can customize these tools or create your own to report on the information you need. You also see how to print reports or save them as PDFs to easily share with others.

Work with Reports

Project comes with about 16 built-in *reports*, not counting dashboards or visual reports. All available on the Report tab, these reports are designed to pull specific types of information from your project plan and display them as a summary, comparison, table, chart, or a combination of these for specific categories.

Depending on its focus, a report can use the following types of information from your project:

- Work (baseline, actual, remaining, variance, cumulative)
- Cost (baseline, actual, remaining, variance, cumulative)
- Start and finish dates
- Percentage complete
- Assigned resources

Because some reports compare current progress against the original plan, the project *baseline* plays a large role in reporting. The project baseline is a snapshot of your project schedule and cost information as they stand when you set the baseline and therefore gives you a standard against which you can compare your project status with your original plan. You get the most useful comparisons when you set the project baseline just after you finish planning and just before you start executing the project. For a refresher, see "Set the Project Baseline" in Lesson 8, "Check and Adjust the Project."

Run a Report

To run a built-in report:

1. Have your project plan open at any view.

2. On the Report tab, in the View Reports group, click the report category, then click the name of the report you want.

   For example, if you want to run the Resource Overview report, on the Report tab in the View Reports group, click **Resources**, then click **Resource Overview**.

   The selected report appears on the screen, as shown in Figure 12.1.

FIGURE 12.1   The Resource Overview report

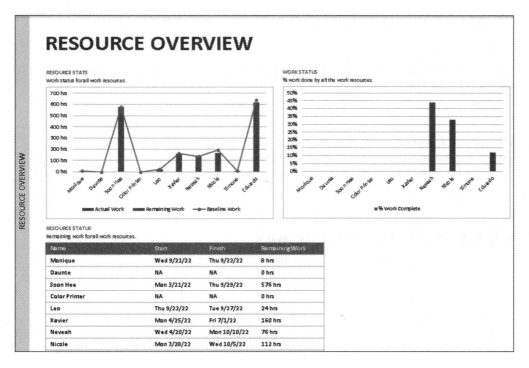

Frequently Used Reports

Explore the following selection of reports to see which might be best for your own use when checking status to make adjustments. Also determine which of these are best to share and communicate progress with the team and other stakeholders.

- Resources, Resource Overview

- Resources, Overallocated Resources

- Costs, Cash Flow

- Costs, Task Cost Overview

- In Progress, Late Tasks

- Task Boards, Current Sprint—Tasks Status

- Task Boards, Sprint Status

Continue to look over the reports in the View Reports group, especially on the Resources, Costs, In Progress, and Task Boards drop-down menus. Even if it looks like a specific report might not be useful to you right now, it's good to know what's available should your reporting needs change.

Note that the reports under Getting Started in the View Reports group are not really reports. Instead, they're mini-tutorials to help you discover how best to set up and use Project, how to analyze the effectiveness of your project information, and how to create a custom report.

Adjust the Design of a Report

When you run a report, Project usually switches the ribbon to the Report Design tab so that you can adjust the report's look or layout if you want.

To adjust the design of a report:

1. Run the report.

2. On the Report Design tab, in the Themes group, click any of the available controls to adjust the look of the report.

   Click **Themes** or **Colors** to browse and select the report's color scheme. Click **Fonts** to change the font style throughout the report. Click **Effects** to apply any one of a variety of effects (like Shaded or Glossy) to the graphic elements in the report.

3. On the Report Design tab, in the Insert group, click any of the available controls to add a graphic element to the report.

   You can add an image (like a logo or photograph) or a shape (like a circle or arrow). You can add a chart or table and specify the data you want included. You can add a text box and enter clarifying text.

4. On the Report Design tab, in the Page Setup group, click any of the available controls to adjust how the report should be laid out on the page.

You can specify page orientation, paper size, margins, and where page breaks occur.

Work with Dashboards

A *dashboard* is a specific type of report that usually shows higher-level summary information. You might think of it as multiple reports within one. It often summarizes three or four types of key information in a single view so that you can see important progress indicators in one glance.

Project comes with five built-in dashboards:

- Burndown
- Cost Overview
- Project Overview
- Upcoming Tasks
- Work Overview

To show a dashboard:

- On the Report tab, in the View Reports group, click **Dashboards**, then click the dashboard you want to see, for example, **Cost Overview**.

The selected dashboard appears, as shown in Figure 12.2.

FIGURE 12.2   The Cost Overview dashboard

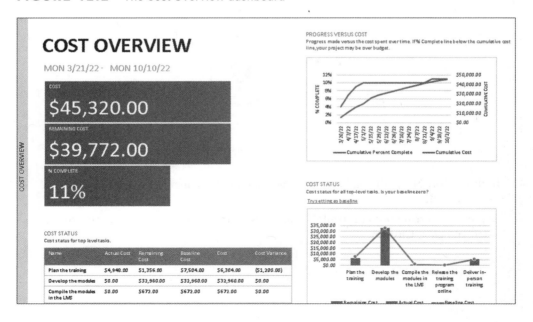

As with reports, you can adjust the design of a dashboard by using the Report Design tab. Use the Themes group to adjust the color scheme or font style. Use the Insert group to add a graphic element, chart, or table. Use the Page Setup group to specify how the dashboard should be laid out on the printed page.

Create a New Report or Dashboard

If you need a report or dashboard beyond the built-in offerings, you can create your own. To create a new report or dashboard from scratch:

1. On the Report tab, in the View Reports group, click **New Report,** then click the template for your new report.

   Format choices are Blank, Chart, Table, and Comparison (see Figure 12.3).

FIGURE 12.3   The New Report templates

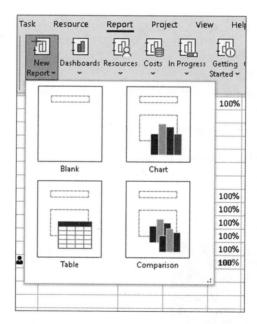

2. In the Report Name dialog box that appears, type the name for your new report, then click **OK.**

   Reports you create become available on the Report tab, in the View Reports group, when you click **Custom.**

3. On the Report Design tab, in the Insert group, click any of the tools available to start creating the elements of your report.

Click **Images, Shapes,** or **Text Box** to create a static element for the report—for example, a logo image or a text box that explains the report.

Click **Chart** or **Table** to identify the interactive data you want the report to draw from in your project plan whenever you run the report. If you started with the Chart, Table, or Comparison template, you already have a chart, table, or side-by-side chart in your new report. Either way, when you click the chart or table embedded in your report, you can specify the data fields in the Field List pane on the right (see Figure 12.4).

FIGURE 12.4   Custom report with the Field List pane

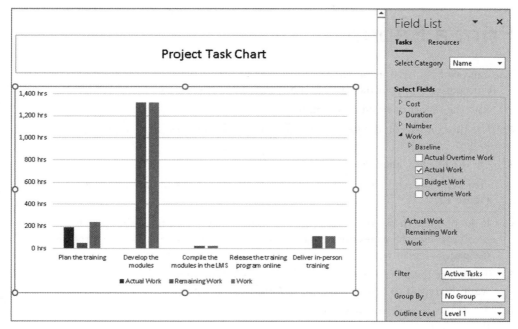

4. On the Report Design tab, use the tools in the Themes group to adjust the report's color scheme or font style. Use the tools in the Page Setup group to specify how the report should be laid out on the printed page.

To run a custom report you've created:

1. On the Report tab, in the View Reports group, click **Custom**.

All your custom reports are listed on this menu.

2. On the menu, click the name of your custom report.

Your report appears.

> **Visual Reports**
>
> With a *visual report*, you export data from your project plan to a report template in Microsoft Excel or Microsoft Visio. If you have either of those programs installed, you can view and manipulate your project data in an Excel PivotChart or Visio PivotDiagram.
>
> To do this, on the Report tab, in the Visual Reports group, click **Visual Reports**. Click one of the templates listed, and then click **View**. Experiment with the various visual report templates available to see how they might be useful for your reporting requirements. These reports are especially useful for analyzing cost and work.

Print a Report

You can print your report on paper or as a PDF file.

To prepare a report or dashboard to be printed or saved as a PDF file:

1. Run the report or dashboard you want to print.

2. Use the controls on the Report Design tab to make any necessary adjustments to the look or format.

3. On the File tab, click **Print**.

    Project shows a preview of the report or dashboard as it will be printed (see Figure 12.5).

4. If the preview shows the report across multiple pages, click the right and left arrows to scroll through the pages horizontally. Click the down and up arrows to scroll through the pages vertically.

5. To change the page orientation, in the Print window, under **Settings**, click whether you want the report to print in **Portrait** or **Landscape** orientation.

6. To set the printed page margins or add a header or footer to the printed report, click **Page Setup**.

    In the Page Setup dialog box, use the tabs to set your preferences for page scaling, margins, header, or footer. When finished, click **OK**.

FIGURE 12.5   Print window with preview and controls

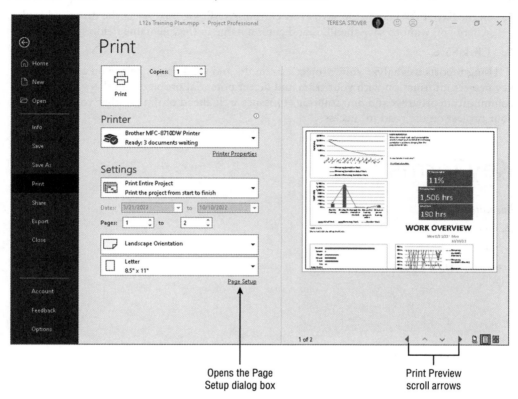

Opens the Page
Setup dialog box

Print Preview
scroll arrows

After the report or dashboard is set up the way you want, you're ready to print it.
To print the report or dashboard on paper:

1. In the Print window, under Printer, make sure the proper device is showing. If not, click the **Printer** button and select the printer.

2. Under Settings, specify whether you want to print the entire report or just specific pages.

3. Click the **Print** button.

If you save the report or dashboard as a PDF file, you can quickly email or share the report in a format that everyone in the team can view.
To print the report or dashboard as a PDF file:

1. In the Print window, under Printer, click the **Printer** button, and click **Adobe PDF** or **Microsoft Print to PDF**.

2. Under Settings, specify whether you want to make a PDF of the entire report or just specific pages.

3. Click the **Print** button.

4. In the Save PDF File As (or Save Print Output As) dialog box, select the drive and folder where you want to save the PDF, and enter a name in the **File name** field.

5. Click **Save**.

Using reports to analyze your project's strengths and weaknesses helps you communicate key project information with your team and detect potential problems. In this way, you can communicate progress and find solutions to issues well ahead of time so that you can keep your project on the road to success.

Key Terms

baseline
dashboard
report
visual report

Review Questions

1. What's the significance of baseline information in reporting?

    A. The baseline shows actual project information as work is completed, and that information is reflected in many reports.

    B. The baseline shows the current state of the project, including work and cost amounts, and compares it with actuals in various reports.

    C. Baseline information indicates the difference in work and cost amounts from your original plan and the current state of the project, and reflects this variance in several reports.

    D. Baseline information shows the project's originally planned schedule, work, and cost information. This is used in various reports to compare with the state of the project.

2. How do you access the built-in reports in Microsoft Project?

    A. On the Report tab, in the View Reports group

    B. On the Report tab, in the Project group

    C. On the Report Design tab, in the View Reports group

    D. On the Report Design tab, in the Insert group

3. How do you change the color scheme of a report?

    A. With the report showing, on the Report tab, in the Themes group, click **Themes** or **Colors.**

    B. With the report showing, on the Report tab, in the View Reports group, click **Color Schemes.**

    C. With the report showing, on the Report Design tab, in the Themes group, click **Themes** or **Colors** to change the report's color scheme.

    D. With the report showing, on the Report Design tab, in the View Reports group, click **Color Schemes.**

4. How do you access and run a custom report you have created for the current project plan?

    A. On the View tab, in the Data group, click **New Report**, then click the name of the report you created.

    B. On the Report tab, in the View Reports group, click **Custom,** then click the name of the report you created.

    C. On the Report tab, in the View Reports group, click **New Report,** then click the name of the report you created.

    D. On the Report tab, in the View Reports group, click **Getting Started,** then click **Create reports.**

5. How do you see what your report will look like when you print it on paper or to a PDF file?

  A. With the report showing, on the File tab, click **Print**.

  B. With the report showing, on the File tab, click **Save As**, then click **Microsoft Print to PDF**.

  C. With the report showing, on the File tab, click **Print**, then click **Preview**.

  D. With the report showing, on the File tab, click **Print**, then click **Page Setup**.

6. How do you save a Project report as a PDF file?

  A. With the report showing, on the File tab, click **Save As**. Click **Adobe PDF** or **Microsoft Print to PDF**.

  B. With the report showing, on the File tab, click **Print**. Click the **Printer** button and click **Adobe PDF** or **Microsoft Print to PDF**.

  C. With the report showing, on the File tab, click **Share**. Click **Go to Save As**, then click **Adobe PDF** or **Microsoft Print to PDF**.

  D. With the report showing, on the File tab, click **Print**. Click **Settings**, then click **Adobe PDF** or **Microsoft Print to PDF**.

Close
Your Project

Lesson 13

Obtain Project Acceptance

LESSON OBJECTIVES

✓ List key elements of presenting the completed project to the sponsor.

✓ Generate Project dashboards to demonstrate project completion.

✓ Adjust the project plan to reflect the final project checklist.

✓ Add a note or a document to a task in the project plan.

✓ Explain the importance of sign-off by the project sponsor and celebration with your team.

Congratulations, your project is nearly finished! At this stage in your project, your team has completed all final project tasks. You've achieved the milestones, submitted all deliverables, and met the project goals. With the completion of the final task, you exit the *monitoring and controlling processes* of the project and enter the *closing process*.

However, there's still a bit of work to be done. As in a construction project, this is the point where the product or service the project has developed is considered "substantially complete." Although all the tasks are done, some fine-tuning and adjusting still must be done before the project sponsor is happy with the end result and can accept the project as finished.

This lesson covers the presentation of the project to your project sponsor, completing the necessary activities to obtain official project sign-off, using Microsoft Project to run reports and document final refinements, and celebrating success with your team.

Present the Project to the Sponsor

Throughout the life of the project, you've been communicating progress to your project *sponsors* or customers. On a regular basis, you probably shared the project's actual costs and schedule performance to date, along with cost and schedule projections. You might have shared prototypes or drafts of the product or service under development, especially if it's an agile project. You also probably announced the achievement of milestones and presented deliverables as they were completed.

Now that you're at the closing process, you want to demonstrate that your project achieved what it was designed to do. Of course, you still want to show how well the project performed on the schedule and budget. For this, present a report or dashboard to your sponsors.

To run a high-level dashboard:

1. Open your project plan.

2. On the Report tab, in the View Reports group, click **Dashboards**, then click **Project Overview**. The Project Overview dashboard displays, as shown in Figure 13.1.

   Your sponsors will also be interested in the Cost Overview dashboard. On the Report tab, in the View Reports group, click **Dashboards**, then click **Cost Overview** to display the dashboard shown in Figure 13.2.

For more information on reports and dashboards, see Lesson 12, "Report Project Information."

FIGURE 13.1   The Project Overview dashboard

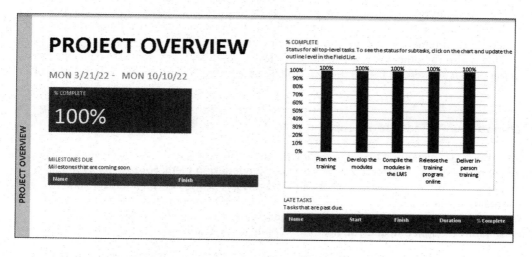

FIGURE 13.2   The Cost Overview dashboard

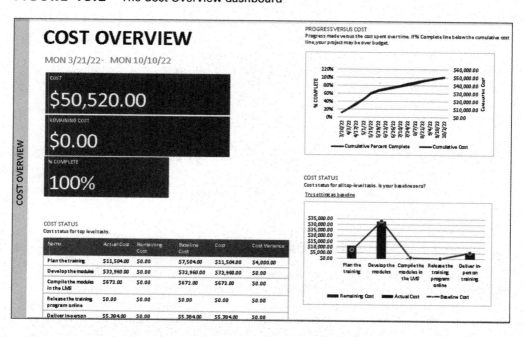

Keep in mind that a project can finish on time and within budget but still be considered a failure if it didn't fulfill its scope or produce the product or service in the way it was intended.

Look to the documents you and your sponsor agreed to during the project's *initiating process*. You can present the original project charter, requirements document, or project scope statement, and systematically offer evidence that the charter was fulfilled, the product or service requirements were met, and the scope was realized.

This is also the time when you and the sponsors can discuss any final refinements needed to the product or service before they are able to accept and sign off on the completed project.

Sometimes Projects Are Canceled

It's a project management reality that sometimes projects are canceled. The reasons are as varied as the types of projects and organizations undertaking them. For example, funding might run out or be rescinded. Maybe a few months into a project, you and your sponsor realize it wasn't a good idea after all. Sometimes market conditions change to warrant the project unnecessary or unwise to continue. Maybe the original premise of the project wasn't fully thought out, and you needed to create a few prototypes to understand this.

Whatever the reason for project cancellation, the organization still learns from the experience, and skills are still built. Everyone involved is more knowledgeable as you all move forward to the next challenge.

In spite of a project being canceled, it's important to carry out the closing processes highlighted in this lesson and in Lesson 14, "Retain Project History." Carry on with the final presentation to the project sponsor, have a last gathering with your team, capture lessons learned, and archive the experience.

Secure Official Project Sign-Off

Getting your sponsor to sign off on *project acceptance* involves completing any final details on the project, then having the sponsor agree to their acceptance of the project.

Complete Final Refinements

Work through any final refining details to ensure the product or service is fully complete and acceptable to the project sponsor. Make sure this final checklist, known as the "punch list" in construction projects, only contains items within the project scope and the original requirements. Nothing new should be on this list; the items should be finishing touches to existing items.

After you agree on the final checklist with the sponsor, confer with your team to determine the time and cost to complete. Make sure you have the resources needed to complete these final tasks, as team members will soon leave for new projects. Completing the final checklist might take a day, a week, or even a month. As always, keep the sponsor informed.

Document the checklist activities in Project and adjust the project plan as appropriate. You might need to insert a refining task, or to add a task covering all the final checklist items.

To insert a new task between existing tasks:

1. Click in the row below where you want the new task to be inserted.

   For example, if you want to insert a new task between rows 3 and 4, click in row 4.

2. On the Task tab, in the Insert group, click **Task**.

   A new row labeled <New Task> appears at your selected location, and the Task Name field is already selected and ready for entry.

3. Type the new task name, then press Enter.

You might need to add a note to your project plan document about the final refinements and the agreement you made with the sponsor as you move toward project acceptance.

To add a note to your project plan:

1. Switch to a task view, like the Gantt Chart or Task Board.

2. Double-click the task to which you want to add the note. This can be a subtask, summary task, or the project summary task.

3. In the Task Information dialog box that appears, click the **Notes** tab.

4. Click in the Notes box and then type your note, as shown in Figure 13.3.

5. When finished, click **OK**.

FIGURE 13.3   Adding a note to a task

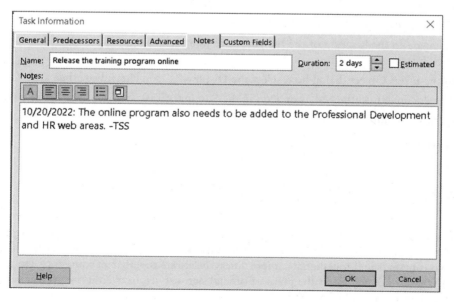

You might need to adjust duration or assign a resource to the final tasks. For more information, see "Respond to Changes" in Lesson 9, "Track Project Information."

Have the Sponsor Sign Off on the Project

After all final checklist items and refinements are completed, obtain in writing that your project sponsor agrees that the project goals have been met and that they accept the project.

This agreement can be a signature on the original project charter, requirements document, or scope statement you developed in the initiating process. It can be as informal as an email stating acceptance. However it's done, make sure your sponsor's acceptance is documented in writing so that it's clear that the project is indeed completed to the satisfaction of the sponsor, who is financially responsible for the project.

Store the sign-off document (or email) with your important project files, whether it's on a network drive, cloud drive, or even a paper binder. It's a great idea to attach the document to the project file itself.

To attach a document to a Project plan:

1. Open your project plan.

2. If necessary, add the project summary task. On the Format tab, in the Show/Hide group, click **Project Summary Task**.

   The project summary task appears as the first task in the plan.

3. Double-click the project summary task to open the Summary Task Information dialog box.

4. Click the **Notes** tab.

5. In the toolbar under Notes, click **Insert Object**.

6. Click **Create from File**, then click **Browse**.

7. Navigate to the location of the file you want to attach to the project plan, then click **Insert**.

8. In the Insert Object dialog box, select the **Display As Icon** check box, then click **OK**.

   The document is attached as an icon in the Summary Task Information dialog box.

9. Click **OK** again.

   A note icon appears in the Indicator field next to the project summary task.

Celebrate With Your Team

The end of a project is often intense and stressful as the final deadline looms, and team members can often feel exhausted and spent at the end. As a result, when the project finishes and while your team is still together, it's important to celebrate together in some way. Do this even if you haven't arrived at the point of official sign-off yet, or even if the project was canceled or did not meet all of its goals.

Whether you have a "ship party," a team dinner at a special restaurant, or just some cake and coffee in the conference room, getting together as a team one last time can help your team members feel valued and that their time on the project was well spent. Consider a few speeches and maybe hand out some "swag" like mugs or t-shirts as project souvenirs. Such an event, no matter how elaborate or modest, can help provide closure to the time spent on the project and give your team members a sense of accomplishment.

Not only did you and your team work on an intriguing project that likely expanded skill sets and even career trajectories, you've all built professional relationships that can live on as you all move on to other projects. Do what you can to make your team members feel good about having worked on this project. The next time you need them for another project, they'll choose yours over others, and they'll look forward to working with you again.

Key Terms

closing process
controlling process
initiating process
monitoring process
project acceptance
sponsor

Review Questions

1. What evidence should you present to the project sponsor to demonstrate project completion?

    A. The prototype of the product or service

    B. The project budget showing all expenses incurred

    C. The project plan showing all milestones and tasks marked as complete

    D. Proof that the product or service produced by the project meets the original charter, requirements, or scope

2. Name two Project dashboards or reports that can best show final project performance.

    A. The Burndown dashboard and Upcoming Tasks dashboard

    B. The Project Overview dashboard and the Cost Overview dashboard

    C. The Cash Flow report and the Late Tasks report

    D. The Overallocated Resources report and the Critical Tasks report

3. What is the purpose of the final project checklist?

    A. To document any final refinements that must be made to the product or service being produced by the project before the sponsor will consider the project fully complete

    B. To add tasks that were considered optional until the end when the project sponsor learns there's more time or budget to complete them

    C. To add new features to the scope of the product or service being produced to improve its effectiveness or marketability

    D. To specify the reasons why the project needs to be canceled, for future archival purposes

4. How do you add a note to a task in the project plan?

    A. In a task sheet view, like the Gantt Chart or Task Usage view, click in the Indicators column for the task, type your note, then press Enter.

    B. In a task sheet view, double-click the project summary task, click the **Advanced** tab in the Summary Task Information dialog box, click in the Notes box, type your note, then click **OK**.

    C. In a task view, double-click the task, click the **Notes** tab in the Task Information dialog box, click in the **Notes** box, type your note, then click **OK**.

    D. In a task view, double-click the task name, type your note, then press Enter.

5. Why is it important to obtain written project acceptance by the project sponsor?

    A. To make sure all project documents are completed and stored properly for future reference

    B. To provide a mechanism for additional features to be added to the project, along with the budget to pay for them

    C. To ensure that the project is indeed completed to the satisfaction of the sponsor, who is financially responsible for the project

    D. To specify the final refinements to the product or service being produced before the sponsor will accept the project results

Lesson 14

Retain Project History

LESSON OBJECTIVES

✓ Define the project review and explain its importance.

✓ Name the types of stakeholders who should participate in the project review.

✓ Specify the three steps for a constructive project review process.

✓ Identify methods for gathering feedback about project challenges and successes.

✓ Define the project archive and explain its importance.

✓ Cite examples of documents that should be included in the project archive.

Now that your project sponsor has signed off on project acceptance, you're really just about finished. There are only a few more tasks to complete the *closing process* of your project. Before you and your team scatter to other responsibilities, take the time to capture lessons learned and archive important project documents.

In this lesson, you learn how to work with your project team in reflecting on the project and conducting the project review to gather lessons learned. You effectively document your project processes and archive its history. These final closing activities ensure that you and your team articulate and record the challenges and successes, not only for your own professional development, but for the success of future project managers and teams implementing similar types of projects.

Document Lessons Learned

You can probably name at least five things you would have done differently in this project if you had the benefit of hindsight. You can probably also count off another five aspects of the project that you're rather proud of and that you'd like to repeat in future projects. As the project manager, you have a unique view of how the endeavor unfolded and its measure of success. Your team members and managing stakeholders likely have other perspectives, because they related to the project from different angles.

One of your final tasks as project manager is to gather and report on the *lessons learned* from these invaluable and varied perspectives. Also known as the *project review*, *postmortem*, or *debrief*, this lessons-learned activity helps you discover and document what could be improved or avoided in future similar projects and what was particularly successful and should be repeated.

Conducting the project debrief sets the stage for future achievements, not only for projects, but also for your team members, your managing stakeholders, and yourself. Articulating challenges helps you mitigate risks in future projects, optimize processes earlier, and improve tools used. Communicating triumphs helps you understand what works and should be replicated when possible.

To conduct a constructive project review, follow these three steps:

1. Identify what you want to know.
2. Gather information from various sources.
3. Write up the lessons learned and share them with everyone involved.

Identify the Information You Can Use

Focus on the types of information that will improve future projects and contribute to the professional development of the people involved. Questions to ask while gathering this information can include:

- What was particularly challenging about this project? What didn't work smoothly? What didn't work at all?

- Why were the hindrances challenging?

- What could have been different or could have created an improved outcome?

- What worked especially well in this project? Was anything easier, faster, or cheaper than expected? Why?

- What contributed to individual task success or overall project success?

- What are the key takeaways about this project that should be recorded?

   In addition to such broad and open-ended questions, you might be interested in homing in on specific aspects of the project. Questions to do this might include:

- How did this project function on the project triangle of scope, time, and cost?

- How successful was this project in terms of the project's stated charter, goal, and requirements? Did the project achieve what it set out to do? How well was this goal achieved? Why (or why not) was it achieved?

- What could have been improved and what went well with the major project management processes of initiating, planning, executing, monitoring, and closing?

- What can be said about the methodology used for the project? Was waterfall project management used when agile project management might have been a better choice (or vice versa)? Why?

- Considering the project management knowledge areas, what can be said about how the project performed in terms of not only scope, time, and cost, but also quality, communication, human resources, risk management, and procurement?

Gather Lessons Learned

After you identify what types of information you want from the project review, you're ready to glean that information.

   Start with the relevant background or supporting information you have on hand. This might include:

- The project charter, requirements document, or scope document

- Periodic status reports, especially the higher-level reports shared with the project sponsor

- Project reports, especially those that compare actual schedule and cost results against the original baseline plan

Then, gather feedback from the people involved with the project. This is where you collect solid information that you and others will be able to assess and act on. The method you choose to gather this feedback depends on whether you want team members to interact and discuss the project with one another, or whether you want them to offer answers individually and perhaps even anonymously. You can gather this feedback with a survey, a group meeting, or interviews.

Surveys

A survey includes developing and distributing a questionnaire to those involved with the project. This method can be especially effective when the survey allows the respondent to rate their opinions on a scale and also enter free-form comments. In this way, surveys enable you to gather meaningful quantitative as well as qualitative data.

You can tailor different lines of questioning based on people's different roles in the project, for example, a developer versus administrative support, or a team member versus a managing stakeholder.

If you use an online tool to develop your survey, you can automatically tally the results, and you can choose whether the survey is anonymous.

Group Meetings

Group meetings in which you gather project participants and ask questions stimulate discussion and ideas. First, determine whether you need separate meetings for different groups of team members or stakeholders. Next, choose the group's makeup to allow for the most open and productive discussion.

Set a clear agenda with a stated meeting goal and time limit. Craft your questions and consider sending them to the participants in advance for thought.

Identify the facilitator and a separate scribe to record all responses. Enforce ground rules for a respectful discussion, ensuring that the discussion remains constructive with a focus on improvement and that everyone has the opportunity to participate.

Interviews

Interviews that are conducted one-on-one or within small groups tend to be more candid and yield more information than a larger group discussion or the more impersonal survey. Interviewing is a good technique to use with key team members or managing stakeholders, or to dig deeper into an aspect of the project that was especially challenging.

Again, prepare your questions and choose your participants intentionally. Let the interviewees know what will be done with the information they share and their level of anonymity.

Document and Share the Lessons Learned

After you've gathered the lessons learned from your survey, meetings, or interviews, write up the results. Determine how broad or detailed the report should be to offer the most benefit to the participants and future project managers. The report should at least include the following topics:

- Project overview
- The project review methodology
- Challenges and weaknesses of the project
- Project successes and strengths
- Solutions and recommendations for future similar projects

Share the report with all project stakeholders, including your team members, managing stakeholders, and the project sponsor. Include this report with the project archives.

Archive Project History

While maintaining the plan in Microsoft Project through all the project phases from initiating to closing, you likely have amassed a considerable collection of reports, charts, tables, financials, and other documents. Your final task as project manager is to organize these documents for future use, probably by someone other than you.

This is not just arbitrary housekeeping. Your project produced a service or product for the organization, and your *project archive* is the official record of how it was accomplished. Because of this, you should leave your archive organized sufficiently to help someone else understand the project's workings, progress, obstacles, and achievements. This becomes vital in case some aspect of the project must be revisited later, or when someone needs to use your project as a model or template for a new project of a similar type.

To do this, review the project plan as well as all your associated project files with an outsider's eye. Consider the following three practices for suitably archiving your project documents for future use:

1. Clean up your project plan.
2. Add key documents to the project plan.
3. Organize the project archive's file structure.

Clean Up Your Project Plan

Much of your Microsoft Project plan served as your day-to-day roadmap through the project. It was your plan, and you tracked actual progress against that plan. You printed views and ran reports based on the information you entered. Sometimes, in the heat of project execution, tracking, and problem-solving, it's not unusual to quickly create some what-if scenarios or enter random notes on a task, resource, or assignment. These were likely what you needed at the time but might be incomprehensible or confusing to someone else later reviewing your project plan.

Go through the project file and remove any tasks or resources that weren't actually part of the project. Edit your notes to clarify them for another reader, add notes if you think they will help explain a situation, and delete notes that are not necessary to the archive.

Documents for Your Project Archive

Together with your project plan in Microsoft Project, the following are examples of landmark documents throughout the project life cycle. These examples can give you ideas on the appropriate items to include in your project archive, whether they're attached to the project plan or prominent in the project's archive file structure.

From the *initiating process*:

- Project charter
- Requirements document
- Scope document

From the *planning process*:

- Work breakdown structure
- Project budget
- Resource plan
- Risk management plan

From the *executing process* and *monitoring process*:

- Deliverable documents
- High-level reports on schedule, milestones, resources, and budget
- High-level status reports, especially to the project sponsor and other managing stakeholders
- Approvals for changes to scope, budget, or schedule
- Issues-tracking document

From the *closing process*:

- Project sign-off acceptance
- Project review (lessons learned) report
- Project archive table of contents or site map

Add Key Documents to the Project Plan

In the *initiating process*, you might have attached the project charter, requirements document, scope document, resource plan, or other key documents to the project file itself. Review your other major documents central to the project and determine whether you should attach them to the project plan as well.

Organize the Archive File Structure

Depending on how you decided to organize your project plan documents at the initiating process (described in Lesson 3, "Establish a Strong Foundation"), your files are likely stored on your organization's network or cloud drive.

Go through these files and organize them in a way that will make sense to someone who did not work on this project, but who might have knowledge of your organization or of the service or product created by the project. Determine the best organization scheme, create folders and subfolders, and move files into the appropriate folders. Delete any duplicate or irrelevant files that might be mystifying or cause unnecessary clutter.

A possible organization scheme is by project process. That is, you could have folders for:

- Initiating
- Planning
- Executing
- Tracking
- Monitoring
- Closing

Build into your archive file structure a way to discern the most important permanent record files from the ones with less value as more time passes, and therefore, can be safely deleted in the near future. Consider separating them into different folders within their categories. Your file structure might reflect the following scheme:

- High-level documents of historical archival significance that should always be part of the project's permanent record
- Mid-range documents that might have importance if a similar project will happen in the next year or two; include in the subfolder name an appropriate expiration date about three years hence
- Day-to-day ephemeral documents that helped to complete tasks or to report on daily or weekly progress; include in the subfolder name an appropriate expiration date about a year hence

Be sure to include an overview page that explains the archives. Either attach the file to your project plan or make it the first, or "readme," file that users see when they open the project archive folder.

Your project archive should tell an accurate story of your project to someone who wasn't involved. With this project history, future projects, project managers, and team members can learn from your hard-won experience and build in more opportunities for success with new projects.

Key Terms

closing process

debrief

executing process

initiating process

lessons learned

monitoring process

planning process

postmortem

project archive

project review

Review Questions

1.   After the project is completed, what is the purpose of a project review?

   A.   The project review evaluates the strengths and weaknesses of individual project team members to then develop incentives and performance improvement plans as appropriate.

   B.   The project review presents the project scope, schedule, and budget, therefore helping the project sponsor determine whether they can accept and sign off on the project as completed.

   C.   The project review gathers feedback from those involved in executing the project to identify challenges and successes throughout the project and help improve performance in future projects.

   D.   The project review shares the product or service created by the project with end users to obtain their feedback for further refinement.

2.   Who participates in the project review to discover lessons learned?

   A.   Immediate supervisors of the team members involved in the project should participate in the project review.

   B.   The project manager and the project sponsor are the key participants in a project review, although other managing stakeholders might also be involved.

   C.   Customers of the product or service created by the project participate in the project review.

   D.   The project team members, project manager, and managing stakeholders should participate in the project review.

3.   Name three methods for gathering information and feedback for the project review:

   A.   Surveys, group meetings, and one-on-one interviews

   B.   Performance evaluations by management, self-evaluations by team members, and peer evaluations

   C.   The project charter, requirements document, and scope document

   D.   The project schedule, project budget, and scope document

4.   What is the project archive and why is it important?

   A.   The project archive is the official record containing the project plan and other key documents that indicate how the project created the product or service. This archive can help someone else understand the workings, progress, obstacles, and achievements of the project.

   B.   The project archive is the organized set of weekly status reports submitted by team members to the project manager and the monthly progress reports presented to managing stakeholders throughout the project life cycle.

   C.   The project archive is the articulated set of initiating documents that got the project started. These can include the project charter, the requirements document, the scope document, and the project budget.

   D.   The project archive is the work breakdown structure that overviews a project's high-level deliverables down to the individual tasks that contributed to completing those deliverables.

5. What are the most important high-level documents to include as part of the project's permanent archive?

    A. Updates from team members that paint the detailed picture of project progress on a daily or weekly basis

    B. PDFs of tracking reports generated in Microsoft Project, like the Overallocated Resources report or Cash Flow report

    C. The project plan, the list of tools and processes used in the project, and the change management procedure

    D. The project plan, any official initiating documents, approvals for changes, project signoff, and the project review report

Appendix

Answers to the Review Questions

Lesson 1. Project Management Basics

1.   B. Although the organization has been working with volunteers for years, the training program is new and unique to the nonprofit and is therefore a project rather than an operation.

2.   C. The branding and marketing materials development was a project, but one of the deliverables of the project was the designed e-newsletter and its process, which is now being used every month. Because editing and disseminating the e-newsletter is a routine task repeating each month, it's considered an operation.

3.   D. Different projects will have different priorities and limitations. The project manager must be aware of which elements are fixed and which are more flexible in terms of time, cost, and scope and then make project adjustments accordingly as needed.

4.   A. There's no flexibility on the finish date and very little flexibility on the budget. This means that when changes happen in the project, you might need to reduce the level of quality or the scope of the project, either of which would save time or money.

5.   B. In the initiating process, the project scope, goals, and budget are framed. From that, the planning process develops the schedule and resource assignments. When the plan is established and the team is set in place, the executing process begins with the project start.

6.   A. In the monitoring process, you gather and enter status about tasks and the budget, then analyze whether the project is on track, ahead, or behind. In the controlling process, you modify project details based on your analysis to maintain the balance of time, cost, and quality within the project scope.

7.   C. All the items mentioned can be an important part of project closing. However, obtaining sponsor acceptance is crucial to ensuring that the sponsor knows the project is complete and signs off on the results and deliverables. Also of vital importance is conducting the project review or lessons learned meeting with the team members to document the project's strengths and weaknesses so that this knowledge can be leveraged for future similar projects.

8.   D. Waterfall project management is best suited for projects in a more physical environment like manufacturing and construction, where early changes can be too expensive, requirements and scope are well defined at the outset, the project team is more independent, or the project sponsor is more remote.

9.   E. Agile or iterative project management is best suited for projects in which the requirements and scope are more vague; in less physical, more knowledge-based creative work like software development; and where iterations and prototyping are a welcome part of the process, the project team is highly collaborative, and the project sponsor is readily available for frequent reviews and feedback.

Lesson 2. Introducing Microsoft Project

1. D. Project is most powerful when creating a schedule and also when adjusting the schedule automatically as task information changes.

2. B. Along with scheduling, Project calculates project costs and helps you communicate progress through its views and reports. It also helps you balance resources and respond to changes.

3. C. Project for the web is designed for basic work management and simple project management. It's best for teams who need to get their projects running quickly and to share information easily with other team members.

4. D. Like Project Professional, Project Online Desktop Client is a professional, full-featured edition of Project. Unlike Project Professional, though, it's an online subscription product, so you get periodic updates.

5. B. The main screen of the Project window is the current view you select, whether it's a Gantt Chart, Resource Sheet, Team Planner, Task Board, or any of several dozen available views of your project information.

6. A. The Tell Me What You Want To Do box gets you quickly to the view, function, or Help topic for which you're looking. You can then click the item to switch to the place, do the activity, or learn about the function.

Lesson 3. Establish a Strong Foundation

1. A. The project initiating process begins with the list of stakeholders and the project charter authorized and signed by the project sponsor.

2. C. Of the five types of project stakeholders, the project sponsor is the executive or customer who signs the project charter and is responsible for funding the project. This person is, therefore, most interested in project progress, deliverables, and outcomes.

3. B. The project charter includes the goal, objectives, high-level requirements, outcomes, overview budget, list of stakeholders, and project approval requirements. It's typically no longer than two pages and is authorized by the project sponsor.

4. D. The project scope statement typically specifies what is and is not included in the project, and includes the requirements, deliverables, constraints, and assumptions. It's a living document that is updated throughout the project life cycle.

5. D. Any of these options are good methods for organizing your project documents and for making them accessible to you and other stakeholders. Review the needs and capabilities of your organization and stakeholders to decide on the best approach.

Lesson 4. Set Up the Project and Tasks

1. Start Microsoft Project. On the Home page, click **Blank Project**. On the Project tab, in the Properties group, click **Project Information**. In the Start Date field, type the project start date. Click **OK**.

2. On the View menu, in the Task Views group, click **Other Views**, then click **Task Sheet**. Or, right-click the **View** bar on the left edge of the Project window, then click **Task Sheet**.

3. Any three of the following:

Backlog Board

Backlog Sheet

Current Sprint Board

Current Sprint Sheet

Sprint Board

Sprint Planning Board

Sprint Planning Sheet

Task Board

Task Board Sheet

4. A. Rearranging tasks in an agile view like the Task Board or Task Board Sheet is considered temporary, largely because of the visual nature of the task cards and because tasks tend to move more in agile projects.

5. C. Outlining your project tasks deconstructs a large project into its component parts, therefore making it easier to manage overall.

Lesson 5. Build the Schedule

1. A. While options B and D will automatically schedule newly entered tasks and option C will change existing tasks to automatic scheduling, option A sets existing as well as new tasks to automatic scheduling.

2. C. For tasks in an automatically scheduled project, the left edge of the Gantt bar represents the start date along the timescale, the duration of the task, and the finish date. Milestones are an exception, which show as a marker at the milestone finish date.

3. B. The four schedule drivers in an automatically scheduled project are the project start date, task duration, task links or dependencies, and any date constraints.

4. B. If you specify a task with a 0 duration, Project marks it as a milestone in the timescale side of the Gantt Chart, noting an important accomplishment in the project.

5. D. To set up dependencies among tasks, select them in the order in which they should be linked, then click **Link the Selected Tasks**. The default Finish-to-Start dependency is applied to the two tasks. You cannot set up links on the Task Board or Timeline view.

6. A. You set up your sprint start date, sprint durations, and the number of sprints in the Manage Sprints dialog box. You can also modify the sprint names and adjust sprint durations if needed.

7. D. For all tasks in a project scheduled from a project start date, the default constraint of As Soon As Possible is applied. This constraint is not associated with a date and therefore offers the greatest scheduling flexibility.

8. C. Set a Must Finish On date constraint on the Advanced tab in the Task Information dialog box.

9. A. A deadline is a reminder that does not affect task scheduling and appears as an arrow on the timescale side of the Gantt Chart. By contrast, any date constraint, including Finish No Later Than, indeed affects the task and project scheduling. Tasks with a date constraint applied are marked with an icon on the sheet side of the Gantt Chart.

Lesson 6. Set Up Resources

1. C. As you add each resource to your project plan, you define each one as either a work, material, or cost resource. Work resource is the default.

2. A. Work resources are people and equipment or machinery, as their effort depends on how much time they can expend in completing a task.

3. B. The Resource Sheet is a table view that contains fields for resource name, resource type, max units, and cost information and is the quickest way to add basic resource information.

4. A. In the Cost Accrual field for each resource, you can choose whether costs are incurred at the start of an assigned task, at the end of the task, or prorated throughout the duration of the task.

5. D. The Max Units field indicates the percent availability for the resource against the full project calendar, and is also referred to as resource units, percent availability, or availability.

6. B. With the Change Working Time dialog box, you can customize the resource calendar by switching the base calendar in the Base Calendar box, define the resource's normal work week on the Work Weeks tab, and set exceptions to that work week on the Exceptions tab.

7.   A. Project looks at the working time in the resource calendar and multiplies it by the max units percentage. This means if a resource calendar shows the resource works 40 hours per week, and the max units show 50 percent, the resource's availability will result in 20 hours per week. If the resource is scheduled for more than 20 hours in a week, the resource will show as overallocated.

Lesson 7. Assign Resources to Tasks

1.   C. The Assign Resources dialog box is the easiest way to assign resources to tasks, especially when you're making several assignments to several tasks in one sitting. You can also use the Resource Names field in the Gantt Chart or other task sheet to quickly assign tasks. A third method is to use the Resources tab on the Task Information dialog box.

2.   B. When you create the material resource in the Resource Sheet, you specify the material label or unit, like boxes or gallons, along with the cost per unit. Then when you assign the material resource to a task, you specify the quantity of that unit needed for this assignment. The default quantity is 1.

3.   A. Because a cost resource—like airfare or conference room rental—can be different when assigned to different tasks, you need to add the cost amount that will be incurred for that cost resource on this task. If you do not enter the cost, it will show as $0.00.

4.   D. An assignment is the intersection of a resource and task—that is, the resource assigned to help accomplish the task. When you assign a resource to a task, you create this new entity or relationship called an assignment, which has its own properties in the Project database.

5.   D. You can use any of these three methods to switch to one of these views to review your assignments in different ways.

6.   A. When you first set up your work resources (people and equipment) in the Resource Sheet, you specify their cost per hour or per day. Then when you assign the work resource to a task, Project multiplies that cost by the number of hours or days of work the resource is assigned to on that task.

7.   B. With the Cost column added to a task sheet like the Gantt Chart, you can see your task costs at a glance. The costs for all assigned resources on this task are added and shown in this field.

8.   C. Work is the amount of time (typically hours or days) that the assigned work resources (people and equipment) are expected to spend on the assigned task. Work is determined by the task duration and the assignment units.

Lesson 8. Check and Adjust the Project

1.   D. Add the Cost column to any task sheet. This column shows the costs for tasks based on the costs of their assigned resources. On the Format tab, select the **Project Summary Task** check box. The project summary task shows rolled-up values for the columns in the current

task sheet. In the project summary task, the value in the Finish field is the finish date of the last task to be completed, and the value in the Cost field is the total of all project tasks.

2. C. The critical path is the longest path through the project, and therefore represents the minimum duration of the entire project. The finish date of the critical path is the finish date of the project. Therefore, focusing on tasks in the critical path is the most effective way to bring in the project finish date.

3. A. In the Gantt Chart view, when you select the **Critical Tasks** check box, the critical path task bars turn red on the timescale side of the view.

4. D. The best way to bring in the finish date is to review tasks on the critical path and see where duration can be shortened or task linking can be improved. If neither of these sufficiently brings in the finish date, discuss the situation with your project sponsor to determine whether project scope should be cut.

5. B. If you need to cut project scope, cut project phases that might be considered optional, cut individual optional tasks, or reduce the duration of tasks so that you're still doing them but not spending as much time on them.

6. C. In the Resource Sheet, focus on work and material resources assigned to the more expensive tasks. Review the base costs of work and material resources and see whether they can be reduced. Review the list of resources and see if less expensive resources with similar skill sets can replace or assist the more expensive resources assigned to tasks. Another technique is to review the material label or unit to make sure it's the most cost-effective unit (like "each" or "cartons") to use for the tasks they're assigned to.

7. C. When checking resource assignments, you want to be sure that resources are assigned at the level of work they have availability for—not too much and not too little. You also want to be sure that all tasks have resources assigned, and to see whether any resources have no tasks assigned. You can check these in a task sheet like the Gantt Chart, and make adjustments there or in Team Planner.

8. B. When you set a baseline for the entire project, Project saves the values in your Duration, Start, Finish, Cost, Work, and other schedule- and cost-related fields into the corresponding Baseline fields, like Baseline Duration, Baseline Start, and so on. Your original project information is saved in this way for helpful comparisons later when your project is in progress and changing in various ways.

Lesson 9. Track Project Information

1. C. The planning process details the goals from the initiating, or preplanning, process and develops the project plan. The executing process is the process for implementing the project plan until it's finished.

2. D. In the monitoring process, you gather and enter status about tasks and the budget. In the controlling process, based on the status you've entered, you analyze whether the project is on track, ahead, or behind, and you modify the project to maintain the balance of time, cost, scope, and resources.

3.   C. Depending on what works best for you and the project, you might ask your team to communicate progress via email, an online tracking method like Project or Microsoft Teams, regular meetings like scrum huddles, or written status reports.

4.   A. Percent complete, actual or remaining duration, and actual start and actual finish dates are the five progress measures most typically used to track and monitor waterfall projects.

5.   A. The Update Tasks dialog box includes fields for percent complete, actual duration, remaining duration, actual start, and actual finish. You can enter one or more of these progress measures for the currently selected task.

6.   B. Agile projects often use Not Started, Next Up, In Progress, and Done on board views indicating progress over time. These are the default columns on the Project Task Board.

7.   D. The best way to update progress on an agile project in Microsoft Project is by using the Task Board or Current Sprint Board and dragging task cards to the correct progress column like Next Up, In Progress, or Done. You can also update agile progress by changing the Status field for a task in the Task Board Sheet or Current Sprint Sheet.

8.   A. Entering actuals like actual duration, actual start, or actual finish can change the scheduled start or finish date for linked successor tasks, depending on the nature of the link, for example, As Soon As Possible or Start No Earlier Than.

9.   B. To see the original scheduled data for your project, review the baseline fields, like Baseline Duration, Baseline Start, Baseline Finish, Baseline Cost, and Baseline Work. These fields show the values of these fields as they were when you first saved the project baseline. They remain unchanged, even as you enter actual information, and the current, scheduled information is changed as a result.

10.   B. After entering progress information, always check the project finish date and overall project cost to make sure they're still within project deadline and budget requirements. Also check that resource allocation is still balanced, without excessive overallocation or underallocation. Check that the project is still within scope, and that any additional scope is accounted for in the updated project.

Lesson 10. View Project Information

1.   D. Use the Zoom slider to zoom any timescale or graphically oriented view to see more or less of the view. Or, on the View tab, in the Zoom group, click **Zoom**, then click **Zoom Out** or **Zoom In**.

2.   A. Sorting a task sheet like the Gantt Chart or Task View by cost is a helpful technique for determining where to focus cost-cutting efforts for the biggest impact.

3.   D. Filtering temporarily removes information from the view, while highlighting shows everything and marks the information that meets the highlight criteria.

4.   B. Click the column labeled **Add New Column**, which is available on the right edge of every sheet view to add a new column. You can drag the new column to the position you want in the sheet. Or, right-click the column heading next to where you'd like the new column, click **Insert Column**, then select the field name.

5. A. On the File tab, click **Print,** then use the controls on the Print page to set your page layout for printing on paper or as a PDF file. Click **Page Setup** to open the dialog box for more print layout controls.

6. C. Use a project plan with enough task and resource data entered to see how a different view arranges project information. Switch to the view by right-clicking the view bar and clicking its name or by using the More Views dialog box. Examine how the view handles your project information, and review the Format tab for this view for options.

Lesson 11. Customize Project Information

1. B. Even though it's a resource sheet, you use the Task tab, Font group to format selected text in the Resource Sheet. Here you can change the font, font size, font color, or make text bold or italic.

2. D. This is the method to change the text style for all text in the current sheet view. The formatting applies to the current sheet view only, and it applies to any new items as they are added to this sheet.

3. D. For the Gantt Chart style you select, the bottom color is the color of the standard Gantt bar, while the top color is the color of the progress line within the Gantt bar.

4. A. Use the Add New Column field on the board view to add a new column. This is helpful if you want the board to show more detailed or incremental stages of completion.

5. D. In the Customize Task Board Cards dialog box, you can add or remove information included on task cards on a board view. In addition to the task name, you can add up to eight fields of task information to each task card.

6. C. Use the Project Options dialog box, available when you click **Options** on the File tab, to set preferences for the Project display, date format, currency format, default file location, spell-check, and more.

Lesson 12. Report Project Information

1. D. Reports such as the Work Overview dashboard and the Cost Overruns report use your project's baseline information to compare currently scheduled cost or work with the original plan, and calculates the variance between the two. This lets you know whether you're running ahead or behind your original plan.

2. A. On the Report tab, in the View Reports group, click the report category, then click the name of the report you want to run. The selected report appears on the screen.

3. C. When you run most reports, Project switches the ribbon to the Report Design tab so that you're already in position to adjust the look of your report. The Themes group contains the Themes and Colors controls you can use to change the report's color scheme.

4. B. You can access any custom report or dashboard you have created for the current project plan on the Report tab, in the View Reports group. Click **Custom**, then click the name of the report or dashboard you created.

5. A. On the File tab, click **Print**. A preview of the report as it will look when printed shows in the window. Whether you print on paper or to a PDF file, this preview shows the report layout.

6. B. On the File tab, click **Print**. Click the **Printer** button and click **Adobe PDF** or **Microsoft Print to PDF**. Click the **Print** button. In the Save PDF File As (or Save Print Output As) dialog box, select the drive name and folder where you want to save the PDF, enter a name in the **File name** field, then click **Save**.

Lesson 13. Obtain Project Acceptance

1. D. You want to demonstrate to your project sponsor that your project achieved what it was designed to do. This is done by showing that the product or service produced by the project meets the goals and objectives originally established during the initiating process of the project.

2. B. The Project Overview and Cost Overview dashboards show final project performance in terms of a high-level schedule with all tasks showing as completed, and a high-level cost report showing the total amount expended on the project.

3. A. The final project checklist, also known as the "punch list" in construction projects, includes the final refining tasks that must be completed before the project sponsor will accept the project as fully complete. These tasks are within the agreed-upon project scope and requirements.

4. C. Enter the note on the Notes tab in the Task Information dialog box. You can also right-click the task and then click **Notes** in the drop-down menu.

5. C. Obtaining final sign-off on project acceptance is important to establish the completion of the project and to ensure that the sponsor will pay project costs. Written project acceptance prevents misunderstandings about project completion or financial responsibility.

Lesson 14. Retain Project History

1. C. The project review—also known as lessons learned, postmortem, or debrief—is among the project manager's final tasks as part of the closing process of a completed project. Its purpose is to discover and document what could be improved in a future similar project and what was particularly successful and should be repeated.

2.   D. Everyone involved in planning, executing, and managing the project should participate in the project review.

3.   A. You can develop and distribute a survey or questionnaire to those involved with the project, facilitate group meetings, conduct one-on-one interviews, or a combination of these three. All of these methods have different ways of discovering the challenges and successes encountered throughout project planning and execution.

4.   A. The project archive starts with your project plan containing all the task, resource, and assignment information. It also includes key documents like the charter, scope document, major updates, and project review report. This record is essential in case some aspect of the project must be revisited later, or when someone wants to replicate this project for a new one of a similar type.

5.   D. The project archive should focus on the high-level project files rather than the day-to-day files like routine status or files outside the scope of the project. The project archive should include the Microsoft Project plan itself, any official initiating documents that specify the charter or scope of the project, the project budget, approvals for changes to the project schedule or budget, project sign-off, and project review report.

Index

A

Account Information command, 30
actual values, 157, 170–172
adding
    columns, 190–192
    Cost column, 145–146
    resource assignments, 129–130
    resources to project plans, 98–100
    sprints to projects, 84–85
    tasks to sprints, 85–86
Agile project management
    about, 10
    rearranging tasks, 63
    reviewing task costs for, 127
    scheduling sprints, 83–87
    task views, 61
    updating status in projects, 172–178
applying task calendars, 91–92
assigning
    cost resources to tasks, 120–121
    material resources to tasks, 118–120
    task names, 55
    work resources to tasks, 116–118, 131
assignment reports, 124–125
assignments
    about, 53
    changing, 128–133
automatic scheduling mode, 70
availability
    of resource units, 104–106
    specifying over time, 105–106

B

balancing resources, 20–21
base calendars
    about, 90, 107
    switching, 108
baseline values, 170–172
board views
    about, 56
    customizing, 212–214
bottom-up approach, 54

browsing
    combination views, 199–202
    graphical views, 195–199
building
    dashboards, 224–226
    projects, 48–49
    reports, 224–226
    resources, 118

C

calculating costs, 19–20
Calendar view, 196
calendars, project and task, 90–92
canceled projects, 236
closing process, of project life cycle, 8
collecting progress information, 167
columns
    adding, 190–192
    board view, 212–213
    changing in sheet view, 190–192
    hiding, 192
    moving, 192
combination views, browsing, 199–202
communicating progress, 21
conciseness, of task names, 55
consistency, of task names, 55
controlling process, of project life cycle, 8
copying projects, 49–50
Cost column, adding, 145–146
cost resources
    about, 100, 103–104, 147
    assigning to tasks, 120–121
costs
    calculating, 19–20
    checking, 145–153
    reducing, 146–153
    resource, 101–104, 147–149, 149–153
creating
    dashboards, 224–226
    projects, 48–49
    reports, 224–226
    resources, 118
Critical Path Method (CPM), 9, 140

critical paths
about, 9, 82
displaying, 140–141
viewing effect of on project finish date, 140
critical tasks
flagging, 141–142
reviewing links of, 143–144
Current Sprint Board, entering progress
on, 176–177
customers, 39
customizing
about, 208
board view, 212–214
Gantt view, 210–212
resource calendars, 106–112
review question answers, 259
review questions, 216–217
setting options and preferences, 214–215
sheet view, 208–210
cutting
resource costs, 149–153
scope, 144–145, 153

D

dashboards
creating, 224–226
working with, 223–224
data, zooming, 184–185
dates, identifying hardwired, 87–89
days, defining, 78
deadline reminders, entering, 89–90
debrief, 242
defining scope, 42–43
dependent tasks, linking, 80–83
descriptiveness, of task names, 55
displaying
critical paths, 140–141
specific outline levels, 186–187
Divider (Gantt Chart), 74
durations
changing on tasks with assignments, 132–133
entering for tasks, 75–78
entering in Gantt Chart, 76–77
estimated, 75–76
relationship with work, 130
shortening for critical tasks, 142–143
viewing on Task Board, 77–78

E

editing
resource names, 139–140
tasks, 139–140
elapsed weeks, 87
end users, 39
entering
actuals in waterfall projects, 168–172
deadline reminders, 89–90
different types of progress
information, 169–170
durations in Gantt Chart, 76–77
progress as expected, 168–169
progress in Task Board Sheet, 173–174
progress on Current Sprint Board, 176–177
progress on Task Boards, 172–173
project finish date, 142–145
resource costs, 101–104
task durations, 75–78
task names, 53–62
equipment resources, 99
estimated duration, 75–76
executing process, of project life cycle, 8

F

Feedback command, 30–31
filtering project information, 188–189
finish date
about, 76–77
changing, 153
checking, 178–179
Finish-to-Start task relationship, 80
flagging critical tasks, 141–142

G

Gantt Chart
about, 56, 73–75
entering durations in, 76–77
Gantt view
about, 56–57
customizing, 210–212
generating
dashboards, 224–226
projects, 48–49

reports, 224–226
resources, 118
graphical views, browsing, 195–199
group meetings, 244
grouping project information, 188

H

hardwired dates, identifying, 87–89
help
    within Microsoft Project, 29–31
    outside Microsoft Project, 31–32
Help tab, 29
hiding columns, 192
highlighting project information, 189–190
human resources, 99

I

identifying hardwired dates, 87–89
initiating process
    about, 38
    authorizing project charter, 39–40
    collecting requirements, 41–42
    defining scope, 42–43
    identifying stakeholders and project sponsor, 39
    organizing plan documents, 43–45
    of project life cycle, 7
    review questions, 46
interviews, 244

K

knowledge areas, 6, 18

L

leveling controls, 155
Linked Learning, 32
linking dependent tasks, 80–83

M

managing
    schedules, 18–19
    stakeholders, 39

manual scheduling mode, 70
material resources
    about, 99–100, 103, 147
    assigning to tasks, 118–120
Max Units, 104, 111
methodologies, of project management, 9–11
Microsoft Project
    about, 18
    app, 24–28
    benefits of, 18–22
    help for, 29–32
    review question answers, 253
    review questions, 33–34
    solutions, 22–24
Microsoft Project app
    about, 24–25
    Backstage view, 27–28
    Browse reports, 26
    Browse task, 25–26
    resource views, 25–26
    ribbons, 26–27
Microsoft Project Blog, 31
Microsoft Project Support Community, 31
Microsoft Project User Group (MPUG), 31
milestones, setting, 79–80
modifying
    assignments, 128–133
    board view columns, 212–213
    columns in sheet view, 190–192
    design of reports, 222–223
    duration on tasks with assignments, 132–133
    finish date, 153
    project calendars, 91
    project templates, 50–51
    resource units, 105
    sprints, 86–87
    task cards, 213–214
    task dependency types, 80
    tasks to automatic scheduling, 71
    Timescale, 185–186
    work week in resource calendars, 108–110
monitoring process, of project life cycle, 8
months, defining, 78
moving columns, 192

N

Network Diagram view, 196
Night Shift base calendar, 107
nonworking times, 90

O

options, setting, 214–215
organizing
    project plan documents, 43–45
    task outline, 63–66
overallocated resources
    about, 122, 153, 179
    resolving in Task Sheets, 154–155

P

percent complete, specifying on Task
    Board, 174–176
perpetual (nonsubscription) editions,
    22
planning process
    about, 40–41
    collecting requirements, 41–42
    defining scope, 42–43
    of project life cycle, 7–8
postmortem, 242
predecessor task, 80, 140
preferences, setting, 214–215
presenting projects to sponsors, 234–236
printing
    reports, 226–228
    views, 193–194
processes, project, 7–8
product requirements, 41
progress, communicating, 21
project acceptance
    about, 234
    canceled projects, 236
    celebrating with your team, 238–239
    presenting projects to sponsors, 234–236
    review question answers, 260
    review questions, 240
    securing official project sign-off, 236–238
project archive, 245–248
project baseline, setting, 157–159
project calendars
    changing, 91
    reviewing, 91
    using, 90–92
project charter, authorizing, 39–40
project cost, checking, 179
project entry bar, 139–140
Project for the Web, 22–23
Project Help & Learning, 31
project history
    about, 242

adding key documents to project plan, 246–247
archiving, 245–248
cleaning project plan, 245–246
croup meetings, 244
documenting lessons learned, 242–245
interviews, 244
organizing archive file structure, 247–248
review question answers, 260–261
review questions, 249–250
surveys, 244
project information
    about, 184
    adding columns, 190–192
    adjusting timescale, 185–186
    browsing combination views, 199–202
    browsing graphical views, 195–199
    changing columns in sheet view, 190–192
    filtering, 188–189
    grouping, 188
    hiding columns, 192
    highlighting, 189–190
    moving columns, 192
    printing views, 193–194
    review question answers, 258–259
    review questions, 204–205
    showing specific outline levels, 186–187
    sorting, 187–188
    viewing data, 184–190
    working with more views, 194–202
    zooming views, 184–185
project management
    about, 4, 11
    methodologies, 9–11
    project managers, 5–6
    project processes, 7–8
    project triangle, 6–7
    projects, 4–5
    review question answers, 252
    review questions, 13–15
*Project Management Book of Knowledge
    (PMBOK)*, 6, 55
project management office (PMO), 23
project managers, 5–6, 39
Project Online, 23
Project Online Desktop Client, 23, 24
Project Online with Portfolio Management
    Features, 23
project plans
    adding key documents to, 246–247
    adding resources to, 98–100
    cleaning up, 245–246
    entering task names, 53–62
    organizing documents, 43–45

organizing task outline, 63–66
review question answers, 254
review questions, 68
sequence tasks, 62–63
setting project start date, 51–53
starting, 48–51
project portfolio management (PPM), 23
Project Professional 2021, 23
project requirements, 41
project review, 242
Project scheduling engine, 70–72
project scope, 42–43
Project Server, 23
project sponsors, identifying, 39
Project Standard 2021, 23
project success
about, 138
adding Cost column, 145–146
changing finish date, 153
checking costs, 145–153
checking project finish date, 138–145
checking resource assignments, 153–157
cutting resource costs, 149–153
cutting scope, 144–145, 153
editing resource names, 139–140
editing tasks, 139–140
entering project finish date, 142–145
flagging critical tasks, 141–142
reducing costs, 146–153
resolving assignment problems in Team
Planner, 155–157
resolving overallocations in Task
Sheet, 154–155
resource leveling controls, 155
reviewing links of critical tasks, 143–144
reviewing project finish date, 139–142
reviewing resource costs, 147–149
reviewing total project cost, 145–146
setting project baseline, 157–159
shortening durations of critical tasks, 142–143
showing critical path, 140–141
surplus budgets, 147
viewing total cost, 146
Project Summary Task, 139, 146
project templates, adapting, 50–51
project triangle, 6–7
projects
about, 4–5
adding sprints, 84–85
canceled, 236
checking finish date, 138–145
copying, 49–50

creating, 48–49
entering finish date, 142–145
reviewing finish date, 139–142
secure sign-off of, 236–238
setting start date, 51–53
viewing effect of critical path on
finish date, 140

R

reducing costs, 146–153
removing
resource assignments, 129–130
work resources from tasks, 131–132
reordering
tasks in Task Sheet, 62
tasks on Task Board, 63
replacing resource assignment, 129
reporting
about, 220
adjusting design of reports, 222–223
assignment and resource reports, 124–125
creating new reports/dashboards, 224–226
frequently used reports, 222
printing reports, 226–228
review question answers, 259–260
review questions, 229–230
running, 221
visual reports, 226
working with, 220–224
requirements, collecting, 41
resolving
assignment problems in Team Planner, 155–156
overallocations in Task Sheets, 154–155
resource calendars
changing work week in, 108–110
customizing, 106–112
max units and, 111
specifying exceptions to, 110–111
resource costs
cutting, 149–153
entering, 101–104
reviewing, 147–149
Resource Form view, 200–201
Resource Graph view, 197
resource names, editing, 139–140
Resource Names field, 119–120
Resource Sheet, reducing costs in, 150–152
Resource Usage view, 202
resources
about, 53, 98, 116

adding to project plans, 98–100
assigning cost resources to tasks, 120–122
assigning material resources to tasks, 118–120
assigning work resources to tasks, 116–118
balancing, 20–21
changing assignments, 128–133
changing units, 105
changing work week, 108–110
checking allocation of, 179
checking assignment of, 153–157
cost, 100, 103–104, 120–121, 147
creating, 118
customizing calendars, 106–112
entering cost of, 101–104
equipment, 99
human, 99
material, 99–100, 103, 118–120, 147
max units, 112
replacing assignments, 129
review question answers, 255–256
review questions, 134–135
reviewing resource assignments, 122–125
specifying availability over time, 105–106
specifying exceptions to calendar, 110–111
switching base calendar, 108
unit availability, 104–106
viewing task costs from assignments, 125–128
work, 102–103, 116–118, 131–132, 147
working times calendars, 107–108
resources reports, 124–125
responding to changes, 21–22, 178–179
review question answers
customizing, 259
initiating process, 253
Microsoft Project, 253
project acceptance, 260
project history, 260–261
project information, 258–259
project management, 252
project plan, 254
reporting, 259–260
resources, 255–256
scheduling, 254–255
review questions
customizing, 216–217
initiating process, 46
Microsoft Project, 33–34
project acceptance, 240
project history, 249–250
project information, 204–205
project management, 13–15
project plan, 68
reporting, 229–230

resources, 134–135
scheduling, 93–95
tracking, 181–182
reviewing
links of critical tasks, 143–144
overall project cost estimate, 127–128
project calendars, 91
project finish date, 139–142
resource assignments, 122–125
resource costs, 147–149
task costs, 126
task costs on Agile planning board, 127
total project cost, 145–146
rolled-up costs, 127
rolled-up values, 139
running reports, 221

S

schedule buffer, 142
scheduled values, 157, 170–172
scheduling
about, 70
adding sprints to projects, 84–85
adding tasks to sprints, 85–86
applying task calendars, 91–92
automatic, 70–72
changing project calendars, 91
entering deadline reminders, 89–90
entering durations in Gantt Chart, 76–77
entering task durations, 75–78
Gantt Chart, 73–75
identifying hardwired dates, 87–89
linking dependent tasks, 80–83
managing, 18–19
manual, 72
modifying sprint information, 86–87
review question answers, 254–255
review questions, 93–95
reviewing project calendars, 91
setting milestones, 79–80
setting up task dependencies, 81–82
sprints for Agile projects, 83–87
using project and task calendars, 90–92
viewing dependencies on Task Boards, 82–83
viewing durations on Task Boards, 77–78
scope
cutting, 144–145, 153
defining, 42–43
scope creep, 42
ScreenTips, 30
sequencing tasks, 62–63

setting
  milestones, 79–80
  new tasks to automatic scheduling, 72
  options, 214–215
  preferences, 214–215
  project baseline, 157–159
  project start date, 51–53
setup, of task dependencies, 81–82
Sheet view
  about, 56, 128
  changing columns in, 190–192
  customizing, 208–210
shortening durations of critical tasks,
    142–143
showing
  critical paths, 140–141
  specific outline levels, 186–187
sorting project information, 187–188
specialized task views, 56
sponsors, presenting projects to, 234–236
sprints
  about, 10
  adding tasks to, 85–86
  adding to projects, 84–85
  costs of, 127
  defined, 83–84
  modifying, 86–87
  moving between, 177–178
  scheduling for Agile projects, 83–87
  updating, 177
stakeholders, identifying, 39
Standard base calendar, 107
Start date, 76–77
starting project plans, 48–51
subscription editions, 22
subtasks, 53, 186
successor task, 80, 140
summary tasks, 53, 186
surveys, 244
switching
  from automatic to manual scheduling, 72
  base calendars, 108
  from manual to automatic scheduling, 72

T

Table Side (Gantt Chart), 73
Task Board
  entering progress on, 172–174
  reordering tasks on, 63
  specifying percent complete on, 174–176
  viewing durations on, 77–78
  viewing task dependencies on, 82–83
  working with tasks on, 60–62
task calendars
  about, 108
  applying, 91–92
  using, 90–92
task cards, modifying, 213–214
task dependency
  about, 80
  setting up, 81–82
  viewing on Task Board, 82–83
Task Entry view, 199–200
task link, 80
task names
  assigning, 55
  editing in Task Sheet, 59–60
  editing on Task Board, 62
  entering, 53–62
  source of, 54
Task Sheets
  reducing costs in, 149–150
  reordering tasks in, 62
  resolving overallocated resources in, 154–155
  working with tasks in, 57–60
Task Usage view, 201
task views, 56–57
tasks
  about, 53
  adding to sprints, 85–86
  adding to Task Sheet, 59
  assigning cost resources to, 120–121
  assigning material resources to, 118–120
  assigning work resources to, 116–118, 131
  changing to automatic scheduling, 71
  deleting from Task Board, 62
  deleting from Task Sheet, 60
  dependent, 80–83
  editing, 139–140
  entering durations for, 75–78
  entering in Task Sheet, 57–59
  entering on Task Board, 60–61
  moving between sprints, 177–178
  organizing outlines, 63–66
  rearranging in Agile views, 63
  removing work resources from, 131–132
  reordering in Task Sheet, 62
  reordering on Task Board, 63
  reviewing costs of, 126
  reviewing costs of, on Agile planning
      board, 127
  scrolling to in timescale, 123
  sequencing, 62–63
  setting new to automatic scheduling, 72

viewing costs from assignments, 125–128
working with in Task Sheet, 57–60
working with on Task Board, 60–62
team members, 39
Team Planner view, 155–156, 197–198
Tell Me What You Want To Do control, 29–30
text wrapping, 58
Timeline view, 195
Timescale
adjusting, 185–186
Gantt Chart, 74
scrolling to tasks in, 123
Timescale Side (Gantt Chart), 74
top-down approach, 54
total project cost, reviewing, 145–146
tracking
about, 166
checking project cost, 179
checking project finish date, 178–179
checking resource allocations, 179
collecting progress information, 167
comparing values, 170–172
entering actuals in waterfall projects, 168–172
entering different types of progress
information, 169–170
entering progress as expected, 168–169
entering progress in Current Sprint Sheet, 177
entering progress in Task Board Sheet, 173–174
entering progress on Current Sprint Boards, 176
entering progress on Task Boards, 172–173
moving tasks between sprints, 177–178
responding to changes, 178–179
review question answers, 256–258
review questions, 181–182
specifying percent complete on Task
Boards, 174–176
tracking, 256–258
updating status in Agile projects, 172–178
Tracking Gantt view, 199–200
traditional project management, 9
24 Hours base calendar, 107

U

underallocated resources, 153, 179
uniqueness, of task names, 55
updating
sprint progress, 177
status in Agile projects, 172–178

V

verifying
costs, 145–153
finish project date, 178–179
project cost, 179
project finish date, 138–145
resource allocation, 179
resource assignments, 153–157
Video Learning Programs, 32
viewing
durations on Task Board, 77–78
effect of critical path on project finish date,
140
task dependencies on Task Board, 82–83
total cost in Project Summary Task, 146
views
combination, 199–202
graphical, 195–199
printing, 193–194
working with, 194–202
visual reports, 226

W

waterfall project management, 9, 168–172
websites
Linked Learning, 32
Microsoft Project Blog, 31
Microsoft Project Support Community, 31
Microsoft Project User Group (MPUG),
31
Project Help & Learning, 31
weeks, defining, 78
What's New command, 30
work, relationship with duration, 130
work breakdown structure (WBS), 8, 41, 55
work resources
about, 102–103, 147
assigning to tasks, 116–118, 131
removing from tasks, 131–132
working times, 90
working times calendars, 107–108
wrapping text, 58

Z

zooming data, 184–185